Take time to love,
To smile, to laugh, to sing.
Because everything passes,
Tires, and breaks.
If you don't have the time,
You forget about love.
Don't be in such a hurry;
Take time to love!

   —a song from Josephine's kitchen

To Dorothy
with prayers, love, and best wishes
Bon appétit
Josephine
30th of October 1980

SOUNDS FROM JOSEPHINE'S KITCHEN

JOSEPHINE ARALDO

Strawberry Hill Press

Copyright © 1978 by Josephine Araldo

Strawberry Hill Press
616 4th Avenue
San Francisco, California 94121

Distributed by Stackpole Books
Cameron & Kelker Sts.
Harrisburg, Pa. 17105

No part of this book may be reproduced by any mechanical, photographic, or electronic process, or in the form of a phonographic recording, nor may it be stored in a retrieval system, transmitted, or otherwise copied for public or private use — other than for "fair use" — without the written permission of the publisher.

First Printing, October, 1978

Manufactured in the United States of America

Edited by Catherine A. Pearsall

Cover designed by Ku, Fu-sheng

Book indexed by Orly Kelly

Book design by Carlton Clark Herrick

Library of Congress Cataloging in Publication Data

Araldo, Josephine, 1897-
  Sounds from Josephine's kitchen.

  1. Cookery, French. I. Title.
TX719.A695   641.5'944   78-10535
ISBN 0-89407-026-6 pbk.

To My Gigolo
To My Friends
To My God

Table of Contents

1	Josephine
3	Notes on the Use of Josephine's Cookbook
4	Metric Conversion Tables
7	*"Barbe à queue"* Money-Saving Menus
21	*"Yes - No - Maybe?"* Appetizers
33	*"Sacramento, California!"* Budget Entrées
53	*"Use Your Noodle"* Vegetables
69	*"Sing While You Cook"* Poultry, Game, and Rabbit
89	*"My Gigolo and Me"* Fish and Shellfish
107	*"An Album of Memories"*
129	*"To Beat the Band!"* Beef, Veal, Lamb and Pork
155	*"Use Your Imagination"* Light Supper or Luncheon Ideas
167	*"One for the Cook!"* Desserts
181	*"Dressed Like a Horse on Parade"* Haute Cuisine
193	*"Know the Fundamentals"* Fundamental Doughs
199	*"The Winning Tricks"* The Fundamental Sauces
209	Glossary
221	Index

Josephine...

The kitchen is bustling with activity and alive with laughter once again, now that Josephine's back with more recipes and helpful hints for her students in her second cookbook. Every day in her kitchen finds it filled with the sounds of creative cookery.

Ripples of laughter . . . Josephine's just told another anecdote about one of the employers she's known: Isadora Duncan; Louis Loucheur, a Minister under Clemenceau; Lily Pons and her husband André Kostelanetz; and such San Francisco notables as the George Oppens, the Mortimer Fleishhackers, the Richard Tobins, the Charles Figgenbaums, the Isaias Hellmans, and others.

Josephine's high spirits and rapid-fire humor are as much a part of her cooking as her thorough mastery of French cuisine. She tells her classes stories of the rich and famous whom she's met head-on in the kitchens of Paris, New York, and San Francisco, stories that not only entertain, but usually impart a lesson in cooking or plain human nature.

Words fly around the tiny kitchen as Josephine advises, "Don't let anything dampen your spirits!" the favorite adage of her teacher at the Cordon Bleu, Henri-Paul Pellaprat. "He was a wonderful man. He gave me my first *toque blanche* and said 'I crown you chef!'" For four years she attended classes, until the Mortimer Fleishhackers met Josephine and brought her to San Francisco to be their cook. Since 1924, she's lived with her husband Charles in San Francisco, cooking in the French style for the American palate.

She's often likely to counsel, "Don't throw anything away!" Bits of foil and brown paper peeking out from below her marble-slab table confirm she's a practitioner of her own advice. Born in Brittany, eighty-one years ago, she's kept close to the teachings of her grandmother, who instilled in Josephine both an imagination and a sense of economy when she cooks.

More sounds from the kitchen. Charles has walked in from the garden with herbs for the cook. He sets aside his black beret, rolls up his sleeves, and prepares to "destroy the evidence" of dirty dishes. Josephine's rapid speech continues as her students scribble in notebooks, and Charles ad libs from the sink. Her stock phrases — which endear her to her every audience – appear here as chapter titles for this book.

Josephine can be heard singing as she whips up the eggs because, she says, "It makes you cook better." We've found this to be true and, following the wisdom of a woman who has devoted nearly sixty years to cooking professionally, have included her favorite songs along with her recipes. You'll find the combination as irresistible as the incomparable Josephine Araldo.

Notes on the Use of Josephine's Cookbook

Many terms used in cooking — especially French terms — are defined in the **Culinary Glossary.** Where these terms occur in the recipes, they are printed in bold-face type.

On Measurement

When you are cooking with me, there are several things to keep in mind as they differ from the standard American cookbook.

Tablespoon and *teaspoon* measurements are always *rounded,* rather than level, unless otherwise specified in the recipe. Measurement of *cups* is done in the usual manner, leveling the surface even with the top of the measure.

If you measure a teaspoon, half-teaspoon, etc., of salt into your palm and carefully observe the amount, you will be able to measure more quickly, without a spoon, from then on — a great time saver.

On Kitchen Aids

Because there is so much interest these days in kitchen aids, I should note here that I have been using for many years the professional model of the Cuisinart. I find it an invaluable addition to my kitchen. But, in my classes, I never use it, because I believe all good cooks should first know how to do all food preparation by hand — and, also, not everyone can afford this equipment.

On Wine

I am also partial to the wines of California — in part, perhaps, because I have lived here for more than 50 years — but also because they are excellent and relatively inexpensive. Of course, my first love in champagnes will always remain *Möet et Chandon.*

On Abbreviations Used

The following abbreviations have been used throughout the book, both in the list of ingredients and in the instructions for preparation:

tablespoon(s) = tbsp(s)
teaspoon(s) = tsp(s)
quart(s) = qt(s)
pint(s) = pt(s)

pound(s) = lb(s)
ounce(s) = oz
envelope(s) = env(s)
package(s) = pkg(s)
piece(s) = pc(s)

Metric Conversion Tables

Volume
¼ tsp = 1.25 ml (milliliters)
½ tsp = 2.5 ml
¾ tsp = 3.75 ml
1 tsp = 5 ml
¼ tbsp = 3.75 ml
½ tbsp = 7.5 ml
¾ tbsp = 11.25 ml
1 tbsp = 15 ml

½ pt = 236 ml
1 pt = 473 ml
1 qt = 946.3 ml
1 gal = 3785 ml

Weight
¼ oz = 7.1 g (grams)
½ oz = 14.17 g
¾ oz = 21.27 g
1 oz = 28.35 g
¼ lb = .113 kg (kilograms)
½ lb = .227 kg
¾ lb = .340 kg
1 lb = .454 kg
2.205 lbs = 1 kg

¼ cup = 59 ml (milliliters)
⅓ cup = 78 ml
½ cup = 118 ml
⅔ cup = 157 ml
¾ cup = 177 ml
1 cup = 236 ml

Fluid Ounces
¼ oz = 7.5 ml
½ oz = 15 ml
¾ oz = 22.5 ml
1 oz = 30 ml

Temperature

200°F = 94°C	325°F = 164°C
225°F = 108°C	350°F = 178°C
250°F = 122°C	375°F = 192°C
275°F = 136°C	400°F = 206°C
300°F = 150°C	425°F = 220°C
	450°F = 234°C

The recipes give all temperatures in degrees Fahrenheit (°F). To convert to degrees Celsius (°C), subtract 32 and multiply by .56. To change Celsius to Fahrenheit, multiply by 1.8 and add 32.

MONEY SAVING MENUS AND RECIPES

"Barbe à Queue"

Part of cooking economically and stretching food dollars is to find a use for everything you buy ~ using beef or poultry "head to tail," for instance. The following budget menus prove that gourmet cooking need not be expensive.

Money Saving Menus and Recipes

A lady once said to me, "You French people eat all the insides of the animal." I said, "Well, madam, what do you think we do with the rest of the beast? We eat the whole beast ~ the barbe à queue. *Incidentally, that is where you get the word barbecue ~ 'head to tail.' The lady said "I didn't know that," and I said, "Well, you can't say that no more." The French way of cooking is similar to the Chinese in the way we use the whole carcass. It's very economical.*

I buy meats for their flavor, not by the price or expensive cut. For flavor and tenderness, I don't think you can beat the top round or top sirloin. They make wonderful tournedos ~ much better than the filet of beef, which is pretty tasteless.

I always shop at several stores in order to compare the prices and the quality ~ but quality always counts first. If I find the same quality of produce in the stores, then I buy the cheapest. But freshness is most important. You may pay a little more but you end up with more nutrients in the fresher meats and produce. And you also know exactly what you are getting when you buy it fresh!

When buying vegetables and fruits, sometimes I take the precaution of soaking them first in water with a little soda added, to take away any pesticides that may be on the skins. Then I drain the water, rinse first in cold, then hot water, before cooking or preparing them.

Petit Dejeuner pour des Invités Inattendus
Breakfast for Unexpected Guests

When someone drops in on you unexpectedly in the early morning, do not let it "dampen your spirits." French toast, or galettes, can be made almost as quickly as you can say their name.

Pain perdu ou galettes   *French Toast or Flapjacks*
Ambrosia   *Fruit Ambrosia*
Café ou thé   *Coffee or Tea*

Pain Perdu   French Toast

2 to 3 eggs	2 pcs of bread per serving
3 tbsps sugar	(French bread preferred)
½ cup milk, wine, beer or cider	4 tbsps butter or more, if needed
1 tbsp vanilla or rum	maple syrup or fruit syrup

Break the eggs in a deep, flat dish. Beat with the sugar using a fork as though making an omelette. Warm the milk or other liquid of your choice and mix with the eggs and sugar. Add vanilla or rum.

Melt the butter in a large, heavy skillet. Dip the bread slices into the egg mixture one at a time and fry on both sides until golden brown. Serve with a fruit syrup or maple syrup.

Galettes   Flapjacks or Griddle Cakes

2 to 3 cups of flour	1½ to 2 cups milk or beer
3 to 4 tbsps baking powder	2 tbsps sugar or maple syrup
½ tsp salt	4 tbsps melted butter
2 large eggs	maple syrup or jam

Stir the flour, baking powder and salt together in a mixing bowl. Beat the eggs, milk or beer, and sugar or maple syrup together until blended. Add to the flour mixture. Add four tablespoons melted butter and mix until well-blended.

With a small ladle or cup, drop the batter on a hot buttered griddle or iron pan. When bubbles appear on the top and edges are dried, turn and brown the other side. Keep hot in the oven until ready to serve with fruit or maple syrup.

Dejuner à quatre   Luncheon for four

Soufflé au fromage et aux herbes du jardin   Cheese Soufflé with Herbs
Salade Verte   Green Salad
Suprême aux Fraises   Strawberry Delight

Soufflé au Fromage et aux Herbes du Jardin
Cheese Souffle with Herbs

4 tbsps butter or margarine	1 tbsp each tarragon and chives
4 level dessert spoons flour	½ tbsp each chervil and parsley
1 cup milk, warmed	1 spring each thyme, marjoram or oregano, summer or winter savory
salt and pepper	
⅛ tbsp nutmeg	1 large sage leaf
½ cup grated cheese of any kind (not processed)	⅛ tbsp fennel
4 eggs separated, plus two egg whites	3-qt buttered soufflé mold coated with grated cheese, Parmesan or other

Melt butter in a double boiler, add flour, stir and let cook two or three minutes; add warm milk a little at a time. Season with salt, pepper, and nutmeg; cover and let cook over simmering water for 15 to 20 minutes. Off heat add the yolks of egg one by one, stirring after each. Add all herbs chopped very fine and fold in the egg whites, stiffly beaten but not dry. Fill mold to ¾ full, set in middle rack of oven on cookie sheet and bake at 375° for 20 to 25 minutes. The center should be very moist. Serve as is without any sauce.

Supreme aux Fraises

½ cup butter, softened
2 cups powdered sugar
1 egg yolk
1 egg white
about 20 butter cookies
   or vanilla wafers

Strawberry Delight

2 baskets of strawberries, cleaned
1 cup walnuts, chopped
½ pt whipping cream
3 tbsps sugar
1 tsp vanilla

Mix butter with sugar and egg yolk until creamy. Beat the egg white very stiff and add to the butter-sugar mixture. Lightly butter a glass dish and line the bottom with a layer of cookies. Spread some of the butter mixture over the cookies.

Crush the strawberries very coarsely, reserving some for decoration. Spread a layer of crushed strawberries over the mixture in the dish, then sprinkle with chopped walnuts. Repeat, adding layers of cookies, butter mixture, strawberries, walnuts, and so on, finishing with a layer of crushed cookies.

Whip the cream, adding 3 tablespoons of sugar and the vanilla, and spread it evenly over the cookie crumbs. Decorate with whole strawberries. Chill until ready to serve.

Diner à quatre

Carbonnade de Boeuf
Riz
Brocoli au Gratin
Crème Renversée à L'Orange

Dinner for four

Spiced Beef Stew
Rice
Broccoli with Cheese
Orange Custard Cream

Carbonade de Boeuf

2 lbs beef chuck, cut in
   2-inch cubes
2 tbsps oil
2 tbsps butter
1 tbsp flour
2½ cups dark beer
2 onions, sliced

Spicy Beef Stew with Beer

2 cloves garlic, chopped
2 tbsps horseradish, drained
1 tbsp Worcestershire
1 tsp fresh thyme, chopped
½ tsp dill seed
½ tsp allspice
salt and pepper

Brown the meat on all sides in oil and butter. Add the flour and mix well. Add the beer, onions, garlic, and spices. Bring to a boil and simmer covered for 2½ hours, adding more beer if necessary. Taste for seasoning.

Or, if using the oven, stew can be cooked at 250° or 300° for 2½ hours. Taste for doneness; if not tender, cook 15 to 20 minutes longer.

Serve with rice, buttered noodles, or mashed potatoes.

Brocoli au Gratin

1 bunch of broccoli
salt and pepper
4 tbsps butter

Broccoli with Cheese

1 recipe **béchamel sauce**
1/3 cup grated Parmesan or
  Swiss cheese

Break apart the flowerets of broccoli. Peel the stems and cut in 1-inch pieces. Drop the flowerets and stems into boiling water. Add salt and boil for 10 to 15 minutes. Remove the flowerets and continue cooking the stems for 5 to 10 minutes more, or until tender when pierced with a fork; drain. In the same pot, add the butter, salt and pepper and mix. Transfer to a fireproof dish. Cover with béchamel sauce, sprinkle with the cheese, and dot with butter. Place in a 375° oven and bake until browned. Serve in the same dish.

Crème Renversée à L'Orange

4 eggs
½ cup sugar
2 cups orange juice, heated
grated rind of one orange

Orange Custard Cream

1 tbsp vanilla
3 tbsps *Orange Curaçao or
  Grand Marnier*
½ pt whipping cream
3 tbsps sugar

Beat the eggs and sugar until lemon-colored. Heat the orange juice to the boiling point. Pour the orange juice slowly over the eggs. Add the rind and stir in the vanilla and orange liqueur.

Pour the mixture into a greased soufflé dish or pyrex dish; set it in a **bain marie** and bake in a preheated oven at 350° for 45 minutes to 1 hour, or until set.

Let the custard cool. Unmold and serve with whipped cream sweetened with sugar.

Diner à six

*Cari à L'Indienne
Riz à la Piemontaise
Petits Pois au Beurre
Gateau de Pommes*

Dinner for six

*Chicken Curry
Piémontaise Rice
Buttered Green Peas
Raw Apple Cake*

Poulet au Cari à l'Indienne

1 chicken, cut into pieces
flour
2 tbsps butter
2 tbsps shortening
salt and pepper

Mirepoix
1 cup chicken broth

Chicken Curry

Curry Sauce:
  4 tbsps butter
  2 tbsps flour
  1 to 1½ cups chicken broth
  1 tbsp curry powder
  1 banana, mashed
  1 apple, finely diced
  1 tbsp raisins
  1/3 cup cream

Cut chicken into pieces. Save the giblets to use in the Riz a la Piemontaise. Roll the chicken pieces in a floured pan, add salt and pepper and brown in the butter and shortening. Cook slowly for 40 to minutes, adding 1 cup mirepoix (equal parts carrot, celery, and onion coarsely chopped) and 1 cup broth. While chicken is cooking, prepare the sauce.

Melt butter in a double boiler and stir in the flour. Add the curry and a little of the broth. Stir and add rest of broth. When chicken is finished cooking, add banana, apple, and raisins to the sauce, and juices from the chicken. Stir well and add the cream. Do not let sauce boil after adding cream. Arrange chicken on platter and serve sauce over it.

Riz à la Piémontaise   Piémontaise Rice

chicken giblets
1 carrot
1 stalk of celery
2 onions
1 sprig of thyme
1 bay leaf
2 to 3 cloves
1 tomato, chopped, or 1 tbsp tomato paste
4 tbsps butter
1½ cups white rice
salt and pepper

Cook the chicken gizzard and neck in 3 cups of water, adding a few slices of carrot, celery and onion. Add thyme, bay leaf, salt, pepper, and 2 or 3 cloves. Simmer until gizzard is tender. Cut gizzard and liver in small pieces and set aside; reserve the broth.

Chop remaining onion and the tomato. Melt the butter and sauté the onion until lightly browned. Add the cut giblets, rice, tomato, and the broth from the giblets (add water to make 3 cups of liquid). Season with salt and pepper. Bring to a boil, then reduce heat and steam for 17 to 20 minutes, or until rice is tender.

Petits pois au Beurre   Buttered Green Peas

1 small onion
4 tbsps margarine, butter or bacon fat
1 pkg frozen peas
1 cup diced raw potatoes
A few leaves of lettuce, shredded
1 cup water or broth
salt and pepper
1 tsp sugar

Chop the onion and sauté in the margarine, butter, or bacon fat until translucent. Add the peas, potatoes and shredded lettuce. Stir them in the butter for a few minutes. Add the warm water or broth and simmer 10 minutes, or until the potatoes are tender. Add salt and pepper and the sugar. Stir to mix and serve.

Gateau des pommes   Apple Cake

1 cup sugar
1 cup flour
1 tsp baking soda
1 tsp cinnamon
½ tsp salt
2 eggs
½ cup oil
2 cups apples, chopped, cored, and peeled
1 cup nuts, finely-chopped

Mix dry ingredients together and stir in eggs and oil. Fold in nuts and apples. Pour into a greased and floured 9-inch baking pan and bake at 325° for 45 minutes, or until done.

Diner à quatre ou six

*Chou Farci~Sauce Brune
aux Capres
Carottes à la Vichy
Salade Verte
Pouding aux Pommes à
l'Orange*

Dinner for four to six

*Stuffed Cabbage with
Brown Caper Sauce
Carrots Vichy
Green Salad
Apple and Orange Pudding*

Chou Farci Sauce Brune aux Capres
Stuffed Cabbage with Brown Caper Sauce

1 medium head cabbage
4 strips bacon
3 to 4 slices stale bread
¼ cup broth
4 scallions or 2 shallots, chopped fine
1 sprig thyme, chopped
1 to 2 tbsps butter

¾ lb ground pork
¾ lb lean ground beef
½ lb leftover chicken, chopped
1 egg
2 pinches allspice
salt and pepper to taste
1 to 2 cloves garlic, minced
brandy (optional)

Preheat oven to 300°.

Blanch cabbage leaves for 7 minutes, then drain. Meanwhile, generously grease a round-bottomed casserole. Crisscross bacon strips in casserole with the ends hanging over the bowl's rim; set aside.

Sauté scallions or shallots and thyme in butter. Combine all meats with bread (soaked in broth), scallions and egg. Season with allspice, salt, pepper and garlic. (To check seasonings, sauté a small amount of mixture in some fat until cooked; taste. Correct seasonings, if necessary.)

To assemble, line bowl with cabbage leaves. Pack some of the meat mixture on top and sprinkle with salt and pepper. Cover with more cabbage leaves and again pack with meat. Season and continue process until all the meat is used. End with cabbage leaves and fold bacon ends over. If desired, flavor the cabbage with a generous splash of brandy. Seal with heavy tin foil and place in a **bain marie**.

Bake in preheated oven for 1½ hours. Remove foil and bake another 30 minutes or until firm to the touch. To serve, invert dish onto a warmed platter. Drain off liquid and incorporate in the sauce.

Brown Caper Sauce

4 tbsps butter
½ onion, chopped fine
⅓ cup flour
1 oz capers with juice

1¼ cups chicken or beef broth, warmed
¼ cup **glace de viande** or 1 tsp beef extract

Prepare a **roux** by melting butter in a heavy-bottomed pan. Sauté onion and add flour. Brown flour until very dark. Slowly add broth, stirring continuously. Cover and cook 20 to 25 minutes over low heat. Before serving add the **glace de viande** and capers. Check for seasoning.

Carottes à la Vichy   ## Carrots Vichy

1 bunch of carrots
½ tsp salt
4 tbsps butter
salt and pepper
1 tsp sugar
chopped parsley

Scrape, wash and slice the carrots. Put the slices in boiling water. Add salt and cook for 15 minutes.

In a heavy pot melt the butter and add the drained carrots, rolling them in the butter. Add the sugar and salt and pepper to taste. Let simmer slowly for 10 minutes until the carrots have absorbed all the butter. Put them in a vegetable dish, sprinkle with parsley and serve.

Pouding aux Pommes à l'Orange   Apple and Orange Pudding

½ cup sugar
½ cup butter
1 egg
1 cup flour
1 tsp baking soda
½ tsp cinnamon
½ tsp salt
½ tsp nutmeg
1½ cups coarsely-grated apples
$1/3$ cup cream
grated rind of 1 orange

Beat the sugar, butter, and egg together until creamy. Add the flour and remaining ingredients and mix well. Transfer to a greased ovenproof soufflé dish or pyrex dish. Bake in a 350° oven for 50 minutes to 1 hour.

Serve with orange custard cream (recipe follows).

Orange Sauce

$1/3$ cup sugar
3 egg yolks
1 tbsp cornstarch
2 cups orange juice, heated
¼ cup orange-flavored liqueur *(Curaçao or Grand Marnier)*

Beat the sugar and the eggs until lemon-colored. Add the cornstarch. Bring the orange juice to a boil and pour slowly over the egg mixture. Pour into a double boiler and cook, stirring, until the mixture coats the spoon. Add the liqueur. Let the sauce cool and serve over the apple pudding.

Diner à six   ## Dinner for six

Timbales aux Champignons et Celeri
Poulet à l'Ail
Céleri Scorvienne
Tarte aux Pommes

Egg Timbales with Mushrooms and Celery Vinaigrette
Garlic Chicken
Braised Celery and Apples with Walnut Sauce
Apple-Applesauce Tart

Timbales

Egg Timbales with Mushrooms and Celery Vinaigrette

4 hard-cooked eggs
¼ cup tomato sauce
  (or ketchup)
¼ cup mayonnaise
2 additional egg whites

1 env unflavored gelatin
salt and pepper
1 tsp prepared mustard
1 tsp chopped parsley

When the hard-cooked eggs are cool, separate the whites from the yolks. Finely chop the whites and combine them with the tomato sauce and mayonnaise. Season with salt and pepper to taste.

Soften the gelatin in ¼ cup cold water, then dissolve it over hot water. Beat the additional egg whites until they are stiff but not dry and combine them with the tomato sauce mixture; stir in dissolved gelatin.

In a separate bowl, mash the yolks and season them with salt, pepper and parsley; moisten mixture with just enough mustard to be able to form a ball. Divide mixture into 8 balls.

Fill 8 timbales or baba molds halfway with the egg white mixture. Drop 1 egg yolk ball into each mold and fill it with remaining egg white mixture. Refrigerate for 45 minutes or more, until set. Unmold timbales and surround with Celery and Mushroom Vinaigrette.

Celery and mushroom vinaigrette: Cut off the base of a stalk of celery 3 inches from the bottom. Peel it and cut into 8 wedges. Boil in water for 15 minutes; drain and toss in Vinaigrette (see recipe). Slice $1/3$ lb mushrooms and toss them in more Vinaigrette. Arrange around egg timbales as an appetizer.

Poulet à l'Ail

Garlic Chicken

2 frying chickens,
  2 to 3 lbs each
salt and pepper to taste
2 tbsps in all: aromatic
  herbs, including oregano or
  marjoram, thyme, savory, sage,
  rosemary (fresh if possible)

3 tbsps butter
3 tbsps olive oil
20 cloves of garlic,
  peeled and crushed
½ cup port
flour

Cut the chicken in serving pieces and put in a large bowl. Toss the chicken with salt, pepper and the chopped herbs.

Sauté the chicken pieces lightly in butter and oil and place in a fireproof casserole. Add all the peeled and crushed garlic cloves. Pour port over it, cover tightly and seal edges with a mixture of flour and water. Set in a preheated oven 350° oven and bake for one hour and 15 minutes. Break the seal of paste just before serving.

Céleri Scorvienne

Braised Celery and Apples with Walnut Sauce

6 to 8 servings

1 bunch celery (about 2 lbs)	1 tsp paprika
1 onion, chopped	¼ cup butter or margarine
1 lb apples, peeled, cored and quartered	1 egg yolk
	$1/3$ cup cream
1 to 1½ cups bouillon	parsley
½ cup ground walnuts	salt and pepper

Peel, wash and cut celery into 2-inch pieces; cook in boiling water about 10 minutes and drain. Melt half of the butter in a heavy pot and lightly sauté the chopped onion. Then add the celery and sauté but do not let it brown. Add ½ cup of broth and simmer for a few minutes. Add salt and pepper. Cut apples into wedges and add to celery. Simmer for 10 to 15 minutes more until the apples are soft, adding more bouillon as necessary.

Melt the remaining butter in a pan and add walnuts, remaining broth, paprika and the egg yolk mixed with cream. Do not let this mixture boil, but when heated, pour over the celery and apples arranged in vegetable dish; sprinkle with parsley and serve.

Tarte aux Pommes

Apple-Applesauce Tart

For the dough:
½ cup butter
1½ cups flour
1 egg yolk
$1/3$ cup sugar

To assemble tart:
2 cups applesauce
4 medium green apples, peeled, halved, and thinly sliced
4 tbsps apricot jam

Combine the ingredients for the dough, forming them into a ball and refrigerate for at least 1 hour. Pat out the dough to a thickness of about ⅛ to ¼ inch, then use to line a 10-inch tart pan. Dough will not hold together like a normal pie dough because it is too "short." Just press it into the pan with your fingers, patting it as evenly as possible.

Spread the applesauce in tart. Arrange the thinly sliced apples on top. Cover with a piece of foil and bake at 375° for 45 minutes. Remove foil and bake 20 to 30 minutes longer, until the crust is crisp. Brush jam over the top and serve tart lukewarm.

Diner à six

Dinner for Six

Potage Breton
Côtes du porc Charcutière
Purée Cherreuse
Croûtes aux Pêches

Breton Soup
Pork Chops
Potato and Turnip Purée
Peaches on Canapes

Potage Breton — Breton Soup

2 pkgs cream cheese
2 cups milk
1 clove garlic, minced
½ cucumber, chopped
a few mint leaves
1 tsp chervil
chopped parsley for
  garnish

Mix all the ingredients together and bring to a boil. Purée in the blender. Serve sprinkled with parsley.

Côtes du Porc Charcutière — Pork Chops

1 pork chop per serving
flour
oil
butter
salt and pepper
½ cup vinegar
1 cup white wine or broth
2 shallots, chopped
2 or 3 **cornichons** (small
  sour pickles)

Flour the chops on both sides and brown in oil and butter. Cook slowly for about 30 to 45 minutes, adding a little broth to prevent burning.

When cooked, add the vinegar, wine or broth, chopped shallots, diced pickles and salt and pepper to taste, sauté quickly, and serve.

Purée Cherreuse — Potato and Turnip Purée

1 lb potatoes
1 lb turnips
4 tbsps butter for each
  vegetable
salt
pepper
½ cup of cream (¼ cup for each
  vegetable)
nutmeg

Peel and wash the potatoes and the turnips. Boil each separately in salted water for 20 minutes, or until tender.

Mash each separately, adding the butter, salt, pepper, cream and nutmeg to taste. Mix the two purées together and serve.

Croûtes aux Pêches — Peaches on Canapes

2 eggs
2 tbsps sugar
⅓ cup cream
1 tsp vanilla
1 pinch of cinnamon
3 peaches
1 cup water, ½ cup sugar,
  for poaching
butter
6 pcs of French bread
Sabayon Sauce

Beat the eggs with the sugar in a deep, flat dish. Add the cream, vanilla and cinnamon.

Poach the peaches in a syrup of one cup of water and ½ cup of sugar. Cut the bread the same size as the peaches. Dip each piece of bread into the egg mixture and fry in butter on both sides, until golden brown. Place on a serving platter and top each with a peach half, hollow side down. Cover all with the Sabayon Sauce.

Sabayon Sauce

3 tbsps sugar
3 egg yolks
6 tbsps sherry or white wine

Beat the egg yolks, sugar and sherry in a double boiler over warm water until very thick. The sauce will keep 2 hours if made ahead of time.

APPETIZERS

"Yes - No - Maybe?"

The word appetizer *always seems to cause confusion when used in the sense of hors d'oeuvre or entrée. If you mean appetizer, yes - no - maybe?, you are planning to serve it before the dinner, probably along with cocktails.*

Appetizers

Henri-Paul Pellaprat was the celebrated chef of the Cordon Bleu in Paris and my teacher for four years. He was a wonderfully kind man and a gifted chef. He is the one who taught me my words of inspiration: Never let anything dampen your spirits! *These are important words to remember in cooking. Even the best chefs have flops once in a while, but they are great chefs because they know how to remedy them.*

Pellaprat had his flops, too. I was helping him in his own kitchen for a dinner party, shortly after I joined the Cordon Bleu. I was honored to assist him at his home, because there he would be himself, cooking the most beautiful dinners for his friends, who included world-famous dignitaries and other chefs. Henri had a soufflé in the oven that was not rising ~ and you know if you have a soufflé that hasn't budged in the first ten minutes, it never will rise.

So Pellaprat called to me to quickly whip up some egg whites. I didn't ask questions then ~ I just did what he said. I gave them to him but then just had to ask, "Henri, what are you doing?" He replied, "I don't know!" ~ but he did, of course, for he folded the egg whites into the soufflé, put it back in the oven, and it puffed up into a beautifully high soufflé.

I remembered Pellaprat when I had my own first disaster. I was preparing an elegant lunch for ten; my employer had requested quail in the nest, trout in jelly, asparagus ~ no expenses spared! And I had suggested for dessert the very showy and delicious Riz à l'Impératrice *(a tall, molded dessert made with sweetened rice, Bavarian cream, and decorated with glacéed fruits to resemble a stained-glass window).*

Everything went well until it came time for the dessert. I unmolded the dish and it went down on the platter like a pancake! The serving maid looked at me in horror ~ "What are we going to do?," she said, "I can't serve something that looks like that!" I kept my wits, remembering, "Never let anything dampen your spirits" and told her to help me fix it. She got out the sherbet glasses, and we spooned the dessert into the glasses and decorated it with the glacéed fruits. The maid looked much happier now, and thought she might be able to serve the

Continued

dessert after all. "Let's give it a name," she said. "Okay, you're so smart, what shall we call it?"

"Well, it was supposed to be an empress anyway, let's call it the Royal Flop!" So we did! It was so successful that later my employer came into the kitchen to get the recipe for one of her guests. I told her, "I can give you the recipe, but your friend will have to make her own flop!"

Pâté de Foie Josephine

Josephine's Best Liver Pâté

1 lb of fresh pork liver
¾ lb of pork **fat back**
1 onion chopped
2 cloves of garlic
2 eggs
2 tbsps of flour
1 cup of cream
1 cup of milk

1½ tsps salt
¾ tsp pepper
½ tsp allspice
¼ tsp of ground cloves
¼ tsp thyme
1 bay leaf
¼ cup cognac (optional)
3 to 4 slices of **fat back,**
   cut ⅛ inch thick or **caul**

Preheat oven to 350°.

Grind liver and fat together or ask the butcher to do it. Chop very fine the onion and garlic; mix all together with the eggs, flour, cream, milk and spices — and cognac, if desired. Line a terrine (meatloaf or pyrex dish) with the thin strips of fat back or with the caul to overlap; place pâté mixture in dish with bay leaf on top. Fold over caul or extra fat back strips, cover dish and place in the center of a large pan filled with water to cover dish halfway. Bake in center rack of oven for 1 to 1½ hours. Remove from oven and take off cover, let it cool and when cool, unmold and chill. May be served in slices as first course, luncheon dish or on bread as an appetizer. This mixture can be put through the blender before baking if a finer texture is desired.

Note: This recipe appears also in my first book, *Cooking with Josephine.* I repeat it here because it is one of the dishes I make most often.

Fondus de Belgique

Cheese Fondue (Belgian Recipe)
8 servings

2 cups Béchamel sauce
   (see recipe)
3½ oz grated cheese (part
   Swiss and part Parmesan)

1 or 2 egg whites
bread crumbs
3 egg yolks
deep fat for frying

Combine Béchamel sauce, cheese, and egg yolks. Spread this mixture in greased rectangular pan. Allow to cool; overnight is all right.

With knife, cut into 2-inch squares. Roll squares in egg white and bread crumbs and fry in deep fat until golden brown. Serve hot with a parsley garnish.

Rissoles de Volailles

Chicken Patties
6 servings

2 cups leftover chicken
1 cup thick Béchamel sauce
salt and pepper to taste
nutmeg to taste
1 tsp parsley, chopped

puff paste or pâte brisée
  (see recipe)
For baked pastries:
  1 egg, beaten with 1 tbsp milk
For fried pastries:
  deep fat for frying

Chop the leftover chicken in very small pieces and add to the Béchamel sauce. Season to taste with salt, pepper, nutmeg, and parsley. Set aside.

Roll out the puff paste to a thickness of ¼-inch. Use a plain or fancy, round or oval pastry cutter to cut out two pieces for each rissole. Put a small mound of chicken filling in the center of one piece, moisten the edges, and put another piece of dough on top of the filling, pressing the edges well to seal. Repeat until all are filled.

To fry the rissoles: Heat deep hot fat and fry the rissoles for a few minutes, until browned on both sides.

To bake the rissoles: Preheat the oven to 375°. Place the rissoles on a baking sheet and bake for 25 minutes. The patties may be glazed with the egg and milk mixture.

Serve warm. These patties may be made in advance and reheated.

Tarte aux Blettes

Swiss Chard Tart
6 to 8 servings

½ lb puff paste or pâte brisée
1 or 2 bunches of Swiss chard
8 tbsps butter
salt and pepper
½ tsp nutmeg

½ lb onions, minced
2 large cloves of garlic, minced
1 tbsp oil
½ lb tomatoes, peeled and seeded
1 large sprig thyme
½ cup Gruyère cheese

Have pâte brisée or puff paste prepared. Preheat oven to 350°.

Roll the paste to ⅛-inch thickness. Grease and flour a pie dish and line with paste. Prick the bottom with a fork. Refrigerate a few minutes (to prevent shrinking when cooking).

Cut the chard greens (the stems can be reserved for another use), wash and cook in 4 tbsp melted butter. Cook very slowly until the leaves are very limp and all the moisture has been absorbed. Add salt, pepper and nutmeg.

Mince the onion and garlic and cook them in 2 tbsp butter and 1 tbsp oil, until they are translucent but not brown. Peel and seed the tomatoes and put them in 2 tbsp butter. Cook gently until all of their liquid has evaporated. Mix them with the onions and the garlic. Add the thyme, salt, and pepper.

Continued

Put half of the tomatoes and onions in the bottom of the crust. Sprinkle with half of the grated cheese and then add the chard, the rest of the tomatoes and onions, and the rest of the cheese. Cook for 20 minutes. Reduce to 300°F and cook 25 minutes longer. The tart can be served hot or cold.

Note: This dish makes an excellent hors d'oeuvre, or an accompaniment for a roast or grilled meat.

Fouace aux Anchois — Anchovy Pizza

This takes less than ¾ of an hour to prepare, and 20 minutes to bake.

1¾ cups flour
1 tbsp yeast
½ cup lukewarm water
1 tsp sugar
2 tbsps olive oil for dough
1 pinch salt
3-4 tomatoes, peeled
chopped ripe olives

2 onions, peeled and chopped
3 tbsps olive oil for sautéing
salt and pepper
1 clove garlic, minced
1 sprig fresh thyme
1 bay leaf
¼ lb Parmesan cheese
12 or more anchovy filets
½ tsp oregano, chopped

Put the flour in a large bowl. In a small bowl dissolve the yeast with a small amount of tepid water and the sugar. Let it ferment a little. Then add the yeast to the flour along with the olive oil, additional warm water, if needed, and the salt. Mix together, knead for a few minutes, then cover with a towel and let it rest in a warm place for ½ hour.

Meanwhile peel and cut the tomatoes, peel and chop the onions, and sauté the onions in olive oil. Add the tomatoes, salt, pepper, garlic, thyme, and bay leaf.

Roll the dough on a baking sheet to form a circle. Make border all around with extra dough or by rolling up the edges. Spread the tomato fondue on the dough, and top with the Parmesan, the anchovies, and the olives. Sprinkle with chopped oregano and bake in a 375°, preheated oven for about 20 minutes.

Trempette — Raw Vegetable Dip

¼ cup butter
1 small onion, minced
2 cloves garlic, minced
2 tbsps flour
1 cup light cream

½ cup white wine
salt and pepper to taste
⅛ tsp cayenne pepper or hot sauce
½ cup Swiss or Cheddar cheese

Melt the butter and sauté the onions and garlic without allowing them to brown. Add the flour and stir for a few seconds, continue stirring and add the cream; then stir in the wine. Season to taste with salt, pepper and cayenne. Cook in a double boiler for about 20 minutes. Remove from the heat, add the cheese and stir until melted.

Serve warm or cold with strips of raw vegetables or with potato or corn chips. Serve with cocktails.

Hors d'Oeuvre Chaud de Tomates
Hot Tomato Hors d'Oeuvres

4 to 6 servings

1 tbsp mustard
1 tbsp brown sugar
3 tomatoes, sliced
salt and pepper
bread crumbs
2 tbsps butter
6 rounds of toasted bread, buttered

Make a paste with the mustard and sugar. Spread the mixture on the tomato slices. Sprinkle with salt and pepper. Dip the coated side of tomatoes in bread crumbs, dot with butter and broil for 5 minutes. Place each on a piece of buttered toast and serve.

Variation:
3 tomatoes, sliced
3 tbsps onion juice
salt and pepper
sautéed mushrooms
juice of 1 lemon
1 egg, beaten
bread crumbs
hot fat for frying

Marinate the tomatoes well in onion juice, salt, pepper, and lemon juice. Dip in egg and then in bread crumbs. Fry in deep hot fat. Drain and serve alongside mushrooms sautéed with chopped garlic and parsley, and moistened with butter and paprika.

Oeufs Farcis
Stuffed Eggs

4 to 6 servings

2 eggs per serving
1 tsp mayonnaise per serving
1 tsp prepared mustard
1 tbsp chives
1 tsp parsley
salt and pepper

Hard cook the eggs for 10 to 12 minutes. Set in cold water. Cut in half lengthwise and remove the yolks. Mix the yolks with the remaining ingredients. If the filling is not soft enough, add a little more mayonnaise. Refill the egg whites and serve on lettuce leaves.

Variations: The yolks can be mixed with a number of different ingredients:
—Butter, Worcestershire, chopped chives, salt and pepper;
—Minced ham, dry mustard, salt and pepper;
—Cold meat or fish, finely minced and seasoned with onion juice, salt, pepper, a little butter and parsley; or
—Pâté, shrimp, lobster spread, spinach, etc.

Beignets Bretons   Brittany Fritters
4 to 6 servings

2 crêpes *(see recipe)* for each serving
½ lb ham, ground
1 onion, chopped
1 tbsp cream

1 egg
1 recipe fritter batter *(see below)*
deep fat for frying

Prepare the crêpes. Mix the ham, onion, cream and egg and use this mixture to fill the crêpes. Fold over and fasten with toothpicks. Dip filled crêpes in batter and fry in deep hot fat for 2 to 3 minutes. Drain on paper towels. Serve hot.

Pâte à Beignets   Fritter Batter

1 cup flour
¼ tsp salt
½ tsp cinnamon
⅓ cup milk

2 eggs, separated
2 extra egg whites
1 tbsp oil
3 tbsps sugar (if batter is for dessert fritters)

Sift together the flour, salt and cinnamon. Mix the egg yolks and the milk. Beat the 4 egg whites well.

Add the yolks and milk to the flour, then quickly add the well-beaten egg whites. Mix well, then add the oil and sugar.

Let the batter stand at room temperature at least 20 minutes or longer (1 to 2 hours if time permits).

Drop spoonfuls of the batter into hot fat, cooking until brown on all sides.

Les Feuilles d'Oignons Farcis   Stuffed Onion Leaves

1 or 2 large onions
leftover meat of any kind:
   veal, pork, beef, chicken, game, etc.
1 tbsp herbs in all, a mixture, or one of the following: thyme, parsley, tarragon
½ lb mashed potatoes

1 egg
1 green onion
pinch of cayenne, cloves, and allspice
salt and pepper
slightly beaten egg
bread crumbs
2 tbsps butter
2 tbsps oil

Remove outer skins of onions, immerse in water, and boil the onions for 5 minutes, reduce the heat and simmer for 15 minutes more. Drain and let them cool, then separate the layers one by one (it is very easy to do this if the onion is not overcooked), laying the leaves on paper towels. The heart will be too small to be used and may be saved for other purposes.

Prepare the stuffing: put the meat, herbs, and green onion through a grinder. Mix with the mashed potatoes, the egg, spices and salt and pepper.

Put a tsp of stuffing on each of the leaves and roll each up in the form of a small sausage (sometimes it may require two leaves). Fasten with a piece of toothpick or tie with thread. The **bouchèes** may be prepared ahead of time to this point. They will keep two days in the refrigerator, covered, or for several months in the freezer.

When ready to use, roll each little sausage in flour first, then in slightly beaten egg (egg whites can be used if they are on hand), then in bread crumbs. Sauté them in butter and oil, turning them over very carefully. Before serving as an appetizer, dip them in melted butter mixed with mustard. Serve on a tray with toothpicks.

They also make a very good first course. Follow the same procedure for stuffing the onion leaves. Lay them in an ovenproof dish, cover with a sauce: tomato, mousseline, Béchamel, etc. Sprinkle with cheese and bake at 375°, until the sauce bubbles.

 **JOSEPHINE SAYS:**

You Americans confuse the terms entrée, appetizer, and hors d'oeuvre. An appetizer is served with the drinks, but the hors d'oeuvres come either before or after the soup course, traditionally speaking. Several kinds of hors d'oeuvres are usually passed together on a tray. An appetizer can be a canapé or bouchée.

Canapés

Thoughts turn to canapés when planning get-togethers with friends. Here are several canapés with enough originality to be pleasing to the eye as well as to the palate — your guests may be almost more interested in the food than in the drinks!

Canapés au Roquefort   ### Roquefort Canapés

4 oz Roquefort or any blue cheese
2 tbsps butter
½ tsp Worcestershire
⅛ tsp pepper
2 oz ground walnuts
parsley or walnut pieces
toast rounds or fried bread

Mash the cheese with the butter and add the Worcestershire, pepper and walnuts. Spread this mixture on toast rounds or fried bread. Sprinkle with parsley or put a piece of walnut in the center of each canapé. For a more decorative look, soften some butter and use a fluted tube and pastry bag to form a ring around the edges.

Canapés Hollandais   Dutch Canapés

mustard, mixed with butter
1 pinch cayenne pepper, or
  few drops of hot pepper
  sauce
toasted bread
grated Edam or Gouda
  cheese
4 oz cream cheese
chopped parsley
capers (optional)

Blend the mustard butter with a little cayenne pepper (or a few drops of hot pepper sauce) and the cream cheese. Spread the mixture on round pieces of toasted or fried bread. Grate some Edam or Gouda cheese and sprinkle over each canapé. Surround with a ring of chopped parsley.

For a fancier pattern, cut a few strips of cheese in fine julienne strips and criss-cross them on the butter-cheese mixture. Put a caper in the intersections.

Canapés de Camembert   Camembert Canapés

4 oz Camembert cheese
2 oz butter
⅛ tsp pepper
black olives
toast rounds

Mix the ingredients well and spread on round pieces of bread which have been toasted or fried. Use a small fluted tube and pastry bag filled with the same mixture to make a ring around the outside of each canapé. Put half a black olive in the center of each.

Canapés de Gruyère   Gruyère Canapés

4 oz Gruyère cheese
4 oz butter
⅛ tsp prepared horseradish
pepper
slices of salami
bread rounds

Grate the cheese and set aside. Mix the butter and horseradish thoroughly. Spread rounds of bread with this mixture. Put a round of salami on top of each and sprinkle with pepper and grated cheese. Put under the broiler until the cheese is browned.

Canapé au Concombre   Cucumber Canapés

4 oz blue cheese
4 tbsps butter
toast rounds
1 pinch cayenne
cucumber slices, seeded
red radishes, sliced

Blend the cheese and butter thoroughly and add the cayenne. Spread this mixture on toast rounds and put a slice of seeded cucumber on each one. Decorate with a slice of red radish.

Canapé de Brie

Brie Canapés

4 tbsps butter
4 oz Brie

$1/3$ cup toasted almonds, powdered
toast rounds

Mix butter and cheese, add the powdered almonds and mix well. Spread on round pieces of toasted or fried bread. Dust tops with additional almond powder.

Croutons au Fromage

Open-Faced Sandwiches

1 pkg cream cheese
4 oz blue cheese
¼ cup butter
1 cup sour cream
1 clove garlic, chopped
1 tbsp chives or scallion green, chopped

1 tbsp lemon juice
1 tbsp fennel or fresh dill leaves, chopped
½ tsp pepper
a little salt, if needed
½ cup walnuts, ground
rye or white toast

Mix the cream cheese, blue cheese and butter together thoroughly until creamy. Add the remaining ingredients and chill. Spread on slices of rye bread or slightly-toasted white bread.

Other suggestions:
—Whole wheat bread, buttered and topped with thin slices of apple and the cheese mixture.
—Tomato slices topped with the cheese mixture and one rolled anchovy.
—Salami slices topped with chopped, marinated cabbage. Top with a slice of small sour pickle.
—Liver pâté topped with a thin slice of onion.

Champignons Marinés

Marinated Mushrooms
6 servings

1 lb mushrooms, sliced if large, otherwise left whole
1 tbsp vinegar
3 tbsps oil
1 shallot, minced

1 tsp mustard
few drops of Worcestershire
1 clove garlic, minced
1 tbsp chopped parsley
salt, pepper

Combine all the ingredients above except the mushrooms. Mix well and add the mushrooms. Cover and let marinate overnight or longer. If this is not to be served within 24 hours, it would be better to blanch the mushrooms for five minutes in lemon water and drain well before adding them to the marinade. Serve as an hôrs d'oeuvre with crackers or french or rye bread.

Champignons Farcis   Mushrooms Stuffed with Crab Meat

1 pkg (8 oz) cream cheese,
   Camembert, or Brie
½ lb crab meat
1 tbsp lemon juice
1 tsp Worcestershire
½ tsp salt
¼ tsp pepper
1 tbsp in all of chopped
   parsley and chives
2 to 3 doz large mushrooms

Whip the cream cheese until fluffy; mix in the crab meat. Add the lemon juice, seasonings and herbs. Wash the mushrooms, removing the stems, which can be saved for another use. Fill the caps with the cheese-crab meat mixture. Store in the refrigerator until serving time.

Note: Shrimp or fish can be used in place of crab.

JOSEPHINE SAYS:

I use a Cuisinart at home, but I never use one in my classes. I don't want students to think they must have one. I used to spend so much time pounding fish, pounding nuts, pounding things for Pellaprat when I was at the Cordon Bleu; now I finally got wise and use both a Cuisinart and a blender.

BUDGET ENTREES, SOUPS, MEATLESS DISHES, LEFTOVERS

"Sacramento, California!"

One of my former employers highly disapproved of my saying "Sacre bleu!" when I worked in his kitchen. Ever since then, I've used "Sacramento, California!" The next story is about another one of my employers, followed by some economic recipes for entrées. I must point out here that this word, entrée, is one of my pet peeves. In France it means ~ and that is how I mean it ~ a dish served between *the chief courses. In America, for many people, it has come to mean* the *chief course.*

Budget Entrées: Soups, Meatless Dishes, Leftovers

Some of my happiest days were spent working for Mrs. George Oppen. She was my favorite boss and was very kind to me. I still pray for her daily.

I worked for her from 1927 to 1935, in her beautiful house in San Francisco. She was only eight years older than I and very petite ~ we were just about the same size ~ and I think that's why she liked me so much! She used to say "My Josephine." Her house was decorated in the delicate Louis XV style which matched her small size.

I used to wear her clothes. When she was tired of one of her dresses, she would say to me, "Josephine, why don't you take this dress?" She was very extravagant with her clothes and with her money. If she gave a big dinner party and everything went well (and it usually did), she would come to me afterward, always with a bottle of champagne ~ because she knew how much I liked it ~ and $10 or $20, never less than that.

But she wasn't that way with everyone. She could be very temperamental with her help. I remember Mae, our serving maid, who was a very pretty, very tall Irish girl. She hadn't been at the Oppens too long when she broke one of Mrs. Oppen's crystal glasses while putting them away. Mae came in to see me in the kitchen, all in a fluster, and in her very thick Irish voice she said she didn't want to tell anyone what had

Continued

happened. I knew the glasses were expensive because I had been with Mrs. Oppen in Venice when she bought them. Over $1,500 a set, a lot of money in those days. But I told her to tell Mrs. Oppen ~ that would be better than letting someone else get the blame. So when Mrs. Oppen came home that day, Mae went to tell her. Even in the kitchen I could hear Mrs. Oppen as she flew into a rage ~ she was furious! "My lovely Venetian glass! How did it happen?"

Mae took Mrs. Oppen into the pantry and showed her. "This is how it happened," and she dropped another glass on the floor in a demonstration. I don't need to tell you that Mrs. Oppen fired Mae on the spot. I'd never seen her so angry! I asked her why she fired Mae so soon, for now there was no one to serve the meals. "Well," she said, "I didn't like Mae anyway. She was too tall for my furniture."

JOSEPHINE SAYS:

Learn to cook so that you don't have to measure everything; then your meals will have the flavor of originality. But some measurements, such as those for pastry or baked desserts, must be exact in order for the product to come out right.

Don't be too precise when adding wine to your cooking. It should be as much or as little as you like, according to your taste. By all means, taste your cooking as you go along. I do!

Langue de Boeuf Bagnette

Beef Tongue with Parsley Sauce

1 beef tongue
1 carrot
1 onion
1 stalk of celery
1 laurel (bay) leaf
2 – 3 sprigs of thyme
salt and pepper
Sauce Bagnette *(below)*

Soak the tongue for several hours to take all the blood out. Put it in a large pot, cover with cold water, and add the vegetables and herbs. Bring it to a boil, add the salt and pepper, and simmer for at least 2 hours.

Remove the tongue, trim and skin it, put it back in the broth and cook for ½ hour longer, until tender. Leave it in the broth until ready to serve.

Sauce Bagnette

1 cup chopped parsley
2 cloves garlic, chopped
1 tbsp mustard
6 tbsps oil
2 tbsps vinegar
salt and pepper
1 tbsp Worcestershire

Chop the parsley very fine, add the chopped garlic, the mustard, oil, vinegar, Worcestershire, and salt and pepper. Mix well and serve with the tongue, which may be served either hot or cold.

Fricadelle de Boeuf Sauce Tomate
Cake of Beef with Tomato Sauce

leftover beef
mashed potato
salt and pepper
½ stick butter

one large onion
1 egg
parsley
thyme
chervil or tarragon

Grind meat in the fine grinder and mix with half its weight of mashed potato, add salt and pepper to taste. Chop the onion and sauté in butter, add meat, the herbs, one sprig of thyme all chopped, then add the egg and let it cool. Divide into balls, flatten to make like a very small pancake, fry them in butter, and serve with tomato sauce or another sauce of your choice.

Poisson Especial
Leftover Fish

about ½ lb or more
   leftover fish
2 green onions
1 tbsp tarragon
1 boiled potato chopped
2 fresh tomatoes
vinaigrette sauce

3 tbsps oil
1 tbsp vinegar
1 tsp mustard
few drops of Worcestershire
salt and pepper
2 hard cooked eggs
parsley for sprinkling over

Cut potato and fish in small pieces or dice, season with the vinaigrette sauce, mix oil, vinegar, mustard, Worcestershire, salt and pepper, toss fish and potato in the sauce, add green onion and tarragon chopped. Set on a platter, surround with tomato and stuffed eggs.

A Demain Ma Mere
Leftover Fish
4 servings

1 lb spinach, chopped
⅛ stick margarine
⅛ tsp nutmeg

salt, pepper
whatever fish you have
   leftover
Béchamel sauce

Cook spinach, add margarine, nutmeg, salt and pepper to taste. In a fireproof casserole put all the spinach, arrange fish over and top with Béchamel sauce. Sprinkle with grated cheese. Bake in oven 300° for 20 minutes or until brown.

 **JOSEPHINE SAYS:**

Every morning I take everything out of the refrigerator to see what I have. Then I decide what to make. That way I don't waste anything.

Potée Nancéenne (Lorraine)   Nancéene Casserole

4 to 6 servings

1 lb sauerkraut
  (or one large can)
2 tbsps bacon drippings or
  oil
1 cup rice
2 cups broth
2 onions
2 green peppers
1 lb leftover roast pork
¼ lb raw veal
salt and pepper
½ cup white wine or broth
¼ cup butter
2 stalks of celery

    Soak the sauerkraut with enough water to cover (if using canned sauerkraut, drain the water and wash.) Heat 2 tbsps bacon drippings or oil and sauté the sauerkraut.
    Cook the rice in the broth for 15 minutes. Peel and slice the onions and sauté in butter until translucent. Do the same with the celery and green pepper. Mix the vegetables together.
    Grind the leftover roast pork and the raw veal. Season with salt and pepper.
    In a fireproof dish make layers of sauerkraut, meat, rice, vegetables until all the ingredients are used. Finish with a layer of sauerkraut. Pour the wine or broth over. Cover and bake in a 300° oven for 1 hour.

Garbure de Mais   Corn Soup

½ lb bacon in one piece
2 medium tomatoes
2 medium potatoes
1 large onion (sliced)
3 ears of corn or
  1 can creamed corn
salt and pepper to taste
½ tsp nutmeg
2 tbsps butter
½ cup cream
3 cups bouillon or water
1 slice of french bread for
  each soup plate

    In a large pan, cover bacon with water and boil for ¾ of an hour; take water out if too salty and remove the grease. Add the bouillon or water. In a frying pan sauté the onions in the butter and add to liquid; add potatoes cut in dices, tomatoes, the corn, the cream, salt and pepper. Simmer ½ hour and serve with a piece of toasted bread in plate. Sprinkle with grated cheese.

Potage Geminy   Sorrel Soup

This soup is named after Charles-Gabriel LeBegue, Comte de Geminy, who was Governor of the Banque de France during the 19th Century.

2 qts beef broth
2 cups fresh sorrel leaves
1 rounded tbsp tapioca
⅓ cup heavy cream
2 egg yolks
2 tbsps fresh butter
salt, pepper, and a pinch of
  cayenne

    Bring the beef stock to a boil and cook the chopped sorrel leaves until tender. Thicken the broth with tapioca and enrich with a mixture of the cream, egg yolks and butter. Season to taste with salt, pepper, and cayenne. Usually served cold.

Bisque de Crevettes   Shrimp Bisque

1 onion, chopped
4 tbsps oil
2 cups tomato soup
   (canned, or made with
   fresh tomatoes)
salt and pepper
½ lb shrimp, cleaned
½ cup sherry
⅓ cup cream
croutons

Sauté the onion in oil. Add the soup, salt and pepper, the shrimp and sherry. Add the cream just before serving, and serve hot with fried croutons.

Soupe aux Cerises Montmorency   Cherry Soup Montmorency

¼ cube butter
1½ tbsps flour
3 cups pitted black
   cherries
¾ cup sugar
1½ qts hot water
4 tbsps Kirsch

Melt butter, add flour and little by little the hot water. Add sugar, stir until melted and cook about 10 to 15 minutes, gently, not galloping. Add cherries and cook for 25 to 30 minutes more, then add Kirsch and pour over slice of French bread sautéed in butter. Serve warm or cold.

Soupe aux Cerises   Cherry/Lemon Soup

1 lb cherries
1 stick cinnamon
juice of lemon and rind
¼ lb sugar
1 qt water
1 cup red wine (Bordeaux)
1 tbsp of tapioca or
   cornstarch

Stone and wash cherries and boil, with water, sugar, cinnamon and lemon for 8 to 10 minutes. Dilute tapioca or cornstarch in a little water and add to cherries.

Boil wine and crushed cherry stones for 5 minutes and add to cherry soup. Put through blender for a finer texture, pour over pieces of French bread *toasted*. Serve warm or cold.

 **JOSEPHINE SAYS:**

For an accent to soups, try adding a *chiffonade:* **a garnish made of finely chopped greens — lettuce, sorrel, chives, parsley, watercress — mixed together or used separately and added to the soup at the last minute.**

Nouilles d'Isigny

Noodles with Sour Cream

6 to 8 servings

This recipe was used at the White House at the time of President Kennedy by Chef Julius Spessot.

10 oz noodles, medium size
4 tbsps butter
½ pt sour cream
½ pt heavy cream
½ cup grated cheese
  (Parmesan or Gruyère)

2 tbsps finely chopped chives
1 tbsp basil or *pesto*
salt and pepper
½ tsp nutmeg

Cook the noodles in a big pot of hot water for 7 to 8 minutes until cooked *al dente*. Drain.

Melt the butter in the same pan. Add the noodles and mix well. Add the sour cream, mix, and add the heavy cream, the cheese, and the herbs. Season with salt, pepper and nutmeg and mix thoroughly. Let it heat through over low heat.

Put on a serving platter and sprinkle with additional cheese.

Nouilles Sauce Marinara

Noodles with Marinara Sauce

4 to 6 servings

1 medium onion, finely
  chopped
3 tbsps olive oil
1 clove garlic, finely
  chopped
5 anchovies, chopped
2 lbs fresh tomatoes,
  peeled and chopped
2 oz white wine
1 tsp oregano, chopped

6 green olives, finely
  chopped
2 bay leaves
½ tsp thyme, chopped
salt and pepper
8 oz noodles or spaghetti
1 tsp salt
4 tbsps butter
2 oz Parmesan cheese

Sauté the onions in olive oil until golden brown. Add the garlic and anchovies and stir for one minute. Add the tomatoes, wine, oregano, olives, bay leaves, thyme, salt and pepper to taste. Simmer for 30 minutes over very low heat.

Cook the spaghetti or noodles in boiling water to which 1 tsp of salt has been added. Cook rapidly for 7 to 10 minutes (or *al dente* — crisp to the bite). Strain and rinse with cold water.

In the same pot, melt the butter, add the pasta and mix thoroughly. Add some sauce and some of the Parmesan cheese. Put in a terrine or large platter. Pour the remaining sauce over and sprinkle with the remaining cheese. Serve at once.

Nouilles Cécile

1 pkg of spinach noodles
1 tsp salt
4 tbsps butter
salt, pepper
nutmeg
2 oz prosciutto, cut
   in small pieces

Noodles Cécilia
6 to 8 servings

1½ cups light cream
⅓ cup Parmesan cheese,
   or any grated cheese
cheese slices for the
   topping
tomato sauce *(see recipe)*

Put the spinach noodles in salted boiling water and boil for 6 to 7 minutes or until cooked *al dente*. Drain and add the butter, salt, pepper, nutmeg, prosciutto, cream and the grated cheese.

Divide the mixture among 1½-cup individual baking dishes or put in a casserole. Top each serving with a small slice of cheese and cover the cheese with tomato sauce. Bake in a preheated 400° oven for 15 minutes.

Gnocchis Verts

2 lbs potatoes (about 6)
1½ cups cooked spinach
⅓ cup sifted flour
3 tbsps grated cheese
   (Parmesan or Gruyère)
2 eggs, lightly beaten

Green Potato Dumplings

⅓ tsp nutmeg
4 tbsps butter
½ tsp salt
¼ tsp pepper
additional butter and
   Parmesan cheese

Peel, cook and mash the potatoes. Cook the spinach, drain thoroughly and chop coarsely. Combine the spinach, potatoes, flour, cheese, eggs, nutmeg, butter, salt and pepper. Mix thoroughly. Roll into cigar-shaped portions on a lightly floured board. Cut into 2-inch lengths.

Drop a few at a time into salted boiling water. Boil the water until the gnocchi rise to the surface, about 5 minutes. Drain well.

Serve with grated Parmesan cheese and melted butter in a flat ovenproof dish, which has been placed in the oven for a few minutes, until the sauce begins to bubble. Serve at once, piping hot.

Note: Gnocchi can also be served with tomato sauce or with a Béchamel.

Salade du Vergeret Potager en Gelée
Cucumber-Pineapple Gelatin
6 to 8 servings

2 envs gelatin
½ cup cold water
1 can (8 oz) of crushed
   pineapple (with juice)
1 tsp salt
¼ cup sugar

3 tbsps vinegar
¼ cup lemon juice
1 cup shredded cucumber
1 cup seedless grapes
frosted grapes (optional)
mayonnaise

Continued

Soften the gelatin in cold water. Stir to dissolve. Drain the crushed pineapple well and heat 1 cup of the juice to boiling. Pour juice over the softened gelatin and stir to dissolve thoroughly. Add the salt, sugar, vinegar, lemon juice and remaining pineapple juice if some is left. Mix well and set aside until syrupy.

Fold in the fruit and cucumber. Put in a ring mold or individual molds. Chill completely. Unmold on salad greens. Fill the center with frosted grapes and mayonnaise.

"Soup makes a very cheap main dish. Just ask the butcher for some bones to make a good basic broth. That makes a meal in itself because the broth is extract of meat. Adding beans gives additional protein. Some of my favorite soup recipes follow."

Crème d'Haricots Bonne Femme

Cream of Bean Soup

6 servings

½ lb dried beans or 1 lb fresh shelled beans
1 medium onion, minced
2 small carrots, sliced
1 rib of celery or small celery root, diced
2 tomatoes (medium), peeled
2 qts broth or water (cold)
salt and pepper
1 bay leaf
thyme
1 tsp sweet basil, chopped
1 thick slice of bacon
2 slices of stale bread (for croutons)
2 tbsps butter
⅓ cup **crème fraiche** or heavy cream

If dry beans are to be used, soak them overnight. Prepare all vegetables: peel and mince the onion; slice the carrots; peel and dice the celery; peel and chop the tomatoes.

Place all in a deep pan with the dried or fresh beans. Add the broth or water, and bring to a boil slowly, removing the scum that forms in the top. Add the salt, pepper, bay leaf, and thyme. Cover and simmer very slowly for 45 minutes (dried beans may take a little longer to cook). Remove the bay leaf and the thyme. Purée the soup in the blender or Cuisinart; then return to the pot and add the chopped sweet basil.

Dice the bacon and fry. Cut the bread into large cubes and fry in butter. Bring the soup to a boil and add the bacon. At the last minute add the cream. Serve hot, adding the croutons.

Aigo Bouido

Garlic Soup
6 to 8 servings

20-25 garlic cloves, peeled, about 1½ heads *(see note)*
1 tsp salt
⅛ tsp cloves
⅛ tsp allspice
½ tsp thyme
1 bay leaf, crumbled
1 tbsp parsley, chopped
1 tsp tarragon
3 tbsps oil
1 tsp chervil
1 tsp fennel
1 tsp sorrel (if available)
2 qts water or broth (veal or chicken broth preferred)
1-2 potatoes, diced
2 egg yolks
6-8 slices toasted bread
Parmesan cheese, grated

Place the peeled garlic and add the herbs, finely chopped, in a saucepan. If you do not plan to strain the soup, add the potatoes also. Cook for 30 minutes over low heat. (If you plan to strain the soup, cook the potatoes separately, mash, and add to the completed herb bouillon.)

Beat the egg yolks for about 1 minute in the soup tureen or serving bowl. Add the oil drop by drop while continuing to beat eggs as in making mayonnaise. Just before serving, slowly beat in a cupful of soup, gradually adding the rest.

Serve immediately on the toasted bread slices, sprinkled with grated cheese.

Note: To make peeling the garlic cloves easier, drop them into boiling water for ½ minute.

Soupe au Crabe Josephine

Crab Soup Josephine
6 to 8 servings

4 medium onions, chopped
4 tbsps butter
1 lb crab meat
1 qt chicken broth
2 tbsps butter
1 tbsp flour
1 qt cream (or milk), heated
salt and pepper
1 tbsp curry (rounded)
1 tbsp paprika
parsley

Peel, chop, and sauté the onions in 2 tbsps butter until translucent. Add the crab meat, mixing well and stir in the chicken broth. Simmer 5 to 10 minutes.

Prepare a thin sauce with the remaining 2 tbsps butter and the flour. Stir a few minutes and add the hot cream. Mix with the crab mixture. Add the seasonings, sprinkle with the parsley, and stir. Serve very hot.

Potage Crème de Cresson

Cream of Watercress Soup
8 servings

1 small onion, sliced
2 white of leeks, chopped
2 medium potatoes, sliced
¼ cup butter or margarine
2 qts chicken or veal broth
2 tbsps flour

1 bunch watercress, coarsely chopped
pinch of nutmeg
salt and pepper
1 or 2 egg yolks
1 cup heavy cream
extra leaves of watercress

Melt butter in a heavy saucepan, and add the sliced onions and leeks, sautéing them lightly but not browning them. Add sliced potatoes. Mix in the flour, adding a little of the stock at a time. Cover and bring to a boil, then reduce heat, and simmer for 15 minutes. Then add watercress.

Cook soup for 20 minutes more, adding the nutmeg, salt and pepper. Strain through a fine sieve or mix in blender; return to heat. (Up to this point, the soup can be made in advance. Reheat when ready to serve.) In a mixing bowl, beat egg yolks and cream; add to soup at the last minute without letting it boil. Decorate with minced watercress leaves and serve hot. (Can also be chilled before serving.)

Soupe à l'Oignon

Onion Soup

This wholesome onion soup from Auvergne is quite different.

1 lb onions
¼ cup butter
1 tbsp flour
1 qt broth or water
1 bottle of champagne
salt and pepper
½ tsp cinnamon

½ lb Camembert cheese, grated
6 egg yolks
½ cup cream
1 liquor glass of cognac or sherry
pieces of French bread, fried in butter

Mince the onions and sauté them in butter until browned. Add 1 tbsp of flour, stir, and add broth, champagne, salt and pepper and cinnamon. Bring to a boil slowly, then lower heat, and simmer for ¾ to 1 hour.

In a bowl, beat the egg yolks with the cream. Add the cognac or sherry. Add this mixture to the soup, being careful not to let it boil again.

Set the fried pieces of bread in an ovenproof **terrine,** and pour the soup over them. Sprinkle with grated cheese and set under the broiler until browned. Serve immediately.

Omelette au Poulet Sauce aux Nois
Omelet with Leftover Chicken and Walnut Sauce

6 servings

Sauce:

1 cup walnuts
1 shallot or white part of
   a green onion, chopped
¼ cup butter
1 tbsp flour

1 cup bouillon or chicken
   stock
1½ to 2 cups leftover chicken,
   in small pieces
¼ cup Gruyère or Parmesan
   cheese, grated
½ cup cream

Put the walnuts in a blender and reduce them to a fine pulp. Sauté the chopped shallots in butter. Add the flour and pulverized walnuts. Stir and add the warm bouillon to make a sauce, with about the same consistency as a Béchamel. Add salt and pepper. When thick enough, stir in the chicken and cheese. Remove from the heat, add the cream and mix well. Keep warm.

Omelet:

12 eggs
½ cup butter

salt and pepper
2 tbsps chopped tarragon

Beat the eggs slightly and add the chopped tarragon and salt and pepper. Melt 2 tbsps butter in a small heavy skillet and pour in ½ cup of the beaten eggs. Cook over moderate heat until set but not dry. The egg should be *baveuse* which means moist or mellow. Turn out and keep warm. Repeat until six omelets are made. To serve, pour the sauce over each omelet.

Note: If desired, the eggs can be beaten two at a time and each omelet prepared separately.

Oeufs Farcies aux Epinards
Stuffed Eggs with Spinach

4 to 6 servings

3 slices Virginia ham
   or 1 can deviled ham
1 small onion, chopped
2 hard-cooked eggs
   per serving
1 tsp prepared mustard
1 tsp mayonnaise
salt and pepper to taste

2 to 3 cups of cooked
   spinach, puréed
3 tbsps butter
3 tbsps flour
1½ cup veal or chicken
   broth
nutmeg to taste
⅓ cup grated cheese

Preheat oven to 350°.

Chop the ham and onion with the finest blade of a food chopper or in a Cuisinart. Cut the eggs in half lengthwise. Remove the yolks and mix with the ham, adding the mustard, mayonnaise, salt and pepper to taste. Refill the whites with this mixture.

Continued

Spread the puréed spinach on the bottom of a flameproof dish and arrange the eggs on top to cover.

In a double boiler, prepare a roux with the butter and flour. Add the hot broth and season to taste with salt, pepper, and nutmeg. Allow it to cook 15 to 20 minutes. Remove from heat and pour over the eggs. Sprinkle with cheese and put in the oven to warm through. Then place it under the broiler just long enough to brown it on top.

La Timbale du Roi René

¼ cup butter
1 hard cooked egg
2 tbsps French mustard
½ lb green olives, pitted
2 cups Béchamel sauce
  (see recipe)

Timbale of Leftover Veal and Olives

1 or 2 envs Knox gelatin
  to 2 or 4 cups broth
1 to 2 lbs leftover veal
1 small bottle of capers

Work ¼ cup butter until soft and then add the hard cooked egg yolk and mustard. Fill the olives with this mixture and chill them in the refrigerator. Prepare Béchamel sauce and allow to cool.

Prepare the gelatin, by bringing the broth to a boil. Dissolve one package of gelatin if using 2 cups of broth (2 pkgs gelatin if using 4 cups of broth) in a little cold water. Stir into the boiling broth and let it cool in the refrigerator. Also chill the mold.

Chop the veal finely. Cut the olives in slices, chop the capers and the remnants of olives. Line the bottom of the chilled mold with some gelatin. Cover the bottom and sides with slices of olives and return to the refrigerator to set. Repeat with another coat of gelatin on the bottom and return to the refrigerator for a few minutes. Then mix the Béchamel with the meat, capers and chopped olives and white of egg. Add the remaining gelatin. Season to taste with a little more mustard, salt, pepper and nutmeg. Fill the mold with this mixture. Tap the mold on a table so as not to leave any air between the layers. Put it in the refrigerator for 3 hours or until set.

To unmold, dip the mold in very hot water for a few seconds. Serve cold with or without a sauce: a vinaigrette, highly seasoned with mustard; or a mayonnaise, seasoned with mustard.

 **JOSEPHINE SAYS:**

Brains, sweetbreads, tripe, etc. are the best bargains and so nutritious. Americans eat liver, but even less expensive is tongue, which will make 2 to 3 meals.

Ris de Veau Lorraine

Sweetbreads, Lorraine Style
4 to 6 servings

2 lbs sweetbreads
¼ cup butter
2 shallots
2 cloves garlic
¼ lb bacon

1 tbsp parsley
1 lb mushrooms
salt and pepper
¹/₃ cup cream
fried croutons

Soak the sweetbreads in cold water to remove all the blood. Rinse and put in a pot with cold water. Let the sweetbreads come to a boil, simmer for 10 minutes. Remove, saving the cooking liquid. Rinse sweetbreads with cold water and remove the skin and fat.

Sauté them in the butter until lightly browned. Take out the sweetbreads and keep them warm while sautéing the shallots and garlic in the same pan. Cut the bacon into small dice and add to the shallots and garlic and sauté. Reserve some of the fat for frying the mushrooms; then moisten the pan with ½ cup of sweetbread liquid. Add the parsley.

Cut the mushrooms into quarters and sauté them in another pan in the fat. Add to the mixture, along with the sweetbreads. Simmer for 10 to 12 minutes. At the last minute add salt and pepper and the cream. Warm through.

Arrange on a platter and sprinkle with parsley. Arrange triangles of fried bread around the dish.

Beignets de Foie

Liver Fritters
4 to 6 servings

1 lb liver
½ tsp salt
½ tsp pepper
1 pinch nutmeg
1 pinch cinnamon
2 onions, chopped
1 tbsp butter

1 tbsp parsley, chopped
2 cups bread crumbs
2 egg yolks
2 egg whites, stiffly beaten
1 tbsp flour
fat for deep frying
   (see note)
Soubise sauce *(see sauce recipes)*

Grind the liver and add the salt, pepper, nutmeg, and cinnamon. Chop the onions and sauté in butter until soft and add to liver, along with the parsley, bread crumbs and egg yolks. Beat the egg whites until very stiff and add the flour. Fold into the liver mixture. Mix well and form into balls on a floured dish.

Drop the balls into heated deep fat and cook until brown, which should take about 15 minutes. The fat should not be too hot, but rather maintain the heat as the fritters cook. Serve with Soubise sauce.

Note: The fritters can also be boiled and served with noisette butter, surrounded by bread croutons, and sprinkled with additional parsley.

Foie de Veau à l'Orange

Calves' Liver with Orange
6 servings

4 tbsps butter
6 slices calves liver
  (see note)
flour to coat the liver

salt
pepper
3 oranges

Melt several tbsps of butter in a heavy pan. Roll slices of liver in flour, and fry them in the butter about 2 minutes on each side (the liver should be a little pink). Add salt and pepper.

Squeeze one of the oranges and use the juice to deglaze the pan, scraping all the bits of liver from the bottom. Peel the other oranges, slice them rather thickly and put them in the orange juice to warm. Melt the rest of the butter in the sauce, stirring very quickly.

Arrange the liver on a serving dish and pour the orange juice over it. Arrange the orange slices around it.

Sprinkle with parsley and serve at once.

Note: Other liver can be used, providing it is tender.

La Beuchelle de Nignon

Sweetbreads and Veal Kidneys
6 servings

A recipe of Edward Nignon.

3 veal kidneys
¼ cup butter
3 sweetbreads
1 liquor glass cognac
  or brandy

1 cup **crème fraiche**
  (heavy cream)
¼ lb fresh morels
  (or mushrooms)
2 truffles (optional)
parsley, chopped

Cut the kidneys in thin slices and toss them in 2 tbsps butter. Flambé them with half of the cognac and put them aside.

Blanch the sweetbreads in boiling water for 10 minutes (having first soaked them in water and cleaned them). Drain, trim, and sauté them in the rest of the butter. Flambé them with the cognac or brandy and bind them with half the cream.

Clean and wash the morels (a particular type of French "mushroom"). Sauté in butter, and add the thinly sliced truffles, if desired. Bind them with the other half of the cream. Put all of the ingredients in a heavy pan. Mix together gently, but thoroughly.

Serve hot on a platter sprinkled with parsley. Puff paste **fleurons** can be made and added around the dish.

Cervelle d'Agneau Cardinal Richelieu
Lamb Brains Cardinal Richelieu

4 to 6 servings

6 lamb brains
Court bouillon:
   ½ cup white wine
   1 cup water
   1 onion
   1 carrot
   ½ cup celery
   salt and pepper
   thyme
laurel or bay leaf
3 tbsps butter
1 tbsp oil
1 rounded tbsp flour
1 cup milk, heated
1 tbsp tomato paste
bread crumbs
butter for sautéing
grated cheese

    Soak the brains in cold water for at least 1 hour. Remove the skin. Prepare the court bouillon with the wine, water, vegetables, salt and pepper, and herbs. Let it come to a boil and simmer for 20 minutes. Cool slightly, then add the brains and simmer for 7-10 minutes.
    While the brains are simmering, melt the butter and oil, add the flour and stir for a few seconds. Add the warm milk and the tomato paste and simmer very slowly for 10 minutes. Add the salt and pepper. Preheat oven to 375°.
    Remove the brains from the court bouillon, drain; roll in bread crumbs and sauté in butter until golden brown. Arrange them side by side in an ovenproof dish, cover with the sauce and sprinkle with grated cheese. Bake in a 375° oven for 10-15 minutes.
    Note: Strain and save the court bouillon. It will keep in the refrigerator for at least one week. This court bouillon will make an excellent sauce base for meat or fish.

Marmite du Jardin Potager
Vegetable Marmite

8 to 10 servings

This dish is named for the pot it cooks in. The real "trick" to the preparation is in cooking the vegetables to just the right point.

2 medium onions and
   2 large onions
4 cloves garlic
2 tbsps oil and 2 tbsps butter
1 bunch carrots
1 bunch turnips
1 bunch leeks, cut in
   2-inch lengths
½ bunch celery, cut in
   2-inch pieces
2 qts bouillon or broth
½ bunch swiss chard,
   coarsely chopped
1 small green cabbage,
   in quarters
1 small red cabbage,
   in quarters
1 tbsp each parsley and
   chervil
1 lb potatoes
½ lb peas
1 bunch radishes, cut in
   thick slices
2 or 3 tomatoes, chopped
¼ lb mushrooms, sliced

Continued

Peel, wash, and cut all the vegetables (cut carrots and turnips in two; chop garlic and onions). Sauté onions and garlic in the oil and butter until golden brown; add carrots and turnips, gradually adding medium onions and leeks. Do not let it brown, but add broth and bring to a boil. Reduce heat to simmer, and add celery, swiss chard, and both cabbages (first blanch them in boiling water for 10 minutes and drain). Season vegetables with salt, pepper, parsley and chervil.

Now the potatoes can be added. Wait 10 minutes and add peas, tomatoes, and mushrooms. Cook 5 minutes more. All the vegetables should be cooked the right amount now. Arrange them on a platter. Then rapidly reduce juices by half — over a high flame. Pour over vegetables. If you wish to add leftover pork or beef, the dish is then referred to as a **garbure**.

Boeuf Bouilli — Sauce Piquante

Boiled Beef with Piquante Sauce

2 servings

¾ lb leftover boiled beef
2 or 3 shallots
½ to 1 cup bouillon
4 to 5 tbsps vinegar

salt and pepper
1 tbsp chopped parsley
cornstarch

Cut leftover meat in thin slices and remove extra fat. Layer in a flat fireproof dish. Chop shallots and add to bouillon. Warm, adding vinegar, salt, pepper, and parsley. Mix a small amount of cornstarch with a few tbsps of bouillon, then add to rest of sauce. Add to beef and warm in the oven.

Piquante Sauce:

2 to 3 shallots
5 to 6 tbsps red wine
  vinegar
1 tbsp of chopped small
  sour pickle or gherkin

1 tbsp chopped parsley
1 cup strong consommé
1 tbsp **glace de viande**
salt and pepper

Peel and chop shallot; in a small pot, add vinegar and shallots and reduce mixture to almost 1 tbsp. Add consommé, **glace de viande,** pickle, salt, pepper, and parsley. Bring to boil and then pour over meat; serve.

Boeuf Bouilli Gratiné

Leftover Beef au Gratin
2 servings

¾ lb leftover boiled
  or braised beef
6 mushrooms, chopped
1 or 2 onions, chopped
2 tbsps flour
½ cup white wine
½ cup milk or bouillon

2 tbsps grated Parmesan,
  Gruyère, or Cheddar cheese
¼ cup butter
1 tbsp chopped parsley
1 tbsp bread crumbs
1 clove garlic, chopped

Eliminate the fat from meat; slice in even slices. Chop the onions and sauté in butter until lightly browned. Add mushrooms, garlic, and parsley. Add flour and stir, then add milk or broth (either should be warmed first), the wine, salt, pepper. The sauce should be slightly thick. Simmer for 10 minutes.

Arrange beef on fireproof dish. Pour mushroom - onion sauce over it. Mix bread crumbs and cheese together and sprinkle over meat. Set in oven to warm through, then brown top under the broiler. Accompany with brussel sprouts, turnips, parsnips, or mashed potatoes.

VEGETABLES

"Use Your Noodle!"

In Brittany, I learned a lot about cooking from my grandmother ~ especially about the preparation of vegetables. She had a very plentiful garden and with her wonderful imagination, she would combine many varieties of fruits and vegetables. Use your noodle when you cook and don't be afraid to try something different.

Vegetables

Some Considerations on Cooking Vegetables

Whether boiled, braised, or steamed, vegetables have nothing to gain from overcooking. Most vegetables can be eaten raw; therefore cooking should add to their gastronomic quality, not destroy it.

GREEN VEGETABLES: As an example, when cooking green beans, many people think they have to use a chemical, such as soda, to keep the beans green. However, this is not true if one does the following:

1. Choose *very fresh* vegetables.
2. Wash and drain them well.
3. Use a pot big enough that the vegetables are not overcrowded.
4. Never put salt in the water before putting in the vegetables. (When the water boils with the salt there is a chemical reaction which is not good for the vegetables.) But vegetables may be sprinkled with salt *before* they are plunged into the boiling water.
5. Cook on high heat so the water is boiling the entire time.
6. Do not over-cook. Ten to 15 minutes should be sufficient to cook them (many vegetables require only a few seconds of cooking). They should be crisp to the bite.
7. Drain the vegetables as soon as they are cooked.

(Potatoes and white vegetables should be treated in this same manner.)

DRY VEGETABLES: When cooking dry beans (for example), if you are planning to use them as a vegetable, again, *do not put salt into the cooking water.* The salt will cause them to burst and they will not be as presentable as when they are whole. (As a rule, salt pork will not burst the beans because the salt in the pork is absorbed slowly as the beans simmer.)

If you are planning to purée the beans or to make soup of them, then *do* put salt in the water when you cook them. This will make them easier to purée.

 **JOSEPHINE SAYS:**

Spinach has been called the "broom of the stomach" because of its high digestibility. It is also high in food value, delicate in flavor, and adaptable to a number of uses.

When cooking spinach, it is preferable to use either pyrex, enamel, or stainless steel cookware; otherwise, the spinach will absorb any metallic taste from the pot.

Artichauts Lyonnais

Artichokes Stuffed with Pork and Spinach
6 servings

1 artichoke per serving
1 bunch spinach
2 onions, chopped
4 tbsps butter
salt and pepper

½ lb sausage meat
thin slices of backfat
  or bacon
1 cup white wine
additional butter
½ cup **glace de viande**

Pare and trim the artichokes, and cut the leaves about 2 inches at the top. Blanch for 10 minutes in boiling water. Then rinse under cold water to cool; drain, and remove the choke.

Cook the spinach in boiling water for 5-6 minutes. Drain and chop coarsely. Chop the onions and sauté in butter. Add the spinach, salt and pepper, and the sausage meat. Preheat oven to 350°.

Salt and pepper the inside of the artichokes. Fill with the spinach-meat mixture. Wrap each with a slice of backfat or bacon and tie with string. Place the artichokes side by side in a large, fireproof dish and pour the wine around them. Dot with a few pieces of butter and bake in a 350° oven for 50 to 55 minutes.

Drain the artichokes and remove the strings. Take off the fat and put the artichokes on a dish. Strain the juice. Add the **glace de viande** to the juices; boil down a little and pour over the artichokes.

Topinambours Sauce Ravigote

Jerusalem Artichokes with Ravigote Sauce
4 to 6 servings

1½ lbs Jerusalem artichokes
2 egg yolks (hard-cooked)
2 tbsps oil
1 to 2 tbsps lemon juice
½ cup homemade (or
  commercial) mayonnaise
¼ cup sour cream

1 tbsp mustard (Dijon
  preferred)
1 tbsp capers or sour
  pickle
1 clove garlic, finely chopped
½ tsp each chopped herbs:
  tarragon, parsley, chives

Wash, peel and slice the Jerusalem artichokes. Boil in water for about 4 minutes; drain.

Mash the hard-cooked egg yolks and gradually add the oil and lemon juice, stirring until the mixture is a little thick and well blended. Add the mayonnaise, sour cream, mustard, capers, and garlic. Add the chopped herbs.

Pour the dressing over the artichokes. Toss and chill for several hours before serving.

Note: This sauce is delicious with regular artichokes, cauliflower, broccoli, cabbage, as well as with poached fish and meat.

Topinambours à la Provençale / Jerusalem Artichokes Provençale

4 to 6 servings

1½ lbs Jerusalem artichokes
2 cups stock
2–3 tomatoes, sliced
2 cloves garlic, chopped
1 onion, finely chopped
4 tbsps butter

salt and pepper
nutmeg to taste
1 large pinch chopped fresh thyme and oregano
1 tbsp chopped parsley

Wash and peel the Jerusalem artichokes, dice them and add to boiling stock. Cook for 7 to 10 minutes and drain (but keep the stock for another use). Slice the tomatoes and chop the garlic and onion. Melt the butter in a skillet, and sauté all the vegetables until the onions are slightly browned. Add seasonings. Serve sprinkled with parsley.

Asperges au Vin Blanc / Asparagus in White Wine

6 servings

3 lbs asparagus, peeled
4 oz butter or margarine
1 cup dry white wine

⅓ cup grated cheese, Swiss or Gruyère
salt, pepper

Tie asparagus in a bundle. Melt the butter in a large pot, add the wine, and stir. Place the asparagus on end in the pot and season with salt and pepper to taste. Simmer for 5-7 minutes. Remove the asparagus, untie and lay them in a shallow baking dish. Sprinkle with cheese. Place on a middle rack of a preheated 425° oven, or under a broiler, until cheese has browned.

Asperges en Petit Pois / Asparagus Slices and Peas in Cream

6 servings

2½ to 3 lbs asparagus, peeled and washed
4 tbsps butter or margarine
salt, pepper, cayenne

½ lb tiny peas
greens of 3 to 4 scallions
2 tbsps heavy cream
juice of ½ lemon

Continued

Break off the small tough ends from the asparagus stalks with your fingers; cut the tender part of the stalk into pea-sized pieces, saving the tips for another use. Melt the butter in a heavy pan and add the asparagus. Season with salt, pepper, and a dash of cayenne. Lower the heat and add the peas and scallions. Cook for about 7 minutes; then stir in the cream. Remove from the heat and gently mix in the lemon juice. Serve on a heated platter.

Mousse d'Avocat

Avocado Mousse

6 servings

6 avocados
1 tbsp cognac or brandy
juice of ½ lemon
salt and pepper
1 cup heavy cream, whipped

For decoration:
chopped parsley
pimiento
lettuce leaves
1 lemon

Cut the avocados in half and remove the seeds. Use a tsp to remove some of the pulp, leaving a small coating on the shell.

Make a fine purée of the pulp. Add the cognac, lemon juice, salt and pepper and whipped cream. Fill the avocado shells. Decorate each with chopped parsley in the center and a speck of pimiento at each end. Set them on lettuce leaves. Cut a lemon in half, scalloping the edges. Set one half in the middle of the platter, surround with avocados, and decorate with parsley.

Chou à la Nivernaise

Cabbage with Bacon

6 servings

1 small cabbage (about
  1½ lbs)
salt and pepper
1 clove garlic, shopped
3 to 4 slices of bacon

3 tbsps oil
1 tbsp vinegar
1 tsp mustard
1 tsp Worcestershire

Remove core and heavy ribs from cabbage and shred the cabbage very thinly. Sprinkle with salt, pepper, and chopped garlic. In a skillet heat the bacon, oil, vinegar, mustard and Worcestershire over moderate heat until the bacon has rendered its fat.

Put the cabbage in a warm salad bowl, pour the bacon mixture over it and toss well. Serve at once.

Chou Rouge Forestière

Red Cabbage with Mushrooms and Blueberries

6 servings

1 head red cabbage
½ lb mushrooms
¼ cup butter
1 cup red wine
salt, pepper

1 tbsp each oil and butter
2 cloves garlic, chopped
1 tsp chopped parsley
1 basket blueberries

Wash and clean cabbage; then shred. Melt the butter in skillet; add cabbage, salt and pepper, and stir over heat. Add the wine, cover and cook slowly for 10 to 15 minutes. Wash and slice mushrooms; sauté in the butter, oil, garlic and parsley. Mix with cabbage. Just before serving, coat blueberries in a small amount of melted butter and mix into cabbage and mushrooms.

Carottes Clamart Carrots with Purée of Peas

6 to 8 servings

2 bunches carrots	2 lbs fresh peas or
½ tsp salt	2 pkgs frozen peas
4 tbsps butter	2 or 3 slices of bread
salt and pepper	¼ cup sour cream
½ tsp nutmeg	¼ cup milk or sweet cream
1 tbsp parsley and tarragon, chopped	1 tsp sugar

Fry the slices of bread in butter and cube them. Set aside.

Peel, wash and cut the carrots in thick slices. Cook them for 15 minutes in boiling water, adding ½ tsp salt. Drain. Sauté the carrots in butter, adding a little salt, pepper, nutmeg and the herbs.

Cook the peas in very little water for 10 minutes; purée. Mix the purée of peas with the sour cream and the milk or sweet cream. Add the sugar and a little salt and pepper. Arrange the carrots on a vegetable dish and put the purée of peas over them. Cover with croutons and serve.

Note: This can also be done with other vegetables such as cauliflower, cabbage, or any other vegetable of a contrasting color.

Chou-Fleur en Xephir Cauliflower Soufflé with Sauce Aurore

6 servings

This dish is not the typical soufflé, but a light, delicious way to prepare cauliflower.

	Sauce Aurore:
1 to 2 heads of cauliflower	½ onion, finely chopped
8 tbsps butter	2 tbsps butter
¼ cup cream	1 tsp flour
3 eggs, separated	8 oz tomato sauce
salt, pepper, nutmeg	1 tbsp tomato concentrate
	4 oz **crème frâiche** or sour cream
	2 tsps fresh oregano or marjoram, finely chopped
	¼ cup dry white wine

Continued

Break cauliflower into flowerets and cook in a **blanc** for 15 minutes. Remove from liquid and mash thoroughly. Melt butter and add cauliflower along with salt, pepper, and nutmeg; simmer gently until fairly dry. Stir in the cream and the yolks, one at a time. Beat the whites stiff and fold into cauliflower.

Place in a buttered soufflé dish and bake in the upper half of preheated 375° oven for 20-25 minutes.

Serve with **Sauce Aurore**: Sauté the chopped onion and herbs in the butter. Add the flour and cook for a minute. Add tomato sauce, tomato concentrate and wine. Before serving, stir in the cream and heat thoroughly. Spoon sauce over individual servings.

Aubergine à la Nimoise

Eggplant with Tomato and Herbs

2 servings

1 eggplant, halved
flour
2 to 3 tbsps oil
3 to 4 tomatoes, skinned
    and seeded

1 tbsp chopped parsley
1 clove garlic, minced
½ cup bread crumbs
1 to 2 tbsps grated cheese
1 tsp chopped fresh herbs
    (try rosemary, basil, thyme)

Sprinkle surface of eggplant with flour. Heat the oil and sauté the cut surface for 5 to 10 minutes. Carefully scoop out the flesh and sauté it with the tomatoes, garlic, parsley, and herbs. Add the bread crumbs. Fill the eggplant shells with this mixture and sprinkle with grated cheese. Place in a 375° oven until the top has browned — about 20 minutes.

Laitues au Nid

Lettuce Nests

6 to 8 servings

8 heads of Boston lettuce
2 cups fresh peas or
    1 pkg frozen
4 to 5 small onions

salt and pepper
¼ lb bacon (4 slices)
3 tbsps butter
½ cup broth or water

Choose a pot that will hold the lettuce comfortably. Cut bacon in large pieces and sauté in the pot along with the onions; stir a few seconds and add the lettuce. Let it simmer about 10 minutes. Add the salt, pepper, and broth and simmer for 30 minutes, checking to make sure there is always enough liquid.

Cook the peas separately. After 30 minutes, open the lettuce leaves delicately and spoon peas into the heart of each lettuce. Simmer 15 to 20 minutes more. Remove from pot and arrange on a warm platter. Surround with the bacon, onions and remaining juice.

Poireaux au Gratin

Leeks au Gratin
4 to 6 servings

2 – 3 bunches of leeks (white part)
½ tsp salt
4 tbsps butter
2 rounded tbsps flour

1½ cups warm milk
½ cup Gruyère cheese, grated
additional cheese and butter for topping

Clean the leeks thoroughly; blanch them in boiling water with ½ tsp of salt for 10-15 minutes.

Prepare a roux with the butter and flour. Let it cook 1 minute and moisten with the milk, stirring. Mix in the Gruyère. Arrange the leeks in a greased, fireproof dish, cover with the sauce and sprinkle with additional grated cheese. Dot with butter and brown in a preheated 375° oven or under the broiler until golden brown.

Flamiche aux Poireaux

Leek Tart
4 to 6 servings

1 recipe pâte brisée (see recipe)
½ lb leeks (the white part)
2 tbsps butter
2 tbsps oil
salt and pepper

½ tsp nutmeg
1½ cup Béchamel sauce (see Sauces)
2 – 3 slices of bacon
1 egg
1 extra egg white

Prepare and precook the pâte brisée. Preheat oven to 375° and prepare the filling.

Clean the leeks and slice them thinly. Sauté them in the butter and oil until soft. Season with salt, pepper, and nutmeg. Mix with the Béchamel sauce.

Fry the bacon, but do not let it become too crisp. Stir the bacon into the Béchamel mixture. Beat the whole egg and the additional egg white and add to the mixture. Fill the precooked crust. Dot with butter and bake in a 375° oven for 20 to 25 minutes. Serve immediately.

Poivrons au Riz

Peppers Stuffed with Seasoned Rice

2 tbsps oil
½ cup rice
¼ lb bacon, diced
¼ lb ham, diced
¼ lb fresh mushrooms, sautéed in butter
1 clove garlic

1 shallot, finely chopped
1 sprig of thyme
1 bay leaf
1 cup bouillon
4 green peppers
salt
additional oil

Continued

Heat the oil in a heavy pot, add the rice, bacon, ham and mushrooms which have been washed and sautéed in butter. Add the garlic and shallot, thyme, bay leaf and bouillon. Cover and simmer for 15-17 minutes.

*Meanwhile, place 4 green peppers in boiling water. Add salt and boil for 5 minutes. Drain, remove the seeds, and stuff the peppers with the rice mixture. Arrange them in a fireproof dish. Sprinkle them with oil and bake covered at 375° for 40 minutes.

Petits Pois Bergerac — Peas with Greens

6 to 8 servings

A favorite dish of Gruyenne province.

1-2 lbs fresh shelled
  or frozen peas
4-6 tbsps butter
2-3 large onions, chopped
2-3 cups lettuce, spinach,
  or any other greens,
  washed and sliced

salt, pepper
thyme
1 tsp sugar
½ bay leaf, crumbled

Melt butter in a heavy-bottom pan. Let the butter brown slightly (beurre noisette) and sauté the onions. After 1 or 2 minutes, add the greens and stir. Season with the salt, pepper, thyme, sugar, and bay leaf. Add the peas, stir, and cook covered for 7-10 minutes, or until done to taste.

 **JOSEPHINE SAYS:**

I know at least 200 ways of preparing the potato. It is as important as bread to the average Frenchman's diet. Parmentier grew them in France in 1771, and a short while after he had his first successful crop, he sent a bouquet of potato flowers to Louix XVI, setting the fashion for potatoes.

Pommes de Terre Marseillaise — Potatoes with Garlic

6 servings

2 lbs small potatoes,
  peeled
5-6 cloves garlic,
  minced

2-3 tbsps parsley, chopped
oil for deep frying
salt, pepper
1 cup **glace de viande**

If using large potatoes, cut into small ovals. Partially deep fry potatoes for 5-7 minutes, depending on size. Drain and remove to a pan and add **glace de viande,** garlic, parsley, salt and pepper. Bring to a boil, cover and simmer 15 to 20 minutes, or until done.

Soufflé de Pommes de Terre

Potato Soufflé
4 to 6 servings

2 cups potatoes (1½ lbs), cooked
¼ cup cream
salt, pepper, nutmeg
¼ cup butter
3 egg yolks
4 egg whites, beaten stiff

Grease a soufflé mold and mash the potatoes. Mix in butter, cream, salt and pepper, and nutmeg to taste. Add the yolks one at a time. Then fold in the beaten egg whites. Fill soufflé mold and bake at 375° for 20 to 25 minutes, until nicely browned on top. Serve hot.

Pommes de Terre Rôties

Roasted Baked Potatoes

1 medium potato per serving
salt and pepper
4 tbsps or more butter
paprika

Peel medium-sized potatoes. Slice ½-inch thick, cutting only ¾ of the way through, leaving the bottom whole. Parboil for 10 minutes; drain and place in a buttered roasting pan. Sprinkle with salt and pepper; brush with melted butter. Bake in a preheated 375° for about 1 to 1¼ hours until brown and crisp. Baste frequently with butter while baking.

Just before serving, sprinkle with paprika and pour melted butter over them. Serve hot with roast or grilled meat.

Galettes de Pommes de Terre

Potato-Nut Balls

1½ lbs potatoes
¼ cup butter
salt, pepper, nutmeg to taste
2 tbsps sour cream or heavy cream
8 oz cream cheese
2 egg yolks
½ cup powdered almonds or walnuts
chopped chives and tarragon
flour for dipping the **galettes**
¼ cup butter for frying

Peel, wash and boil the potatoes for 20 to 25 minutes, until soft. Mash them with butter and add the salt, pepper and nutmeg to taste. Add the cream and cream cheese and mix until creamy. Add the egg yolks, powdered nuts, and herbs.

Form the potato mixture into round balls and roll in flour. Then fry balls in melted butter until brown. Serve these **galettes** with veal, pork roast, or chops.

Riz aux Champignons

Rice with Mushrooms
4 to 6 servings

3 cups broth or water
1½ cups rice
salt and pepper
1 lb mushrooms

4 tbsps bacon drippings
1 clove garlic, chopped
1 tsp parsley, chopped
1 small onion, chopped

Bring the broth or water to a boil, and add the rice, salt and pepper. Let it come to a boil, stir and reduce to very low heat. Steam the rice for 15 minutes.

Wash and mince the mushrooms. Heat the fat and add the mushrooms, garlic, parsley and onion; sauté. Mix with the cooked rice and serve in a vegetable dish. This dish is a good accompaniment to shrimp or fish timbale.

Rutabagas Agenaise

Rutabagas Stuffed with Prunes and Meat
4 to 6 servings

3 medium rutabagas, halved
2 tbsps butter
1 or 2 scallions, chopped
1 lb meat, fresh or leftover pork, beef, veal or chicken
1 egg, if leftover meat is used

½ cup pitted prunes
salt and pepper
thyme
chopped parsley
melted butter

Use a grapefruit knife or a melon ball spoon to hollow the rutabaga halves, leaving a ½-inch shell. Coarsely grate the rutabaga flesh and sauté in butter with the chopped scallions. Let it simmer 15 minutes, covered. Mix with the meat and the prunes; add salt and pepper to taste. Add the thyme. If leftover meat is used, add the egg to bind the mixture together.

Spoon the mixture into the halves; dot with butter. Wrap the halves in foil and bake in a baking pan in a preheated 350° oven for 1 hour. Remove and discard the foil. Cut each of the halves in two. Arrange the stuffed rutabagas on a serving dish. Pour some melted butter over them and sprinkle with chopped parsley.

Epinards Sauce Aigre

Spinach in Sour Cream
6 to 8 servings

3 bunches of spinach (or 3 pkgs of frozen)
4 tbsps butter
1 cup sour cream

salt and pepper
⅛ tsp nutmeg
1 large onion, chopped and sautéed (or 1 pkg dehydrated onion soup)

Clean and wash the spinach and cook it for 7 to 10 minutes in very little water. Drain well and chop coarsely. Melt the butter in a pan. Add the spinach and onion, salt, pepper and nutmeg. Stir in the sour cream.

Grease a pyrex dish and fill with the spinach mixture. Bake in a 375° oven for 20 to 25 minutes. Serve hot.

Note: Additional nutmeg sprinkled on top of the spinach will add a pleasant spiciness.

Purée des Courgettes aux Herbes — Squash Purée with Herbs

4 to 6 servings

- 2 lbs squash (any kind)
- ¼ cup butter
- 1 tbsp oil
- 1 onion, chopped
- salt and pepper
- 1 tsp parsley, chopped
- 1 tsp tarragon, chopped
- 1 tsp chives, chopped
- 1 tsp sweet basil, chopped
- 1 sprig thyme, chopped
- 1 sprig oregano, chopped
- 1 tbsp potato flour or cornstarch
- 3 tbsps heavy cream
- 2 tbsps butter

If squash is young, such as zucchini or summer squash, do not peel. Cut squash into chunks or slices and wash. Heat the butter and oil in a heavy pot or skillet and sauté the chopped onion without allowing it to brown. Add the squash and salt and pepper to taste, cover and simmer very slowly. Stir often to prevent it from browning and cook about 20 minutes, until tender.

Purée the squash and onions in a blender. Return them to the pot and add the herbs, cornstarch and cream. Taste for seasoning. Add a piece of butter and serve.

Soufflé a la Courge — Squash Soufflé

4 to 6 servings

- 3 cups fresh or canned squash
- 2 tbsps brown sugar
- salt and pepper
- 1 pinch of nutmeg
- ½ tsp powdered cloves
- 1 tsp cinnamon
- 1½ cups molasses
- 3 eggs, separated
- 2 tbsps flour
- 3 tbsps butter
- 1 cup cream
- 1 tsp baking powder
- a little mace

If using fresh squash, cut in half, scoop out the seeds and put in a baking dish. Cover with foil and bake in a 400° oven for 1 hour or less. When tender, measure 3 cups of pulp.

To the squash add the sugar, spices and molasses. Mix thoroughly, then add the egg yolks. Add the flour, butter, cream, and baking powder. Finally, fold in the stiffly-beaten egg whites.

Put the squash mixture in a greased pyrex dish and set in a pan of hot water. Bake for 45 minutes to 1 hour at 350°. If the top becomes too brown, protect with foil.

Blettes Frites au Gratin

Swiss Chard au Gratin
6 to 8 servings

2 bunches swiss chard
1 tbsp bread crumbs
1 egg
1/3 cup grated cheese
1 medium onion, chopped and sautéed

salt and pepper
½ tsp nutmeg
¼ cup **crème frâiche** (heavy cream)
¼ cup butter
1 recipe Béchamel sauce

Clean, wash, and boil the swiss chard in water for 15 minutes; drain and chop. Mix in bread crumbs, egg, cheese, seasonings, and onion. Then add cream. Heat butter and fry mixture by rounded tbsps, until golden brown. Arrange on a fireproof dish and pour Béchamel over it, dot with butter and brown under the broiler.

Tomates à la Provençale

Broiled Tomatoes Provençale
4 to 6 servings

1 large tomato per serving
salt and pepper
½ cup white bread crumbs
1 clove garlic, chopped

4 tbsps basil or parsley, chopped
1 tbsp mustard
4 tbsps butter
1 egg

Cut off the top of each tomato and squeeze out the juice and seeds. Set aside.

Mix the bread crumbs, salt, pepper, garlic, herbs, mustard, egg, and half of the butter. Fill the tomatoes with this mixture. Place them in a greased ovenproof dish, or store in the refrigerator if not ready to use.

Fifteen minutes before serving, dot each with butter. Put the tomatoes in a preheated 400° oven and bake for 5 to 7 minutes. Put under the broiler for a few seconds. Serve around any roast or separately.

Navets de Jean-Marie

Turnips with Lemon and Sour Cream
6 to 8 servings

2 bunches of turnips, with greens if possible
juice of 1 lemon
2 tbsps butter
salt and pepper

1 tsp sugar
½ cup sour cream
grated rind of 1 lemon
chives, chopped
parsley, chopped

Peel the turnips and cut them in bite-sized pieces. Boil them in water with the lemon juice for 10 minutes. Drain.

Heat the butter and sauté the turnips. Add salt, pepper, sugar, sour cream, grated lemon rind and chives. Transfer to a vegetable dish and sprinkle with parsley.

Jardinière de Legumes

Mixed Vegetables Jardinière

4 to 6 servings

1 small cauliflower
½ lb small onions, peeled
1 lb carrots, peeled
½ lb fresh peas
½ lb potatoes, peeled
juice of 1 lemon
1 tbsp flour

2 egg yolks
1 tbsp water
salt and pepper
1 tsp cornstarch
½ cup butter
½ pt cream

Peel and wash all vegetables. Cook the cauliflower whole, for 15-20 minutes in water mixed with the juice of 1 lemon and 1 tbsp flour. Blanch the onions in boiling water for 10 minutes. Cook the carrots, peas, and potatoes, each separately.

Meanwhile prepare the sauce: Put the egg yolks in the top of a double boiler with 1 tbsp water and a pinch of salt and pepper. Stir with a wooden spoon, adding 1 tsp cornstarch. Place over hot water and stir constantly while adding the butter, a little at a time. Keep the heat very low or remove from the heat while adding the butter. When the butter is completely melted, raise the heat and stir until the sauce thickens. Taste for seasoning. Beat the cream until very fluffy and add to the sauce. Keep warm until ready to serve.

Arrange the vegetables on a serving platter. Garnish the top with a bouquet of parsley and a little piece of red pepper or tomato. Serve the sauce separately.

Ratatouille à la Béchamel

Vegetables with Béchamel

6 to 8 servings

1 small cauliflower
½ lb string beans
½ lb carrots
½ lb turnips
2 tbsps flour
4 artichoke bottoms
½ lb zucchini
thyme, laurel (bay leaf)

1 large eggplant
½ stick butter
salt, pepper, nutmeg
1 tbsp chopped parsley
1 qt chicken or veal broth
1 recipe of Béchamel
1 cup heavy cream

Peel and wash all vegetables, cut carrots and turnips in one inch pieces, the egg plant and zucchinis in thick slices, the cauliflower in flowerets, the bottom of artichokes in quarters. Melt half the butter in a heavy pot, add all the vegetables, salt and pepper, thyme, laurel, and stir to coat the vegetables in butter. Add half the broth, close tightly and simmer for ½ hour — by that time the vegetables should have rendered all their water into the broth.

In the meantime, make a Béchamel; melt remaining butter in a heavy pot, add the flour and stir, add the remaining warm bouillon stirring until it becomes thick and satiny and simmer in a double boiler 15 to 20 minutes. Add half the parsley, salt and pepper, nutmeg. Off the fire add the cream, arrange braised vegetables on a hot platter, and cover vegetables with part of the sauce. Serve remaining sauce separately, garnished with rest of parsley.

POULTRY, GAME
AND RABBIT

"Sing While You Cook"

Pellaprat would always sing while he cooked. It made things go better for him ~ and it does the same for me. You'll find delicious recipes here for chicken, turkey, duck, and rabbit.

I hate having to scald lobsters and crayfish, since they must be scalded alive. So, when I am doing that, I sing a little prayer:

> *Sorry for having to do this to you, my friend,*
> *But ~ Mon Dieu, Mon Dieu,*
> *Better to scald you than me.*

Poultry, Game, and Rabbit

Many people ask me about my teacher, Henri-Paul Pellaprat. He was a very modest man who never even allowed his photograph to be taken. He learned to cook from the great Auguste Escoffier, and though I never met Escoffier, Henri introduced me to most of the other great chefs of Paris.

Henri's sense of humor never failed him; he had a pet name for all of his friends in the kitchens of Paris. There was Edward Nignon, the Breton, who was always elegantly dressed, often changing into tails after he finished preparing a dinner; Henri called him "Edward the Elegant." There was Prosper Montagné ~ a very fat man; Pellaprat nicknamed him "Prosper le Bouffi" (the puffed-up).

And there was "Philéas the Sophisticated" for Philéas Gilbert because he was always bragging about himself. Emile Prunier was "Emile the Successful" because his restaurant cooked for the Loucheurs of Paris and many of the wealthy New York families. He served only fish ~ but every variety you could imagine.

Henri also knew Marguery, the chef who originated Filet de sole Marguery. *He had a name for him, too ~ "Marguery the quiet" ~ because he was a very simple, down-to-earth man. I knew Marguery, too, and even have his famous recipe, which he signed and gave to me.*

And, of course, Pellaprat had a name for himself. He was "Pellaprat, the good-for-nothing!"

Continued

At the Cordon Bleu, Pellaprat would use every utensil imaginable ~ le daubière *(for beef)*, le poissonière *(for fish)*, le jambonière *(for ham)*, etc. But in his own house, he dispensed with all the *"ières."* He did what he pleased, using only a few bowls and frying pans ~ just the bare essentials.

I do practically the same thing. I use the roaster and the oven. And I try to show my classes that they don't need to use the expensive equipment in order to cook well. If you can afford a blender or a Cuisinart, they are wonderful machines which make life much easier. Some of my recipes mention their use, but it is never essential to have them. As Pellaprat would say, "Take an extra headache out of your head" ~ use the most convenient utensils you have.

Poulet de Grains Sautés Bordelaise
Fryers with Artichokes and Mushrooms
4 servings

for fryers:

2 fryers, halved or quartered
6 artichoke bottoms, chopped fine
½ lb mushrooms, chopped fine
2 large onions, sliced
chopped parsley

3 tbsps butter (or margarine)
2 tbsps oil

for vegetables:
3 tbsps butter (or margarine)
2 tbsps oil
¾ cup white wine
¼ cup demi-glacé

Sauté chicken in butter and oil and continue cooking until done, about 30 minutes total. Sauté the vegetables in more butter and oil. Transfer chicken to a hot platter and deglaze pan with the wine and demi-glacé. Reduce a little. Place vegetables around chicken and pour sauce over. Sprinkle with parsley. Good with rice or mashed potatoes.

Poulet Parmentier
Fryers with Potato
4 servings

From Marguery

2 fryers, halved or quartered, floured
1 lb potatoes
1 onion, chopped
salt, pepper

for chicken:
3 tbsps butter plus
2 tbsps oil (more if necessary)

for potatoes:
3 tbsps butter plus
3 tbsps oil (more if necessary)
chopped parsley
¾ cup white wine

Brown fryers in the butter and oil. While chicken is cooking, peel and dice potatoes. In a frying pan, sauté the potatoes. When two-thirds cooked, add the chopped onion and finish cooking. Transfer chicken to a platter and surround with the potatoes. Deglaze pan with ¾ cup white wine and pour over chickens. Sprinkle with parsley. Good with Broiled Tomatoes, mushrooms, or Ratatouille.

Poulet de Grain Sauté aux Fines Herbes   Fryer with Herbs
4 servings

2 fryers, halved or quartered, floured
3 tbsps butter
2 tbsps oil

salt, pepper
2 tbsps herbs: tarragon, chervil, chives, parsley, sage

Same as above. When done cooking, deglaze with the wine and add the herbs. Reduce a little and pour over chicken. Serve with any of the above vegetables.

Suprême de Volaille Empire   Chicken Breasts with Mushrooms and Noodles
2 servings

2 chicken breasts
salt, pepper, paprika
2 tbsps butter, margarine or oil
¼ lb medium-sized mushroom heads
1 clove garlic, chopped

1 tsp parsley, chopped
1 cup cooked egg noodles
½ cup heavy cream
½ – 1 cup chicken broth
3 oz sherry
1 egg yolk
flour

Preheat oven to 300°. Season chicken breasts with salt, pepper, and paprika and roll in flour. Sauté in butter until golden browned. Sauté mushrooms in a little oil for about 5 minutes, adding the garlic and chopped parsley. Set aside.

Place the cooked noodles in a buttered ovenproof casserole. Arrange chicken breasts on top along with the mushrooms. Deglaze chicken pan with sherry and broth and let it reduce. Pour over chicken, cover and cook in preheated oven for 30 minutes. Just before serving mix yolk and cream together. Lay chicken breasts on heated platter and mix egg mixture with the noodles and mushrooms. Surround the chicken with noodles and serve at once.

JOSEPHINE SAYS:

Never dry a cut-up chicken with a towel. It robs the meat of flavor. Instead, dry it with a little flour. The flour will also add a little thickening to the juices for a sauce.

Poulet aux Dents du Chat

Chicken with Tomato and Cheese
4 servings

1 medium-sized chicken, cut up
2 tbsps butter
2 tbsps brandy
1 clove garlic, minced
1 small onion, chopped
3 large tomatoes, peeled (2 sliced, 1 chopped)
1 tbsp tomato paste
3 tbsps flour
⅞ cup chicken broth
¾ cup sour cream
½ cup slivered almonds, sautéed in butter
½ tsp salt
1 pinch cayenne
Parmesan cheese, grated
1 pinch dry mustard

Brown the chicken slowly in butter, then moisten with brandy and ignite. Remove the meat from the pan and add the garlic and onion. Cook slowly for 1 minute; increase the heat and add the 2 sliced tomatoes. Cook briskly for 6 minutes, stirring occasionally to prevent scorching.

Remove the pan from the heat and add the tomato paste and flour. Pour in the chicken broth and return the pot to medium heat. Stir until the sauce boils. Again remove the pot from the heat and very carefully stir in the sour cream. If the sauce is too thick it may be thinned with a little light cream. Add the chopped tomato and the sautéed almonds. Season with salt and cayenne. Return the chicken to the sauce and cook very gently, uncovered, on top of the stove for 45 to 50 minutes. (Or it may be baked in a 350° oven.)

Arrange the chicken on a flameproof platter. Add 1 tbsp Parmesan cheese and the dry mustard to the sauce and simmer very briefly, no longer than a minute. Pour the sauce over the chicken, sprinkle with more grated cheese and dot with butter. Put it under the broiler to brown.

Poularde Toulousaine

Roast Chicken with Stuffing
4 servings

1 3-4 lb fryer chicken
1 cup chicken broth and/or wine
salt, pepper
sprig thyme
leaves from sprig rosemary
few leaves fresh tarragon
1 bay leaf
2-4 tbsps chicken fat, butter, or oil (or combination)

Stuffing:
½ lb sausage meat or fresh ground pork
liver from chicken, mashed
2-3 green or black olives, chopped
3 green onions, chopped fine
2 tomatoes, skinned, seeded, and chopped
any desired herbs
1 tsp cornstarch or arrowroot dissolved in wine or water

Season cavity of chicken with salt and pepper. Fill cavity with the stuffing and tie closed. Melt any chicken fat from the chicken and add enough butter or oil to enable you to brown chicken on all sides. Remove chicken and drain off any remaining fat. Deglaze pan with the broth or wine. Place chicken back into the pan. Season with salt, pepper, and the herbs. Cover and place in a 375° oven for 45 minutes. When ready to serve, cut the chicken up and place on a heated platter. Thicken the juices with the cornstarch or arrowroot. Make sure each serving includes some of the stuffing.

Poulet Marengo   Chicken Marengo with Shrimp Garnish

4 servings

1 chicken (3-4 lbs), cut up
flour
butter or chicken fat to
   brown chicken
Mirepoix: finely chopped
   carrot, stalk of celery
   and white of leek
2 - 3 ripe tomatoes,
   coarsely chopped (or 1 tbsp
   tomato paste)
1 cup chicken stock
1 cup white wine (¾ cup for
   chicken, ¼ cup for the
   crayfish or shrimp)
1 sprig thyme for chicken;
   1 for shrimp

chopped truffles and shallots
8 tbsps butter, and 2 tbsps oil
   (half for shrimp, half
   for mushrooms)
1 unshelled crayfish or
   jumbo shrimp per serving
salt and pepper
¼ lb mushrooms, sliced
   if large
2 - 4 tbsps chopped parsley
1 large clove garlic, chopped
1 bread round per serving,
   sautéed in butter
1 poached egg per serving
1 bay leaf for chicken;
   1 for shrimp

Preheat oven to 375°. Dust the chicken pieces with flour. Melt butter or chicken fat in a heavy-bottomed skillet and brown the chicken completely on all sides. Remove to an oven-proof, covered casserole. Sauté the mirepoix and add the chopped tomatoes, adding more butter if necessary. Deglaze the pan with the chicken stock and ¾ cup of wine. Pour over the chicken. Remove the leaves from the sprig of thyme and crumble the bay leaf. Chop together and sprinkle over the chicken. Cover and cook in preheated 375° oven for 15-20 minutes or until done. Do not overcook. Chopped truffles and shallots may be added at the end of the cooking time if desired.

Meanwhile, melt 4 tbsps butter in a pan. Add the crayfish or shrimp, toss in the butter and add ¼ cup of wine. Add bay leaf and leaves from sprig of thyme and season with salt and pepper. Cook until the shellfish takes on a pink color. Remove from the heat and remove the shell when cool enough to handle. Set back into the cooking broth to keep warm. Set aside.

Melt 4 more tbsps and 2 tbsps oil over very high heat. Quickly sauté the mushrooms with 2 tbsps chopped parsley and the chopped garlic.

To assemble and serve: Place the chicken in the center of a large warmed platter. Surround the chicken with the bread rounds. Place a poached egg on each round. Between the rounds place the shrimp or crayfish. Spoon some sauce over the eggs and crayfish. Also spoon some sauce over the chicken. Sprinkle the dish with chopped parsley. Serve remaining sauce separately.

Poulet Carmen / Chicken Carmen

3 to 4 servings

1 chicken, whole or cut up (3 to 4 lbs)
salt and pepper
1 sprig rosemary (or ⅛ tsp)
½ cup butter (1 stick)
¼ lb mushrooms
2–3 shallots
1 small clove garlic
1 cup white wine
1 tomato, skinned and seeded
thyme, bay leaf, salt and pepper
1 tsp cornstarch
½ pt whipping cream

Season the chicken inside with salt, pepper, and rosemary. Sauté on all sides and place in a large Dutch oven or pan and cook for about 45 minutes, until done, basting with the melted butter. (If using a cut up chicken, the cooking time will be less). Meanwhile, sauté the mushrooms, shallots, and garlic. Add the wine, reserving 2 tbsps, and the coarsely chopped tomato. Add the thyme, part of a bay leaf, salt and pepper and reduce slowly to one-third the original volume.

Dilute the cornstarch with a little wine and add to the sauce along with the cream which has been whipped. Serve the sauce with the chicken.

Poularde Savoyarde / Chicken with Herbs and Mushrooms

1 chicken, cut up
Mirepoix (1 small carrot, 1 small onion, ½ stalk celery, all coarsely cut)
¼ cup cognac
¼ lb girolles mushrooms
4 tbsps chicken fat, oil or butter
aromatic herbs: rosemary, thyme, marjoram, sage; one pinch of each
1 tbsp parsley (chopped)
1 cup sherry or madeira
1½ cups broth
salt, pepper

Sauce:
2 tbsps butter
2 tbsps chopped mushrooms
1 pinch aromatic herbs
1 shallot chopped
½ cup whipped cream
1 rounded tbsp flour
1 clove garlic
¼ cup sherry

In a large frying pan, melt the fat, and fry the pieces of chicken that have been rolled in flour; fry them until they are golden brown. Douse chicken with cognac and ignite; when flames die out, then add the aromatic herbs, the *mirepoix* of carrot, onion and celery, the broth, salt, pepper, and half the parsley. Bring to a boil and simmer slowly for 20 minutes. Add the sherry and mushrooms and simmer 10 minutes more. Arrange on a serving dish, pour cream sauce over, sprinkle with remaining parsley.

SAUCE:

In a one qt heavy pot melt the butter, add the rounded tbsp of flour, the garlic, shallots and the aromatic herbs. Add the juice of the braised chicken and ¼ cup of sherry. Add the mushrooms. Simmer for 10 minutes; just before serving mix in the whipped cream. Test for seasoning.

Note: If using dry mushrooms, soak them in water for at least one hour and add 2 tbsps of that juice to sauce.

Les Poulets Reine Chasseur

Chicken with Wine and Tomatoes

4 servings

This dish was served by a chef friend of mine at the White House for President Kennedy and President Ayub Khan.

1 large fryer (3 to 4 lbs), cut up
flour
3 tbsps olive oil
2 tbsps shallots (or white of scallions), cut up
2 tomatoes, peeled and seeded
½ cup dry white wine
¾ cup chicken broth
4 to 5 quartered mushrooms (optional)
salt and pepper
1 bay leaf
1 sprig of fresh thyme
2 oz brandy (optional)

Flour chicken and sauté in oil until browned. Remove to a 3-qt casserole. In the same fat, sauté shallots and tomatoes. Warm brandy and pour over chicken and ignite. Then add wine, herbs, chicken broth, salt and pepper. Simmer for a few minutes. Add mushrooms and pan juices, cover, and bake in preheated 375° oven for 30 minutes.

Arrange chicken on hot platter; strain sauce over it and sprinkle with parsley.

JOSEPHINE SAYS:

When you're at the market, you can test a chicken for tenderness by bending back the tip of the breastbone. Younger, more tender chickens have more resilient breastbones; the older ones will be tougher and the tips won't bend as easily.

Poulet aux Amandes

Chicken with Tomatoes and Almonds

6 to 8 servings

2 whole chickens, 3-4 lbs each
2 tbsps butter
2 tbsps oil
2-3 oz brandy
3 cloves garlic, chopped
2 small onions, chopped
3 large tomatoes, peeled and seeded; 1 chopped, 2 sliced thin
salt, pepper, cayenne
additional butter
1 tbsp tomato paste
3 tbsps flour
1 cup chicken broth
¾-1 cup sour cream
little light cream, if necessary
½ cup blanched slivered almonds (browned in butter)
3 tbsps grated Parmesan or Swiss cheese
½ tsp dry mustard

Continued

Tie chickens carefully and brown them all over slowly in the butter and oil. When nicely browned, pour brandy over and ignite. Remove from pan and sauté the onions and garlic in the same fat for about 1 minute over medium heat. Increase heat and add the sliced tomatoes. Cook briskly for 5-6 minutes, stirring occasionally to prevent scorching. Remove the pan from the fire and add the flour. Pour in the broth and return pot to medium fire. Add the tomato paste and keep stirring until the sauce boils. Again remove the pot from the fire and carefully stir in the sour cream. If the sauce is too thick, you can thin it with a little cream. Now add the chopped tomato and browned almonds. Season sauce with salt, pepper, and dash of cayenne. Cut the chicken up and return it to the sauce. Cook, uncovered, very gently on top of the stove for 45-50 minutes. Do not let sauce boil as sour cream will curdle.

To serve: Remove chicken to a flameproof serving dish. To the sauce add 1 tbsp Parmesan and the dry mustard. Simmer for a few moments and carefully pour sauce over the chicken. Sprinkle the top with the rest of the Parmesan and dot with butter. Run under the broiler to brown.

Poulet Raphael Weill
Chicken with Sherry and Garlic

1 frying or broiling chicken, disjointed
¼ cup butter
salt and pepper
2 shallots, chopped
3 tbsps sherry

10 cloves garlic, chopped
6 to 8 egg yolks
$1/3$ cup heavy cream
parsley
Optional garnish:
  ½ lb mushrooms
  ½ lb artichoke hearts
  1 clove garlic, chopped
  1 tbsp parsley

Cut the chicken into serving pieces and sauté in butter until lightly and evenly browned. Season with salt and pepper. Sauté the shallots in butter until soft but not brown. Cover the bottom of the pan with sherry; add the chicken and shallots. Prepare the optional garnish, if desired. Simmer about 25 minutes. About 10 minutes before the dish is cooked, check to see that it isn't dry (if it is, add a little chicken broth or more sherry). Chop the garlic and add to the chicken.

Mix the egg yolks and cream. Put the chicken on a warm platter. Add cream and yolks to the pan, give it a few shakes to mix and pour over the chicken. Sprinkle the dish with parsley and serve.

Optional Garnish: Cut the mushrooms in quarters and sauté them in oil. Continue cooking and add 1 chopped clove of garlic and 1 tbsp parsley. In this mixture, sauté the artichoke hearts and add to the chicken 20 minutes before it is fully cooked. Serve with the chicken.

Poulet Saigonnaise Indochine

Chicken Saigon
6-8 servings

Marinade:
   3 tbsps olive oil
   1 tbsp vinegar or
      lemon juice
   1 tsp mustard
   a *bouquet garni* of
      thyme & bay leaf
   1 clove of garlic, chopped
   salt and pepper (very little)
   grated rind of 1 lemon

4 squab chickens (Poulet
   de grain)
1 tbsp mustard
1 tbsp powdered ginger
flour, for rolling the
   chicken pieces
¼ cup butter, melted

Prepare the marinade by mixing all ingredients together.

Cut the squab chickens in half and rub them with mustard and ginger. Set the chickens in the marinade and allow them to soak for several hours. Remove the chicken, but do not wipe dry as that will remove some of the delicious marinade. Roll the chicken pieces in flour then brush with melted butter. Put them skin side down under the broiler or barbecue over hot coals about 4 inches away from the heat. Broil 10 minutes on each side, basting once or twice with the marinade.

Reduce the marinade to half and pour over the chicken.

Poulet St. Pierre

Chicken Saint Peter

1 roasting chicken (4-5 lbs)
Marinade:
   1 cup white wine
   juice of 1 lemon
   1 liquor glass of rum
   1 sprig thyme
   1 bay leaf
   ⅛ tsp allspice
   2 tsps paprika
   1 tsp curry powder
   salt and pepper

flour, for rolling the chicken
2 eggs, beaten
bread crumbs
5 tbsps oil
2 tbsps tomato paste
½ cup **crème frâiche**
   (heavy cream)
2 bananas
1 recipe fritter batter
fat for deep frying
additional rum for igniting
   chicken

Cut the chicken into serving pieces and marinate 24 hours in the wine, lemon juice, rum, thyme, bay leaf, allspice, paprika, curry powder, salt and pepper (you'll want to save the marinade to make the sauce later).

Remove the pieces of chicken and roll first in flour, then in beaten eggs, then in bread crumbs. Fry in hot oil, very slowly, for 25 to 30 minutes. Reduce the marinade to half and add the tomato paste and the cream. Strain sauce and set aside until ready to serve.

Cut the bananas in half, dip in fritter batter (see recipe) and fry in the hot fat until brown, then set on a paper towel. Arrange the warm chicken on a serving platter, ignite with warmed rum, and arrange the bananas around it. Serve the sauce separately.

 **JOSEPHINE SAYS:**

If you don't have wine in the house, it's a shame, but no disaster. Substitute $1/3$ cup vinegar and $2/3$ cup water for every cup of wine called for in the recipe.

Suprémes de Volaille Normandie — Breast of Chicken Normandy

4 servings

4 to 5 chicken livers
chicken broth or white wine
bay leaf
sprig of thyme
1 medium onion, chopped
2 tbsps chicken fat, ground or chopped
1 tbsp butter
1 tsp cornstarch
2 tbsps bread crumbs
1 egg, lightly beaten
ground cloves, allspice
4 chicken breasts, boned
Mirepoix of 1 tbsp each of chopped celery, carrot, onion
¼ cup wine (Chablis or Sauterne) for deglazing
parsley

Preheat oven at 375°.

In a small amount of wine or broth, boil chicken livers along with bay leaf and thyme for 5 to 7 minutes. While this cooks, sauté onion in 1 tbsp chicken fat until it is translucent but not brown. When livers are cooked, drain off liquid, mash them with a fork, and combine with onion, butter, remaining fat, bread crumbs, and egg. Season to taste with salt, pepper, allspice and cloves. Smear this mixture over each chicken breast. Fold one half of breast over the other and secure tightly by wrapping it in its own skin, the caul of a pig, or with string.

Brown breasts on all sides in 1 tbsp oil and 1 tbsp butter and then transfer them to a casserole dish. In the same fat, sauté the mirepoix and add to the chicken. Deglaze pan with wine and pour over breasts. Braise in preheated oven for 35 minutes.

Serve with the juices thickened with 1 tbsp cornstarch which has been diluted in cold broth or wine. Serve hot with a sprinkling of parsley.

Note: Breasts may be stuffed with veal, pork, and onion and served with Supreme Sauce, as a variation.

Poulet Sauté Chasseur

Chicken Sautéed Hunter-Style
4 servings

1 chicken (4 lbs) or
   2 chickens (weighing 2 lbs each),
   cut up
2 tbsps oil
2 tbsps butter
2 shallots or white part
   of scallions, chopped
1 cup white wine: chablis,
   sauterne, or graves
¼ cup tomato paste

¾ cup **demi glacé sauce**
1 tbsp brandy
1 tbsp in all finely chopped
   parsley, chervil and tarragon
a **bouquet garni** of thyme,
   bay leaf, and celery leaves
¼ lb mushrooms, sliced
1 clove garlic, minced
parsley, chopped

Preheat oven to 375°.
   Sauté the pieces of chicken in hot oil and butter until brown on all sides. Place them in a 3-qt fireproof casserole and set aside. In the same pan that was used for browning the chicken, sauté the chopped shallots; deglaze the pan with wine, and add the tomato paste, the **demiglacé sauce** and the brandy. Add the herbs and the **bouquet garni.** Pour over the chicken and braise in a preheated 375° oven for 35 minutes.
   Fifteen minutes before the chicken is cooked, sauté the sliced mushrooms and garlic and add to the chicken; bake 10 to 15 minutes more.
   Arrange on a heated platter and sprinkle with chopped parsley.

Poulet au Citron

Chicken with Lemon
6 to 8 servings

2 frying chickens,
   2-3 lbs each
2 tbsps flour
½ cup butter
1 cup white stock (chicken
   or veal broth)

1 cup dry white wine
1 tsp fresh sage
salt and pepper to taste
10 cloves of garlic
2 lemons
parsley, chopped

Cut the chicken in pieces and toss with the flour. Sauté the chicken until lightly browned. Transfer to a fireproof casserole and deglaze the pan with the broth and wine. Pour over the chicken and add the sage, salt, and pepper.
   Poach the garlic cloves in boiling water for 2 minutes. Peel but do not crush them. Cut the lemons in slices. Put the garlic and lemon with the chicken, and bake for 35 minutes in a preheated 375° oven.
   When chicken is tender, mash the garlic into the sauce. Put the juices in a small saucepan, reduce, and pour over the chicken. Sprinkle with chopped parsley.

Poulet Exotique Chicken with Pineapple, Papaya and Ginger

6 to 8 servings

2 fryers, 2 to 3 lbs each
1½ cups pineapple juice
2 tbsps oil
additional oil for frying
 the chicken
salt and pepper
parsley, chopped

1 fresh or canned papaya,
 mashed
1 tbsp chopped ginger
1 clove garlic, minced
1 tbsp soy sauce
2 tbsps brown sugar
juice of 1 lemon
1 tsp cornstarch

Cut each fryer into quarters. Marinate in the pineapple juice and oil for at least 2 hours.

Brown the pieces to a golden brown and set in a fireproof casserole. Sprinkle with salt and pepper.

In a saucepan put the marinade, the mashed papaya, ginger, garlic, soy sauce, brown sugar and lemon juice. Add the deglazed juices from the fried chicken pan. Bring sauce to a boil and pour over the chicken; cover and bake at 350° for 35 minutes.

Arrange the chicken on a serving dish. Dilute 1 tsp cornstarch in a little cold pineapple juice, and mix it into the cooking liquid. Let it come to a boil and pour over the chicken. Sprinkle with parsley and serve.

Foies de Poulet Marie Chicken Livers Marie

4 to 6 servings

(Sauce for rice, pasta, etc.)

2 tbsps butter
2 tbsps oil or chicken fat
1 medium onion, chopped
2 cloves garlic, minced
1 lb tomatoes
1 bay leaf
2 sprigs thyme
1 tbsp in all of rosemary,
 basil, marjoram, and
 oregano

1 tsp salt
1 large pinch cayenne
½ cup sherry
1 cup bouillon
1½ lbs chicken livers
2 tbsps butter
½ lb mushrooms
1 clove garlic, chopped
1 tsp parsley, chopped

Heat the butter and oil in a large saucepan. Add the onion and garlic and sauté over low heat until translucent, but not brown. Add the tomatoes, the herbs and spices, sherry and bouillon. Bring to a boil, reduce the heat and simmer for 25 to 30 minutes.

Meanwhile, sauté the chicken livers in more butter until they are just pink. Set them aside and sauté the mushrooms in the saucepan with more chopped garlic and 1 tsp parsley. Return the livers to the pan and simmer 10 minutes more. Add them to the sauce.

This mixture can be served over an omelet, rice or pasta.

Pigeons Joyeaux

1 squab for each serving
1 cup wild rice, cooked
the squab livers, cooked
   and puréed
1 small can of pâté
   de fois gras (goose liver)
1 tsp chopped crisp bacon

Squabs Stuffed with Liver, Bacon and Wild Rice

4 to 6 servings

1 tsp chives and parsley
½ cup chopped mushrooms
1 clove garlic, minced
1 tbsp parsley, chopped
1 tbsp oil
1 8 oz glass of currant,
   apple, or other red jelly

Mix wild rice with the livers, pâté, bacon, and herbs. Sauté the mushrooms in oil with the garlic and parsley. Add to the other mixture. If too dry, moisten with a little broth.

Fill the squabs with this mixture and close opening securely with toothpicks. Brown the squabs on all sides in oil and butter. Put in a fireproof dish and braise, covered, in a 350° oven for 35 minutes. When half done, add a glass of jelly and mix with the cooking juice. Finish cooking.

Serve with string beans, peas, carrots, endive or other green salad, and with ambrosia (marinated mixed fruit) in lemon halves which have been scooped out and scalloped. For additional jelly sauce, see following recipe.

Jelly Sauce for Squabs

1 jar of currant jelly
   (8 oz) or other red jelly
2 tbsps mustard
½ cup red wine

salt and pepper
1 pinch of cayenne
2 tbsps butter
cooking juice from the squabs

Melt the jelly and add the remaining ingredients. Mix well and serve with roast squab or game.

Pigeons Montmorency

1 squab for each serving
1½ lbs fresh cherries,
   pitted, or 2 small cans
   of pitted cherries
flour to coat squabs
2 tbsps butter

Squabs Stuffed with Cherries

4 to 6 servings

salt and pepper
1 onion, chopped
1 bay leaf
½ cup sherry
⅓ cup cherry juice
1 tsp cornstarch
parsley, chopped

Stuff the squabs with the pitted cherries. Rub the birds with flour and sauté them in melted butter until brown. Place the squabs in a fireproof dish, adding salt and pepper, chopped onion, bay leaf, sherry and ⅓ cup of the cherry juice.

Bake at 350° for 30 to 35 minutes. When finished baking, thicken the pan

Continued

juices with the cornstarch, diluted in a little water. Place the squab on a warm serving dish and surround with additional cherries if you wish. (Fresh cherries should first be put in hot water for a few minutes.) Sprinkle with chopped parsley.

Canard Roti à Ma Façon

Roast Duck, My Way

4 to 6 servings

1 duck, 5 to 6 lbs
salt and pepper
2 stalks celery
5 tbsps butter (part for onions and part for the livers)
½ lb onions, chopped
1 cup red wine (burgundy)
thyme
bay leaf
1 cup **demiglace**
4 to 5 chicken and duck livers
¼ cup cognac, warmed
parsley, chopped

Preheat oven to 375°.

Rub the outside of the duck with salt, and salt and pepper the inside. Place one of the stalks of celery inside the duck. Truss it and place on a rack in a roasting pan. Roast at 375° until done (about 1½ hours).

While the duck is cooking, melt 4 tbsps butter. Add the chopped onions, wine, salt and pepper, 1 stalk of celery chopped, and the thyme and bay leaf. Simmer 10 to 15 minutes. Add the **demiglace** and simmer 10 minutes more over low heat.

In another skillet sauté the chicken and duck livers in 1 tbsp butter and ignite with the warm cognac. Combine with the **demiglace** and wine mixture, and reduce to a purée in a blender.

Carve the duck and arrange on a serving platter. Pour the sauce over and sprinkle with chopped parsley.

Note: Glazed turnips and figs or a purée of turnips and potatoes, go very well with this dish.

Canard Sauvage ou Faison

Wild Duck or Pheasant with Sweetbreads

4 to 6 servings

1 or 2 wild ducks or pheasants
1 slice of pork back fat
½ lb sweetbreads, soaked in water at least ½ hour
butter
1 truffle (optional)
fines herbes: parsley, chives, tarragon, chervil, thyme (chopped fine)
salt and pepper
½ cup butter
2 tbsps flour
½ cup bread, soaked in sweetbreads poaching liquid and squeezed dry
1 lemon, cut in wedges

Tie a piece of pork back fat around each duck and roast 10 minutes at 450°. Meanwhile prepare the soaked sweetbreads by poaching them in water, simmering them for 10 minutes (and reserve the liquid). Remove all the skin and fat and separate meat into small chunks; sauté in butter.

The truffle should be chopped rather fine. Add it to the sweetbreads along with the fine herbs, salt and pepper. Make a roux with the butter and flour. Add 1 cup of the sweetbread liquid, and simmer 5 minutes, then add to sweetbreads. Add the soaked bread. Stuff the ducks with half of this mixture and finish cooking them at 375°, about 10 minutes more. Simmer the remaining sweetbreads ragout.

When the duck is done, arrange the ragout in the bottom of the serving dish. Carve the meat and arrange on top of dish, with lemon wedges.

Le Canard de Pékin

Peking Duck

1 duck (4 to 5 lbs)
½ cup honey
1 stalk of celery, chopped
1 onion, sliced
thyme
1 bay leaf

white syrup:
  ½ cup water, ¼ cup sugar
  cooked together, or
  ¼ cup corn syrup
salt and pepper
1 tbsp soy sauce

Sear duck on top of the stove or in a 500° oven until well-browned. Then prick with a two-tined fork to drain the fat. Pour boiling water over and marinate in the honey, celery, onion, thyme, bay leaf, and the white syrup. Allow the duck to marinate overnight, or for at least 3 to 4 hours to allow the glaze to seep through the duck.

Stuff the duck with the celery and onion from the marinade. Sprinkle with salt and pepper and close the cavity.

Finally, barbecue or bake the duck in a 375° oven. Serve with a sauce made from the marinade with soy sauce added. If the duck has been cooked in the oven, add the juices to the sauce. Cut and serve the duck on round buns or bread like a sandwich.

As one gourmet friend of mine puts it, "Reverend bliss!"

Dinde à la Touraine

Turkey Touraine

8 to 10 servings

¼ lb sausage meat
1 turkey, 10 to 15 lbs
turkey giblets
Mirepoix:
1 carrot, 1 onion, 1 celery stick
2 sprigs of fresh thyme, chopped

1 medium onion, chopped
salt and pepper
8 prunes, pitted
red wine
¼ cup butter

Continued

In preparation, soak the giblets with 1 carrot, 1 onion, 1 stalk of celery, salt and pepper for 1 hour or until tender. Sauté the onion in butter and set aside. Soak the prunes in wine, then cook them until tender but still a little firm; chop into pieces.

Mix the onion, prunes, wine, sausage meat, salt, pepper, thyme, and giblets (chopped). Mix well and stuff the turkey. Sew the cavity closed with thread or skewers and rub the turkey with melted butter. Turkey should roast at 350° at 20 minutes per pound, or until tender. When turkey is well browned, cover with foil or paper and continue cooking. Turkey juices can be thickened with 1 tbsp cornstarch, diluted with a little bouillon, and served separately with the sliced turkey.

Lapin Chasseur

Rabbit in Tomato and Rosemary Sauce

6 servings

1 rabbit, cut up
¾ cup butter
2 large onions, chopped fine
2 heaping tbsps flour
1 cup bouillon
½ cup white wine
½ tsp parsley, chopped fine
2 large sprigs thyme, chopped fine

1 bay leaf
2 cups tomato sauce
2 tbsps Worcestershire
salt and pepper
2 tsps sugar
1 tsp mustard
3 or 4 pinches rosemary

Sauté the rabbit in melted butter, until it is lightly browned. Remove, and sauté the onions until they are golden brown; then add the flour and blend it in. Stir in the bouillon, white wine, chopped parsley, thyme, bay leaf, tomato sauce, Worcestershire, salt and pepper, sugar and mustard. (If desired, this sauce may be started in a regular saucepan and then placed in a Dutch oven.) Pour the sauce over the rabbit in a Dutch oven and add the rosemary. Cook the rabbit in the oven until tender, for about ¾ to 1 hour and serve.

Lapin aux Champignons

Rabbit with Mushrooms

4 servings

1 rabbit, cut into pieces
Marinade:
   1 onion, sliced
   1 carrot, sliced
   1 cup white wine
   sprig of fresh thyme
   1 bay leaf
   1–2 tbsps fresh fennel
     and dill, if available
flour, to coat rabbit pieces
4 tbsps butter
1 tbsp oil
salt and pepper

2 oz cognac
6–8 boiling onions, peeled
4 tbsps butter
½ lb mushrooms, sliced
  or quartered
2 or 3 cloves garlic, finely
  chopped
½ cup parsley, finely chopped
  (reserve a little for garnish)
8 oz fresh bacon or pork,
  in strips
2–3 slices of French bread, cubed
  and fried in butter (croutons)

Marinate the rabbit pieces in the marinade for several hours or, preferably, overnight. When ready to cook, remove the pieces from the marinade and roll in flour. (*Do not* dry them first; the flour will absorb the moisture.) Melt the 4 tbsps butter with the oil in a skillet and brown the rabbit on both sides. Season with salt and pepper, then add the cognac and ignite. Preheat oven to 350°.

Lightly grease a baking dish that has a tight-fitting lid, and place the rabbit pieces inside. Use the marinade to deglaze the frying pan, and add juices to the rabbit, along with the peeled onions. Cook at 350° for 30 minutes.

Melt the remaining 4 tbsps of butter and sauté the mushrooms quickly over high heat. Add the garlic and parsley. Ten minutes before the rabbit has finished cooking, add the mushrooms and the bacon or pork.

To serve: Place the rabbit pieces on a heated platter. Pour the sauce over and garnish with the croutons and fresh chopped parsley.

FISH AND SHELLFISH

"My Gigolo and Me"

The night I proposed to Charles I had prepared fish for dinner. My other fish recipes are all just as delicious!

Fish and Shellfish

When I met Josephine in 1925, she called me her "gigolo" because I was broke and my employment was, at best, sporadic. (I traveled the Orpheum Circuit, playing my accordion, when bookings were available.) I've been Josephine's "gigolo" ever since, though I've worked hard and long at many jobs since.

After Josephine proposed, I went to make the arrangements for our wedding with the Italian fathers at the Church of Saints Peter & Paul. One of them asked me what I did for a living, and when I replied that I played the accordion he remarked to another priest, "Can you imagine that. Another accordion player!" (At that time North Beach, the Italian section of town, was overrun with accordion players ~ most of them out-of-work.) When I added that my intended was a French girl, they suggested strongly that we get married in the French church.

So I went over to Notre Dame des Victoires, where I met with its pastor, Father Libihan, who asked me who I was planning to marry. When I told him Josephine Enizan, he told me to have her come to see him immediately. (It seems she was working for a very wealthy, titled family, who wouldn't permit her *to attend Sunday mass because she was expected to prepare fantastic brunches for them and their guests while* they *were attending mass. Father Libihan had noted Josephine's absence from church, and wasn't pleased.) She saw him, and worked things out ~ including our wedding plans.*

On Sunday, October 4, 1925, we arrived at the church rectory, where we waited, and waited, and waited ~ for almost two hours. Finally, Father Libihan came down ~ for his Sunday dinner. He had forgotten about our wedding. So we had a special nuptial mass ~ almost by ourselves.

We'd arranged to live at 132 25th Avenue, in the basement of a high-toned mansion owned by an English woman named Mrs. Churchill, and it was there that our reception was held. But because of the mix-up at the French church, several of our guests left before we arrived, my father among them. He had walked the 8 to 10 miles from North Beach,

Continued

and had to get back before dark. We did finally arrive, in a jitney bus, courtesy of a friend of Josephine.

We had no honeymoon when we were married ~ in fact, Josephine went back to work the next day ~ but in 1927, when we'd saved the money, we went to Paris, where Josephine attended courses in patisserie while I'd go each day to the Follies Bergere to see the magnificent Josephine Baker sing and dance. Of course, while we were in Europe, and even though Josephine had to work for the Oppens ~ at the Ritz Hotel, between classes ~ we did manage to get to Brittany in France to see her family, and to Piedmont, Italy, to meet my relations. On our return, Josephine traveled first class with the Oppens, while I was in steerage the entire voyage.

Finding work in those days wasn't easy ~ there were so many people out of work, but finally I found a job with Schmidt Lithograph, cutting cardboard. It was just like working in a lumber mill ~ very hard work. Then I worked "here and there" ~ at several small jobs, until I decided to go into business for myself. In 1931 I purchased a small grocery store in the 3800 block of Sacramento Street, behind Childrens Hospital. What I didn't know at the time was that the fellow who sold it to me had been bootlegging from the store, and his groceries were mostly fakes to fool the police. Boy, did I get angry when I discovered that all those spices were filled with bugs, and non-saleable! On top of that, most customers paid me wth bum checks. So I sold the store about six months after I bought it, for $600 ~ just about what I'd paid for it.

As a family, we did rather well, because both Josephine and I worked. When Jacqueline was born (June 22, 1931) we were living in an apartment on Clay Street between Taylor and Mason ~ around the corner from Nob Hill's Fairmont Hotel. On my days off, I'd take Jacqueline around the streets of Nob Hill in her perambulator. A number of the wealthy people livimg at the Fairmont felt sorry for me (they thought, seeing me propel the buggy, rather than a Nanny, that we must be a very poor family), and several brought me suits of clothes ~ some of them of such good quality that I was stll wearing them ten years later.

I had an old Chevrolet, and I'd tuck Jacqueline in the back seat with the blankets all around her, and we'd park in the sunshine and giggle and play games. She was only six months or a year at the time. We had a wonderful time together, and I really loved that little girl ~ and I love her just as much today. But often I think of how she was raised ~ "inside a Chevrolet."

I worked for Yellow Cab Company, "hacking," from 1929 to 1931 ~ and again from August 4, 1934 to July 1, 1962 (for a total of 31 years) and I enjoyed that work best of all because I met so many different types of people. I could write a book about those experiences.

On April 1, 1948, we purchased and moved into an apartment house on the corner of Mason and Filbert. The fellow who sold me the building so regretted selling that he parked in front of the building every day for months afterward, getting drunk, looking at the building he'd sold me for $20,000. I sold the building on April 1, 1962, for $70,000 ~ and thought I'd done well until I learned the building was sold again, a couple of years ago, for $170,000. The building had no garden, so Josephine and I grew our herbs and vegetables in pots on the roof.

These days I keep busy by assisting Josephine with her cooking classes, playing my accordion at the weddings and birthdays of friends, and in meeting the many people who have come to know us through Josephine's books. Life is a joy, and, with Josephine, it will always be so.

Congre à l'Oseille

Conger Eel with Sorrel

6 to 8 servings

2½ lbs of conger eel, sliced into ¼ inch pieces
flour for dusting the conger
8 tbsps butter (1 tbsp for the conger, 4 tbsps for the sorrel and 3 tbsps for the Béchamel sauce)

salt and pepper
2 lbs sorrel
3 tbsps flour (rounded)
½ pt whipping cream, heated
⅛ tsp nutmeg

Roll the slices of conger eel in a little flour and sauté them in the oil and 1 tbsp butter. Do not sauté them too quickly; cook about 7½ minutes on each side. Salt and pepper them and keep warm.

Clean and wash the sorrel. Dry and put it in a pan with 4 tbsps butter (no water). Cook very slowly until the sorrel forms a purée.

Prepare a thick Béchamel with the remaining butter. Melt it in a pot, add the flour, stir a few seconds and add the hot cream. Season with salt, pepper, and nutmeg. Add the sorrel to it. Arrange the sorrel on a hot serving dish. Top with the eel and serve with lemon wedges.

 **JOSEPHINE SAYS:**

To make a most delicious *fumet* of fish (fish stock):
1 lb fish trimmings (heads, tails, bones)
1 qt water
2 cups wine, white or red
1 sliced onion
1 chopped celery stalk
1 bay leaf
thyme
salt
6 crushed peppercorns

Boil ingredients; then reduce to simmer for 30 minutes. Cool and strain. Stock will keep in the refrigerator or freezer.

Praires en Gelée   Clams in Aspic

2 to 3 lbs clams in their shells
¼ cup dry white wine
1 tbsp fines herbs, chopped:
   sprig thyme, 2 to 3 sage
   leaves, spring oregano and
   winter savory
1 clove garlic, chopped
1 tbsp gelatin (1 env)
¼ cup cream
salt, pepper

Scrub clams well under cold water. Place in a large kettle and pour over wine. Add herbs and garlic. Bring to a boil and steam (covered) for 10 minutes. Remove clams from their shells, reserving some of the shells. Strain juices. Soften gelatin in a little cold wine and add to hot broth, stirring until completely dissolved. Add cream. (For 2 cups broth, you need 1 tbsp gelatin. Adjust measurements according to amount of broth you are working with.) Check seasonings, be generous with the pepper. Chill mixture to the syrupy stage. Meanwhile, film shells to facilitate unmolding and place a few clams on each shell. Spoon gelatin over and thoroughly chill until completely jelled. Unmold to serve if desired.

Moules   Mussels
Yield 48

4 dozen mussels
1 small onion,
   chopped fine
10 tbsps butter
2 tbsps chopped parsley
2 cloves garlic, minced
1 piece bread
1 cup white wine
½ cup fresh bread crumbs
Shallow pan with layer of rock salt

Place mussels in a large pot with the wine. Cover and steam for five minutes or until mussels open. Remove mussel meat, saving the bottom shell. Set aside. Sauté the onion 2 tbsps of butter, but do not brown. Combine the rest of the butter, the parsley, garlic, and the sautéed onions. Soak the bread in the mussel juice and squeeze out the excess liquid. Add to butter mixture. Smear a little of this mixture on the bottom of the shell. Place a mussel on top. Cover with more of the butter mixture. Sprinkle with the bread crumbs. Set shells on the rock salt. Place in a preheated 400° oven and cook until hot and bubbly. Serve immediately.

Haddock Poché   Poached Haddock
4 to 6 servings

1½ lbs haddock
¼ cup butter
salt and pepper
1 tsp each fine herbs:
   parsley, tarragon, dill
   or fennel, chives
2 cups milk

Soak the haddock in cold water for at least 1 hour. Drain and wipe off. Film a fireproof dish with butter and place the fish in it. Dot with 2 tbsps butter, add salt, pepper and the chopped herbs. Warm the milk and pour over the fish.

Put the dish in a preheated 375° oven. When the milk starts to boil, lower the heat to 325° and continue baking. When the fish is cooked add the remaining 2 tbsps butter to the milk (which should be reduced to the thickness of cream). Place the fish on a serving platter and pour the milk over it. Sprinkle with additional herbs.

Boiled potatoes may be served with this dish.

Truites en Gelée

Trout in Aspic

6 to 8 servings

Court bouillon:
- 1 large onion
- white part of 1 leek
- 1 rib or a few leaves of celery
- 1 small carrot
- 2 tbsps butter
- 1 sprig thyme
- 1 bay leaf

- salt and pepper
- 1 cup wine
- 8 trout, cleaned
- 1 tbsp unflavored gelatin
- lemon slices
- tarragon leaves for decoration

Prepare a court bouillon as follows: Sauté the chopped vegetables in butter in a saucepan. Add the thyme, bay leaf, salt and pepper. Add the wine and simmer about 5 minutes. Let the broth cool. Preheat the oven to 350°.

Lay the trout in a fireproof dish and pour the cooled court bouillon over them. Bake in a 350° oven for 15 to 20 minutes. Let the trout cool in the court bouillon.

When cool, arrange the trout on a serving dish. The skin may be removed, if desired. Prepare a gelatin with fish stock if you have it or with meat stock if necessary. For 2 cups of liquid dissolve 1 tbsp gelatin in a little cold water. Heat the liquid to boiling and pour it over the dissolved gelatin. Let the gelatin cool until it becomes very syrupy.

Decorate the trout with lemon slices and a few tarragon leaves, or as you choose. Pour the gelatin over the trout. You may have to repeat pouring gelatin over before it sets completely.

Serve with a cucumber or beet salad.

Coquille de Poisson

Scallop Shells Filled with Fish

6 to 8 servings

- 6 to 8 scallop shells
- 1 lb fish (salmon, cod, sole or any other)

- ¼ lb shrimp, and ¼ lb mushrooms
- Mornay sauce (see index)
- bread crumbs

Arrange fish in scallop shells with shrimps and mushrooms, coat with Mornay sauce, sprinkle with bread crumbs and dot with butter. Brown in hot oven or put under broiler.

Continued

Note: If fish is left over, just cut it in dices or small pieces, before putting it in shells or ramequins, cut mushrooms in halves or quarters and sauté in butter for 4 to 5 minutes. If fish is fresh, it should be poached before putting it in shells.

Soufflé aux Crevettes / Shrimp Soufflé

4 – 6 oz baby shrimp,
    coarsely chopped
⅓ cup cooked cereal
    (Cream of Rice or Wheat)
½ cube butter
2¼ cups milk, heated

4 egg yolks
6 egg whites
salt, pepper, nutmeg
butter and Parmesan (optional)
    for soufflé mold

Butter a suitable dish and sprinkle with Parmesan cheese if desired. Set aside. Melt butter in top of double boiler over medium heat. Stir in cooked cereal and hot milk. Season with salt, pepper, and nutmeg to taste. When ready to make soufflé, add yolks to **bouille,** one at a time. Add chopped shrimp. Beat egg whites stiff and fold one third into soufflé base. Gently fold in the rest. Pour into buttered dish and bake in upper half of preheated 375° oven for 20-25 minutes.

 **JOSEPHINE SAYS:**

When you buy fish without bones, you should figure on ¼ to ½ lb per serving. For fish with bones, plan on ¾ lb per serving.

To keep fish fresh for a day or so, wrap it in aluminum foil and keep it in the coolest part of the refrigerator.

Le Bar du Maréchal Joffre / Striped Bass with Chivry Sauce

6 servings

1 whole striped bass (4 to 5 lbs)
2 3 tbsps mustard
sorrel leaves
fresh fennel or dill
2 coups court bouillon
2 tbsps olive oil
salt, pepper
Garniture:
    1 lb asparagus, cut into
        ½-inch pcs
    juice of 1 lemon
    1½ lbs small potatoes
    ¼ lb butter
    ¾ cup chopped parsley
        and/or chervil

Chivry Sauce:
    4 tbsps butter
    ¼ cup flour
    ½ cup stock (fish or
        chicken), warmed
    ½ tsp total of equal parts
        oregano, sage, marjoram,
        thyme, rosemary
    1 tsp each chives, parsley,
        tarragon, chervil
    salt, pepper, nutmeg
    walnut-size **beurre manié**
    2 egg yolks mixed with
        ½ cup cream

Smear cavity of bass with mustard and season generously with salt and pepper. Place sorrel leaves and fennel or dill in cavity. Place fish in a fish poacher and cover with the court bouillon. Place wax paper, freezer paper or parchment filmed with olive oil over the fish and seal with foil. Bake in a preheated 350° oven for 35-45 minutes, being careful not to overcook.

Prepare sauce: Melt the butter and stir in flour. Slowly add the stock. Season with salt, pepper, and nutmeg. When ready to serve fish, strain the **fumet** (juices from the fish) and stir into the sauce. *If* the sauce becomes too thin, add the **beurre manie** and cook until sauce thickens. Add herbs and correct seasoning. Enrich sauce with the egg/cream mixture.

Garniture: Melt the butter and add 4 tbsps to the asparagus pieces, coating them thoroughly. Season with salt and pepper and add lemon juice. Cover and cook for 5 to 10 minutes — just enough to cook the asparagus. Boil potatoes in salt water until cooked through; drain and add the remaining melted butter along with the parsley and chervil. Asparagus and potatoes can be served separately in tartlet shells or simply arranged around the fish.

To serve: Remove the fish from the poacher, and carefully place on a heated platter. Remove the skin from the top side and cover fish lightly with the sauce. Surround with vegetable tartlets and sprinkle fish and sauce with parsley. It is an elegant meal.

Truites au Grand Marnier / Trout with Grand Marnier

6 servings

Court bouillon:
- ½ cup white wine
- ½ cup water
- 2 tbsps vinegar
- 1 sprig thyme
- 1 bay leaf
- 1 carrot
- 1 onion
- salt and pepper

- 1 orange rind
- 1 lemon rind
- 6 trout
- 2 shallots, chopped
- 1 cup heavy cream (or **crème fraîche**)
- 4 tbsps butter
- 1 liquor glass of **Grand Marnier**
- parsley, chopped

Prepare the court bouillon with the wine, water, vinegar, thyme, bay leaf, carrot, onion, salt and pepper. Bring to a boil and simmer 20 minutes. Cut the orange and lemon rinds into thin strips and blanch in water about 3 minutes. Drain and add to the court bouillon.

Preheat oven to 375°.

Place the trout side by side in a fireproof dish and sprinkle with chopped shallots. Pour the court bouillon over the trout, cover with buttered waxed paper and bake for about 10 minutes. Remove some of the liquid, strain, and reduce it to ¼ cup. Add the **crème fraîche**, the butter and the **Grand Marnier.** Let it reduce if necessary, to reach a sauce consistency.

Put the trout on a serving platter and cover with the sauce. Sprinkle with chopped parsley and serve.

Note: If you have fish stock on hand it may be used instead of the **court bouillon.** And, the the orange and lemon rind may be chopped rather than cut into strips.

Tranches de Saumon—Sauce à l'Oseille
Salmon Steak with Sorrel Sauce
2 servings

2 salmon steaks
1 tbsp flour
1 tbsp oil
1 tbsp butter

2 oz vermouth
1½ bunches sorrel
4 tbsps whipping cream
salt and pepper

Dredge both sides of salmon steaks with flour. Add a touch of salt and pepper. Melt the butter and oil in frying pan; warm it at low heat for 2 to 3 minutes. When it is hot, add the salmon and place in the oven for 3 minutes each side at 375°.

Sauce: Put vermouth and sorrel into sauce pan and reduce mixture over low heat for 3 - 4 minutes; strain. Whip the cream and add to the sauce, stirring until it gets thick. Add salt and pepper to taste.

When the salmon steaks are ready, remove the skin and debone. Place fish on platter and pour the sauce over it. If you wish, you may serve with rice and a white Bordeaux.

Sole Normandie
Fillet of Sole Normandy
6 to 8 servings

8 fillets of sole
salt and pepper
1 cup white wine
1 sprig parsley
1 sprig thyme
1 bay leaf
2 lbs mussels or clams
¼ cup butter

1 rounded tbsp flour
¼ lb mushrooms, sliced
¼ lb shrimp, cooked
juice of 1 lemon
2 – 3 egg yolks
¼ cup cream
parsley to garnish

Preheat oven to 350°.

Wash and dry the sole fillets and lay them in a fireproof dish. Sprinkle with salt and pepper and add the wine and herbs. Cover with a piece of buttered wax paper, set in preheated oven, and bake 15 to 20 minutes.

Meanwhile steam the mussels or clams and remove them from the shell. Make a roux with the butter and flour. Remove the sole fillets from their liquid and keep them warm. Strain the liquid and add gradually to the roux to make a sauce. Stir until thickened.

Sauté the mushrooms in a little butter and add them to the sauce, along with the shrimp and mussels or clams. Add the lemon juice. At the last minute before serving, stir in the egg yolks and cream and pour the sauce over the sole. Sprinkle with parsley and serve.

Filet de Carrelet Bordelaise

Flounder in Mushrooms and Wine
2 servings

1 flounder
½ lb mushrooms, sliced
2 shallots, chopped
1 to 2 tbsps parsley, chopped
1 tbsp **aromatic herbs:** thyme, bay, savory, sage, rosemary (use more sage than any of the others)

1 clove garlic, minced
bread crumbs
flour
¼ cup white wine
½ cup fish **fumet**
butter
⅓ cup grated cheese

Melt about 2 tbsps butter with a little oil in a pan. Sauté mushrooms with garlic quickly over high heat. Add shallots.

Butter a baking dish large enough to hold the fish. Place half of the mushroom mixture on the bottom as a bed for the fish. Sprinkle with bread crumbs, parsley and chives, some of the herbs and 1-2 tsps flour. Place fish on top, then sprinkle with salt and pepper, and place pinches of herbs, parsley, and chives in the cavity of the fish. Cover fish with rest of mushrooms, and sprinkle with breadcrumbs, herbs and flour. Cover all of this with about ⅓ cup grated cheese. Dot with butter. Put wine and fish fumet in the baking dish, cover and bake at 350° for 25-30 minutes or until done. Remove cover for the last 5-10 minutes to brown fish.

Perches Pochées Champenoise

Perch Poached in Champagne

Court bouillon:
   1½ cup champagne
   1 cup veal or chicken stock
   1 carrot
   a few leaves of celery
   1 onion, chopped
   1 sprig each: parsley and thyme
   2 or 3 cloves garlic
   salt and pepper
   2 tbsps oil

1 perch per serving
Beurre manié:
   1 tbsp butter
   1 tbsp flour
   1 tbsp parsley, minced
juice of ½ lemon
2 tbsps butter
¼ cup heavy cream
parsley for garnish

Prepare a court bouillon with the champagne, broth, vegetables, spices and oil. Let it come to a boil and simmer for 25 minutes. Allow to cool.

Preheat oven to 375°. Put the fish in a shallow, fireproof dish and pour the court bouillon over them. Cover with a buttered piece of wax paper and tinfoil. (Do not allow foil to touch the fish directly.) Bake at 375° for 15 minutes or until tender. Drain the fish very carefully and take the skin off. Arrange the fish on a heated platter and keep warm.

Continued

Strain the court bouillon and reduce it to 1½ cups. Stir in the beurre manié (made by kneading the butter with the flour and parsley). When the sauce has thickened a little add the lemon juice. At the last minute enrich the sauce with 2 tbsps butter and the heavy cream. Spoon the sauce over the fish, sprinkle with parsley and serve at once.

Poisson de Saison Meurette — Fish Meurette

any fish, ½ lb for each serving
1 to 2 cups red wine
3 tbsps oil

herbs: parsley, thyme, sage and sorrel
(2 tbsps of herbs in all)

Marinate the fish in the wine and oil for at least ½ hour, longer if possible. Remove the fish and bake at 375° until half done. Cover with the herbs and return to the oven to bake until done, about 15 minutes. Serve with one of the following sauces:

Sauce #1

yolks of 2 hardcooked eggs
parsley, chopped
vinegar
oil

salt and pepper
1 tsp mustard
1 tbsp purée of sorrel

Mash the egg yolks and beat the other ingredients into them.

Sauce #2

2 tbsps butter
1 rounded tbsp flour
juices from the fish (1 to 1½ cups)

1 egg yolk
$1/3$ cup cream

Melt the butter in a pan and add the flour. Stir for a few seconds without allowing it to brown. Add the fish juices and simmer for 10 minutes. Mix the egg yolk and cream and add to the sauce at the last minute. Do not allow the sauce to boil after adding the cream.

JOSEPHINE SAYS:

A suitable fish poacher can be improvised by placing a wooden board on the bottom of the baking pan. Place fish on a piece of cheesecloth on the board and cover fish well with the cheesecloth. Tie with string.

Poaching liquid can be poured over fish and then the entire dish covered with oiled, waxed paper, parchment, or freezer paper (with the waxed side down). Seal with tin foil.

Filets de Sole Escoffier

A recipe of Auguste Escoffier

Poached Sole Fillets Escoffier

4 to 6 servings

1 lobster
court bouillon for boiling
   lobster
¼ lb mushrooms
¼ cup butter
1 clove garlic
1 tbsp parsley
Marinade:
1 onion, minced
juice of 2 lemons
1 cup white wine
salt and pepper

4 to 6 sole fillets
1 or 2 eggs, beaten
2 tbsps flour
½ tsp nutmeg
2 egg yolks
1 cup cream
Sauce:
3 tbsps butter
2 tbsps flour
1 tbsp paprika
chopped parsley

If starting with a live lobster, boil the lobster in the court bouillon, for 10 minutes (dropping it head first into the pot). If already cooked, put the meat through a fine chopper or Cuisinart, reserving the coral for another use (it is the very best part). Reserve mushroom caps and sauté the stems in 2 tbsps butter. Add the chopped garlic and parsley and set aside.

Mix the minced onion, lemon juice, wine, salt and pepper and marinate the fillets for 20 to 30 minutes. Then dip each first in egg, then in flour, and sauté in butter. Do *not* cook completely, however.

Grease a baking dish and line with the fillets. Place whole mushroom caps on top. In a bowl, mix the puréed lobster meat with salt, pepper, and nutmeg. Beat in the egg yolks one at a time and add half of the cream. Cool in the refrigerator for 20 to 30 minutes. Form mixture into little balls, roll them in flour and poach in the sole marinade for 10 to 20 minutes, adding more wine or water if needed. Drain the balls, and place in the baking dish with the sole and mushrooms. Pour the remaining marinade over the sole. Cover dish with buttered wax paper, then with foil. Bake at 375° for 15 minutes. Remove the fillets and keep warm while preparing the sauce.

Sauce: Make a roux with the butter and flour, stirring well. Moisten with about 2 cups of the poaching liquid. Add the chopped mushroom stems, paprika, salt and pepper as needed, and ½ cup cream.

Arrange the sole on a serving platter. Surround with mushroom caps and lobster balls. Pour sauce over fish and garnish with parsley. Spinach au gratin or asparagus with vinaigrette and parsley-buttered potatoes are excellent accompaniments.

 **JOSEPHINE SAYS:**

Never **wrap a fish in foil if it is resting in a wine or court bouillon. Foil will turn the fish an unappetizing black. Instead, use cheesecloth or buttered butcher paper** *before* **covering with foil.**

Filets de Sole ou Cabillaud Epinette   ## Sole or Cod Epinette
6 servings

1 large fillet of sole or cod per serving	4 egg yolks
6 crushed peppercorns or 1 tsp coarse pepper	2 tbsps heavy cream
	2 tbsps fish stock
salt	1 tbsp minced chives
cayenne pepper	2 tbsps milk mixed with 1 egg
2 shallots chopped fine	¾ cup steamed clams, oysters, or mussels
¼ cup vinegar	
¼ cup fish stock	2 tbsps lemon juice
¼ cup butter, melted	1 crushed clove garlic

First prepare sauce: Combine in a small saucepan vinegar, fish stock, chopped shallots, salt and pepper, and reduce to about 3 tbsps. To the reduction, add the yolks, and 2 tbsps fish stock, stirring in a double boiler that is not too hot. Stir until creamy, then add the melted butter (lukewarm) gradually, leaving the butter residue in the pan. Add lemon juice, chives, and crushed garlic. Remove crushed garlic clove before serving. Cream should be stirred into the sauce at the last minute when you are ready to serve.

Salt and pepper the fillets lightly; dip each one in the egg and milk, and lay them in a lightly greased baking dish. Place under the broiler (oven temperature of 300°), 4 inches from flame, and cook slowly until brown. Then distribute shellfish over dish, and pour sauce over all. Place under broiler again to lightly brown. Serve with remaining sauce.

Turban de Sole en Soufflé   ## Sole Fillets with Fish Mousse
6 to 8 servings

1 cup ground fish	6 to 8 sole fillets with skins
1 cup **panade**: Pâte à choux made with ½ **fumet** and ½ water	2 to 4 tbsps heavy cream
	ring mold, 2 qt capacity
	salt, pepper, nutmeg
1 egg white	

Prepare the **panade** (see recipe for Pâte à choux) using the fish stock and water. Combine **panade** with ground fish and season with salt, pepper, and nutmeg. You may wish to add tarragon, and chervil also. This mixture is easiest to work with if kept chilled. You can place the mixing bowl in a larger bowl that is filled with ice. Then you can add the egg white and mix thoroughly. The cream may be added a little at a time, mixing continuously.

Generously salt and pepper the underside of each fillet. Place them skin side down in a well-greased ring mold, so that the ends extend over the sides of the mold. Fill the mold with the fish mousse and then fold remaining fillet ends over the top. Cover mold with a cover or buttered wax paper. Place in a **bain marie** of almost boiling water and bake in the lower third of the oven at 375° for 45 minutes to an hour. To test, insert a knife which should come out clean when done.

Note: Mold may be prepared ahead of time and cooked just before serving.

To serve, unmold ring and drain off the excess liquid. Add a few tbsps of the juices to the sauce you are serving with it, such as Suprême, Mousseline, or Nantua (see *Sauce* recipes). Fill center of the mold with any kind of cooked vegetable (broccoli, carrots, cauliflowerets) or shellfish (shrimp, prawns). Coat the turban with some of the sauce.

Ecrevisses Colombines

Crayfish with Tomato and Heavy Cream

Court bouillon:
  1 cup white wine
  1 cup water
  2 tbsps vinegar
  ½ carrot
  ½ onion
  ½ stalk celery
  1 bay leaf
  2 sprigs thyme
  salt and pepper

12 crayfish per serving
¼ cup butter
2 tbsps **coulis** (light tomato sauce)
$1/3$ cup heavy cream
1 tbsp **fine herbes:** tarragon, chives, and chervil, chopped
parsley, chopped

Make a **court bouillon** by simmering the ingredients together for 25 minutes. Poach the crayfish in this **court bouillon** for 10 minutes and let them cool in their juice.

Take the fish out of their shells. Melt the butter and sauté the crayfish. Season with salt and pepper and add 2 tbsps **coulis,** the heavy cream, and chopped fine herbs. Put the fish back in their shells and arrange on a warmed platter. Sprinkle with parsley and serve.

 **JOSEPHINE SAYS:**

How to Prepare Shrimp

1 lb shrimp, in shells
Court bouillon:
  1 qt boiling water
  1 stalk celery, cut in pieces

1 onion, cut in pieces
1 tsp black pepper
1 tsp salt
3 slices lemon

Wash the shrimp and set aside.

Prepare a *court bouillon* with the water, vegetables, and seasonings. Let it simmer for 25 minutes. Add the shrimp and simmer slowly for 10 minutes. Peel the shrimp before using in the desired way.

Note: **Delicious served with tomato sauce and spaghetti or noodles.**

Gratin d'Ecrevisses

Crayfish au Gratin
4 servings

12 crayfish per serving
2 cups **court bouillon**
   (see preceding recipe)
¼ cup butter or margarine

3 tbsps flour
salt, pepper, nutmeg
½ to 1 cup grated cheese

Cook crayfish in **court bouillon** and remove the shells. Reduce the **court bouillon** and strain it. Make a Velouté sauce in a double boiler by melting the butter and stirring in the flour. Add 1½ cups of the broth and season with salt, pepper and nutmeg. Cook, covered, for 15 to 20 minutes. Butter a shallow, ovenproof dish and arrange the crayfish in the bottom. Pour sauce over and sprinkle top with cheese. Place in a hot oven or under the broiler to brown slightly.

If you cannot find crayfish, you may substitute lobster tails or jumbo shrimp. For a variation, serve with Nantua sauce (add some finely chopped shrimp and 1 tsp tomato paste to the Velouté sauce).

WHEN YOU SING WHILE YOU COOK, YOU COOK BETTER!

Grenouilles Sautées à Sec

Frogs Legs with Sherry/Butter Sauce
4 to 6 servings

2 pair of frogs' legs
   per serving
flour
2 eggs, beaten
1 cup bread crumbs
2 tbsps butter and
   2 tbsps oil

salt and pepper
parsley, chopped
for **Sauce au beurre:**
½ cup butter
2 shallots, chopped
juice of 1 lemon
¼ cup sherry

Roll the frog legs well in flour, then in beaten eggs and then in the bread crumbs. Sauté in the hot butter and oil for 5 to 6 minutes. Sprinkle with salt and pepper and arrange on a platter. Sprinkle with parsley and serve separately with **Sauce au beurre.**

Sauce au Beurre

Melt the butter in a small pan. Add the shallots and let them cook until the butter has turned a nice hazelnut brown. Add the lemon juice and sherry and bring to a boil. Serve hot alongside frog legs (or with poached fish).

Oeufs Leontine

Baked Eggs with Shrimp and Haddock

4 to 6 servings

½ lb shrimp
½ lb haddock
1 – 1½ cups milk
¼ cup flour
⅓ cup butter
⅓ cup grated cheese

1 can of truffles, chopped
  (optional)
nutmeg, salt, pepper
1 small onion, chopped
2 eggs per serving
1 can tomato paste

Boil shrimp in salted water (enough to cover) and poach the haddock in milk for 10 minutes. Reserve the milk and shrimp water. Put the haddock and *half* of the shrimp through the fine blade of a good chopper, and season lightly with salt and pepper. Preheat oven to 350°.

In a double boiler make a roux with the butter and flour. Stir a few minutes and add the heated milk and the shrimp water. Stir until thick. Cook a few minutes more and add the optional chopped truffles, salt, pepper, and nutmeg. Set aside ⅓ cup of sauce. To the rest add the chopped fish and shrimp mixture and the chopped onion.

Butter a pyrex dish and put the fish mixture into it. Set in the oven and bake at 350° for 20 minutes. Meanwhile sauté the remaining cooked shrimp in butter and spread over the baked fish mixture. Dot with butter and break the eggs over it. Put back in the oven about 7 to 8 minutes, until eggs are set.

Meanwhile, dilute the tomato paste with the remaining ⅓ cup of the cream sauce. When the eggs are set, dollop some sauce on each egg and then sprinkle with grated cheese. Put under the broiler for a few seconds, and serve in the same dish.

Bouquets au Cari

Prawns with Curry Sauce

4 to 6 servings

1½ lbs prawns
2 tbsps butter
1 recipe of curry sauce
1 cup rice

2 cups broth or water
salt and pepper
parsley, chopped

Sauté the shrimp in 1 tbsp butter. Prepare the curry sauce and add the sautéed shrimp to it.

Put 1 cup of rice, 1 tbsp of butter and the broth or water in heavy pot. Add seasonings. Bring to a boil; stir the rice once. Reduce the heat and let the rice simmer for 15 minutes. When rice is cooked press it into a ring; then unmold it on a warmed platter and place the prawns in the center. Sprinkle with chopped parsley and serve hot.

Curry sauce: Follow recipe for Hollandaise sauce. Add 1 tbsp curry powder.

Bouquets au Potiron

Prawns in Pumpkin
4 to 6 servings

¼ piece of pumpkin
1½ lbs prawns
1 onion, chopped
1 clove of garlic,
    minced
2 tbsps butter

1 small tomato, chopped
⅛ tsp nutmeg
⅛ tsp cloves
1 sprig thyme, chopped
1 tsp parsley, chopped
salt and pepper

Preheat oven to 375°.

Scoop some of the flesh from the pumpkin, and chop it very finely. Sauté the prawns, onion, and garlic in butter; then add the finely chopped pumpkin and tomato, along with the spices. Finally add the chopped shrimp. Return mixture to the pumpkin shell. Cover with foil and bake ¾ of an hour.

Langouste à la Parisienne

Lobster Salad

1 lobster, cooked and cooled
shredded lettuce
Vinaigrette dressing:
    3 tbsps oil
    1 tbsp vinegar
    1 tsp mustard
    salt and pepper

mayonnaise
Garnish:
    anchovy fillets
    capers or olives
    beet salad
    celery root salad
    chopped parsley

Cut out the underside sections of the lobster and reserve the shell. Place the shell on a platter and line it with shredded lettuce which has been seasoned with French dressing. On this foundation line up the scallops of lobster, horseback-like. Season with vinaigrette and cover with mayonnaise. Decorate with anchovy filets and capers or olives. Garnish each side with beet salad and celery root salad, and top with parsley.

Calmars

Squid
6 to 8 servings

2 dozen squid
1 onion
¼ cup butter
2–3 tomatoes
1 piece of french bread,
    moistened and squeezed
    dry (about 1 cup)
2 cloves garlic
2 tbsps white wine or bouillon
2 to 3 egg yolks or 1 whole egg
oil for frying

Sauce:
    1 onion, chopped
    1 clove garlic, chopped
    2 tbsps butter
    1 rounded tbsp flour
    ½ cup white wine
    salt and pepper
    1 bay leaf
    1 sprig thyme
    bread crumbs

Remove the black ink bags and cartilage from the squid. Separate bodies and tentacles and wash thoroughly. Lay the bodies flat on a cloth.

Chop the onion and fry in butter. Cut the tentacles in small pieces and add to the onion. Peel and chop the tomatoes and fry them with the onions. Add the squeezed bread, chopped garlic and moisten with wine or bouillon. Add the egg yolks or whole egg. Remove from the heat and fill the squid bodies. Close them with thread and fry in oil.

To make the sauce, sauté one chopped onion and one garlic clove in butter. Add the flour and stir. Stir in the white wine and seasonings. Simmer for 15 minutes.

Pour the sauce over the fried squid. Sprinkle with bread crumbs and brown lightly under the broiler.

Calmars en Salade   Squid Salad
4 servings

1 lb calamaris (squid)	salt and pepper
3–4 tomatoes	2 cups white wine
2 cloves garlic	6 tbsps oil
3 to 4 onions	2 tbsps vinegar
3 tbsps oil	1 tsp mustard
Bouquet garni: 1 sprig thyme and 1 bay leaf	few drops of Worcestershire
	1 small can of pimientos
1 pinch saffron	chopped parsley

Clean the calamaris, removing the ink sack and cartilage. Cut in slices and cook in boiling water for 10 minutes. Drain the calamaris and refresh them in cold water.

Peel the tomatoes and cut them in pieces. Chop the garlic and two of the onions. Heat the oil and sauté the chopped garlic and onion until translucent. Add the tomatoes, **bouquet garni,** saffron, salt, pepper and wine. Bring to a boil and simmer, covered, for 20 minutes. Remove the **bouquet garni** and strain the liquid. Return it to the heat, add the calamaris, and simmer 20 minutes more. Allow the calamaris to cool in the juices.

Meanwhile make a vinaigrette with the oil, vinegar, salt, pepper, mustard and Worcestershire. Cut the pimientos and the remaining onions. Remove the calamaris from their juices and put them on a serving platter. Add the onions and pimientos. Add a little of the cooking juice to the vinaigrette and pour over the calamaris. Sprinkle with chopped parsley.

**AN ALBUM
OF MEMORIES**

My mother – in her favorite Breton costume.

1923 – Paris, with my sister.

1925 – My Gigolo.

My favorite employer – Mrs. Oppen.

All dressed up–in Mrs. Oppen's clothes.

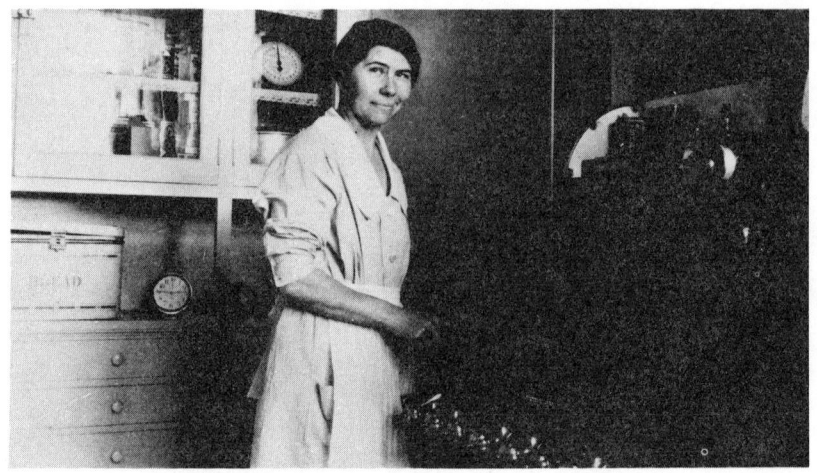

A new stove (about 1930).

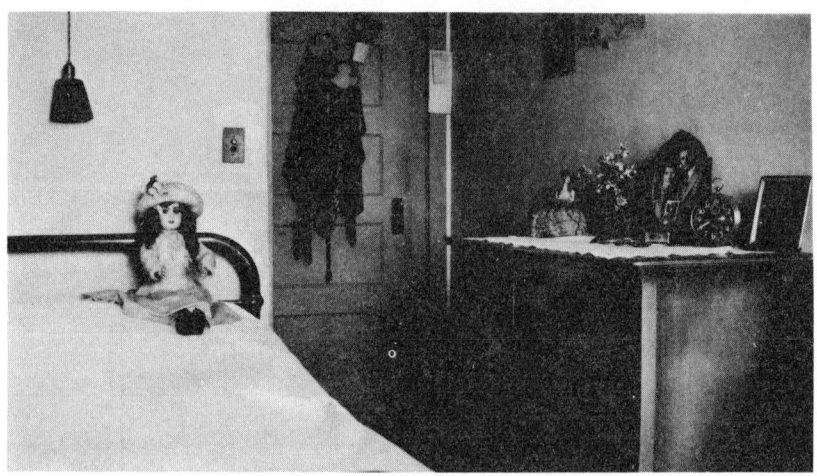

1928 – My room at the Oppen's.

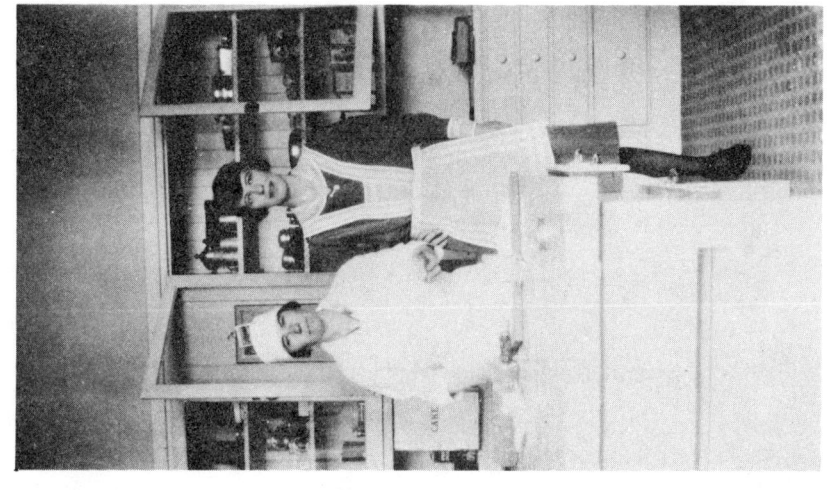

With Mae, the Irish girl, in the Oppen's pantry (I'm standing on a box).

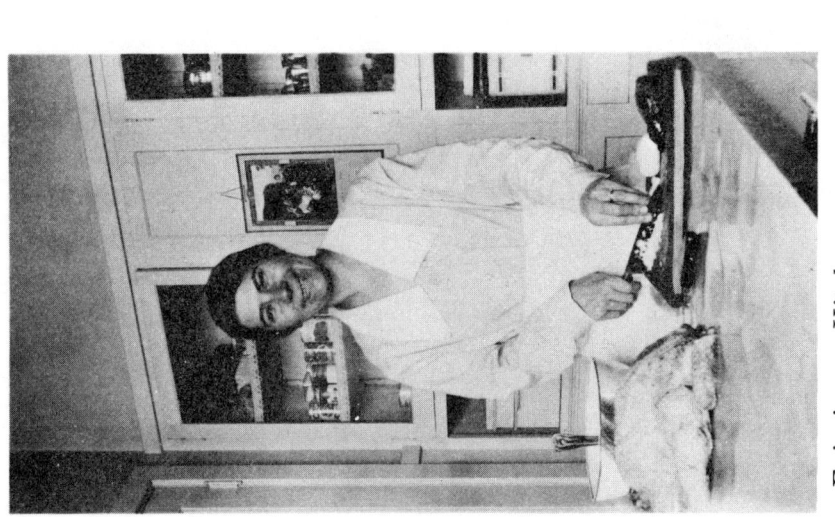

Enjoying my Kitchen.

My *diplome* from the Cordon Bleu.

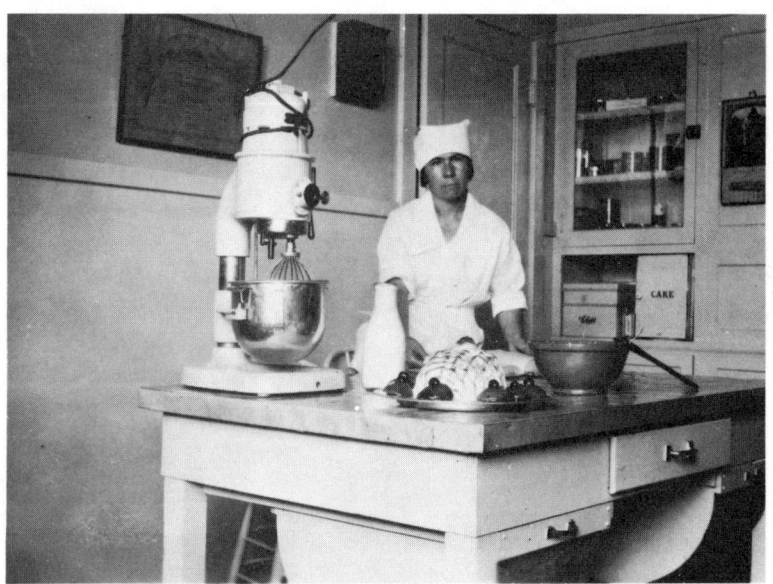

In the Oppen's kitchen.

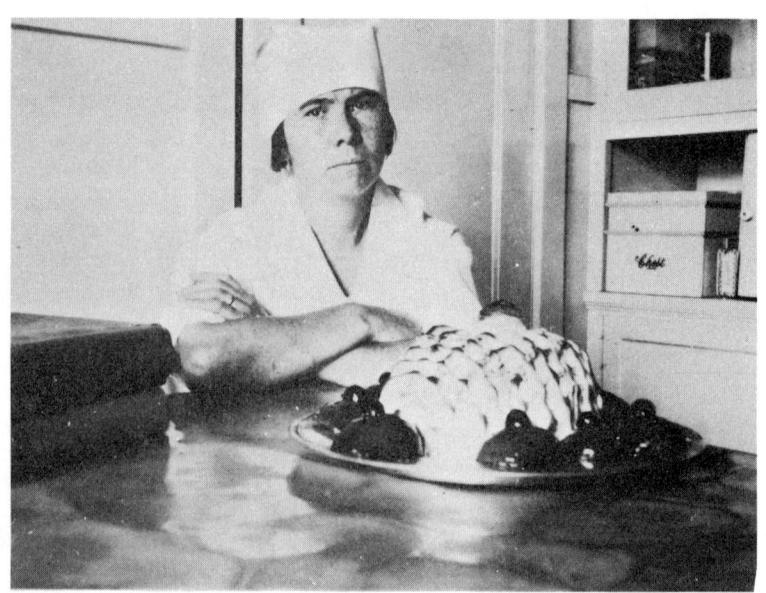

An early success.

1927 – On shipboard.

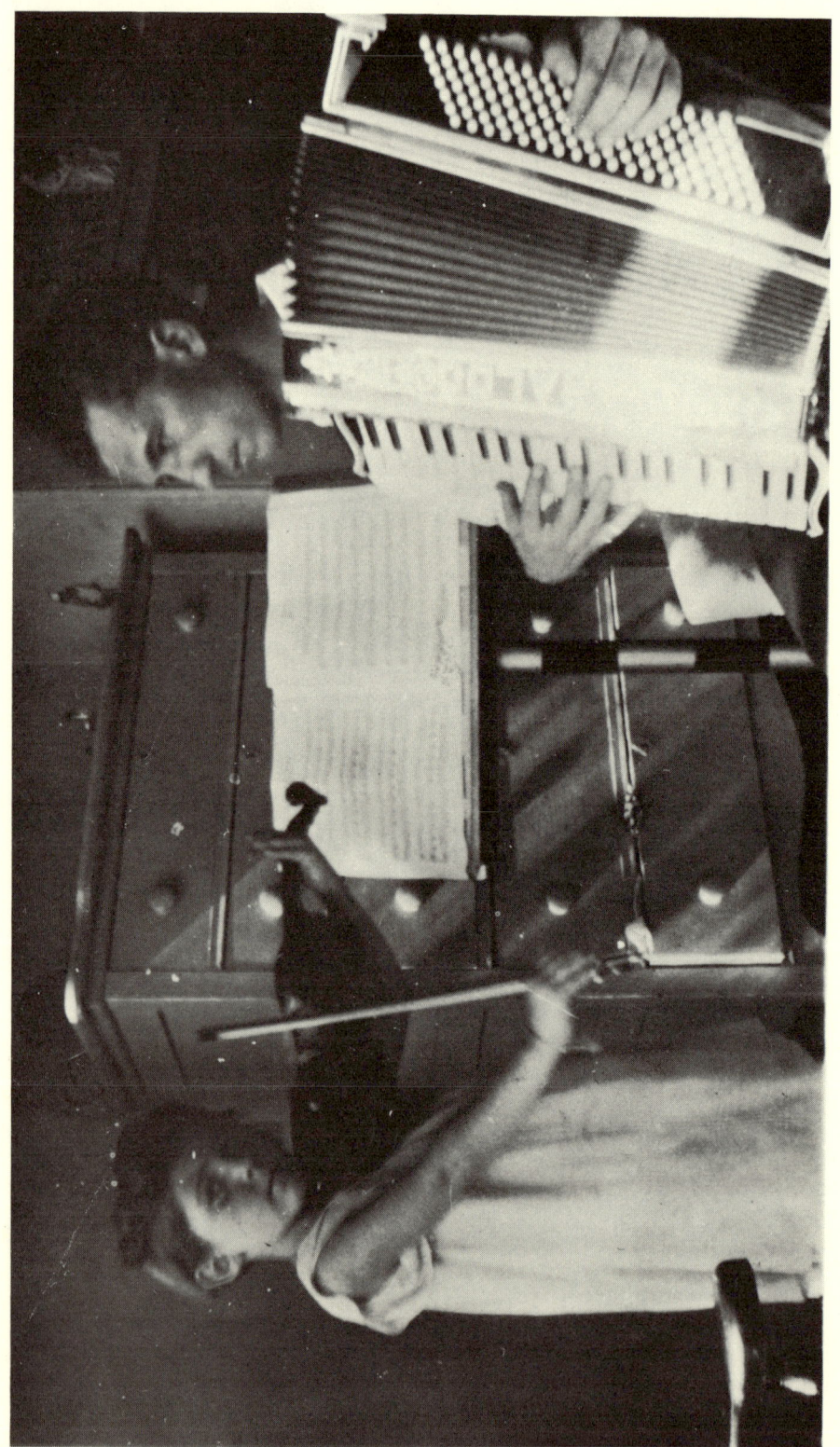

1937 – Jacqueline and Charles practicing their music.

We're on an outing.

Charles near Santa Cruz. 1923

Relaxing near Santa Cruz. 1927

Then... 1925

...Now 1978

Dinner with Fr. Leonard Ferringo, present pastor of Notre Dame des Victoires.

BEEF, VEAL, LAMB AND PORK

"To Beat the Band!"

These recipes for beef, veal, lamb and pork ~ served in their own juices or with a sauce ~ have flavor to beat the band! Remember, "la sauce c'est toute."

Beef, Veal, Lamb, and Pork

I have always been very religious. I grew up in the Church, and attended school at the convent, until I decided the life of a nun was not for me. But religion is still very important to me ~ religion and cooking are all I know! For more than fifty years, I have cooked the meals for the Fathers at Notre Dame des Victoires. And for more than ten years I have taken theology classes at the University of San Francisco, because of Father Connolly. When he was president at U.S.F., he gave me a lifetime scholarship to take classes there. All these years I've gone to class every week after work to study religion.

When Charles and I moved into our apartment on Mason Street, I had already begun cooking classes for a few of the women for whom I worked and their friends. One day a student wanted to come visit me ~ I told her I lived "on the corner." Of course, there are four corners, and, I'd forgotten to tell her which *corner. But she found my apartment anyway ~ she simply figured out which room was mine. "When I got to the street, I looked up at all the windows, until I saw one with a crucifix hanging. That must be Josephine's!" And she was right! I told her I was very glad that someone knew me by the sign of the cross.*

SONG TO COOK BY ~

*Keeper of the round table
Let us know if the wine is good.
If I die I want to be buried
In a cellar where there's good wine.
With my feet on the wall
And my head under the spigot!*

Aiguillettes de Boeuf à la Flamande

Braised Fillet of Beef with Vegetables

6 servings

3 lbs fillet of beef
   or top sirloin
strip of pork back fat
butter and oil, or
   chicken fat
2 onions, sliced
2 carrots, sliced

1 cup white wine, warmed
1 cup demi-glacé sauce
   (brown sauce)
bouquet garni of thyme,
   bay leaf, celery stalk
   and leaves

Lard the beef with a larding needle or have your butcher do it for you. Brown meat on all sides in the butter or fat. Remove from pan and in the same fat sauté onions and the carrots for a few minutes. Return meat to the pan, add salt and pepper, **bouquet garni,** warm wine, and demi-glacé sauce. Boil, then place in a 300° oven for 2 hours.

Vegetable garnish:

1 cabbage
1 lb garlic sausage
   (saucisson)
½ lb lean fresh bacon
   (or smoked)
1 onion studded with
   4–5 cloves
2 bunches of carrots
1 bunch turnips
¼ cup butter

bouquet garni of bay leaf,
   parsley, thyme, celery
   leaves
1 tsp sugar
1 cup bouillon
1 lb potatoes

Cut cabbage into quarters and blanch in boiling water for 7 minutes. Drain and place in a fireproof casserole, adding salt, pepper, and bouillon. Boil the bacon 10 minutes to remove the salt, then add to cabbage along with sausage, onions, and **bouquet garni.** Cook for 1½ hours in a 350° oven.

Prepare carrots and turnips by using a round melon spoon to make marble-size vegetables. Sauté in half of the butter and enough bouillon to barely cover them. Add salt and pepper, and the sugar and cook until the bouillon is absorbed and sugar forms a glaze.

Prepare potatoes by peeling and washing them; dry and cut thick ½-inch slices. Use a fluted knife to give a waffle look across the sides. Sauté in the remaining butter for a few minutes; add bouillon and cook until bouillon is absorbed and potatoes begin to brown.

To serve: Arrange sliced beef on a platter and garnish with the cabbage, carrots, and turnips. Place potatoes at both ends of the platter. Skim off fat from sauce and pour sauce over meat and vegetables.

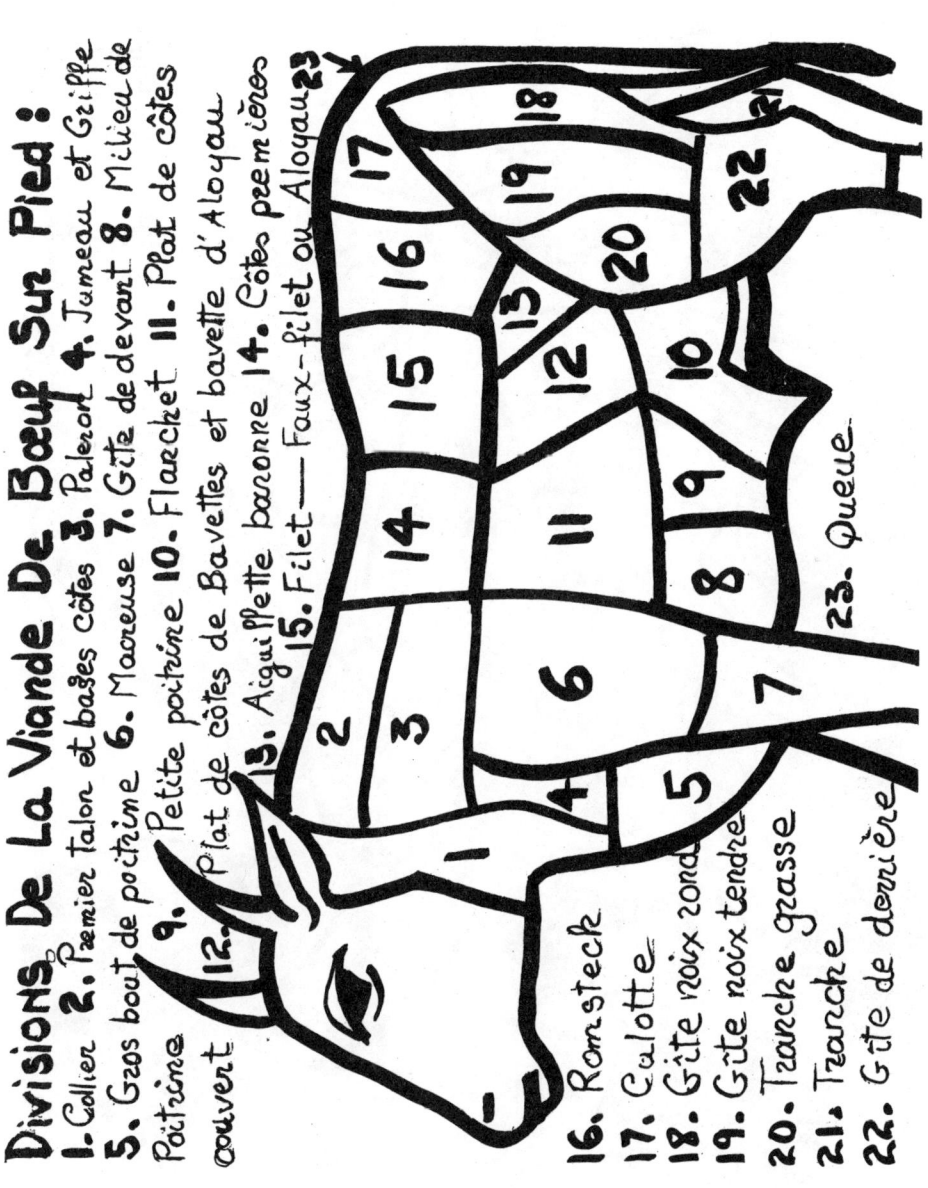

Divisions De La Viande De Bœuf Sur Pied :

1. Collier
2. Premier talon et basses côtes
3. Paleron
4. Jumeau et Griffe
5. Gros bout de poitrine
6. Macreuse
7. Gîte de devant
8. Milieu de Poitrine
9. Petite poitrine
10. Flanchet
11. Plat de côtes couvert
12. Plat de côtes de Bavettes et bavette d'Aloyau
13. Aiguillette baronne
14. Côtes premières
15. Filet — Faux-filet ou Aloyau
16. Romsteck
17. Culotte
18. Gîte noix ronde
19. Gîte noix tendre
20. Tranche grasse
21. Tranche
22. Gîte de derrière
23. Queue

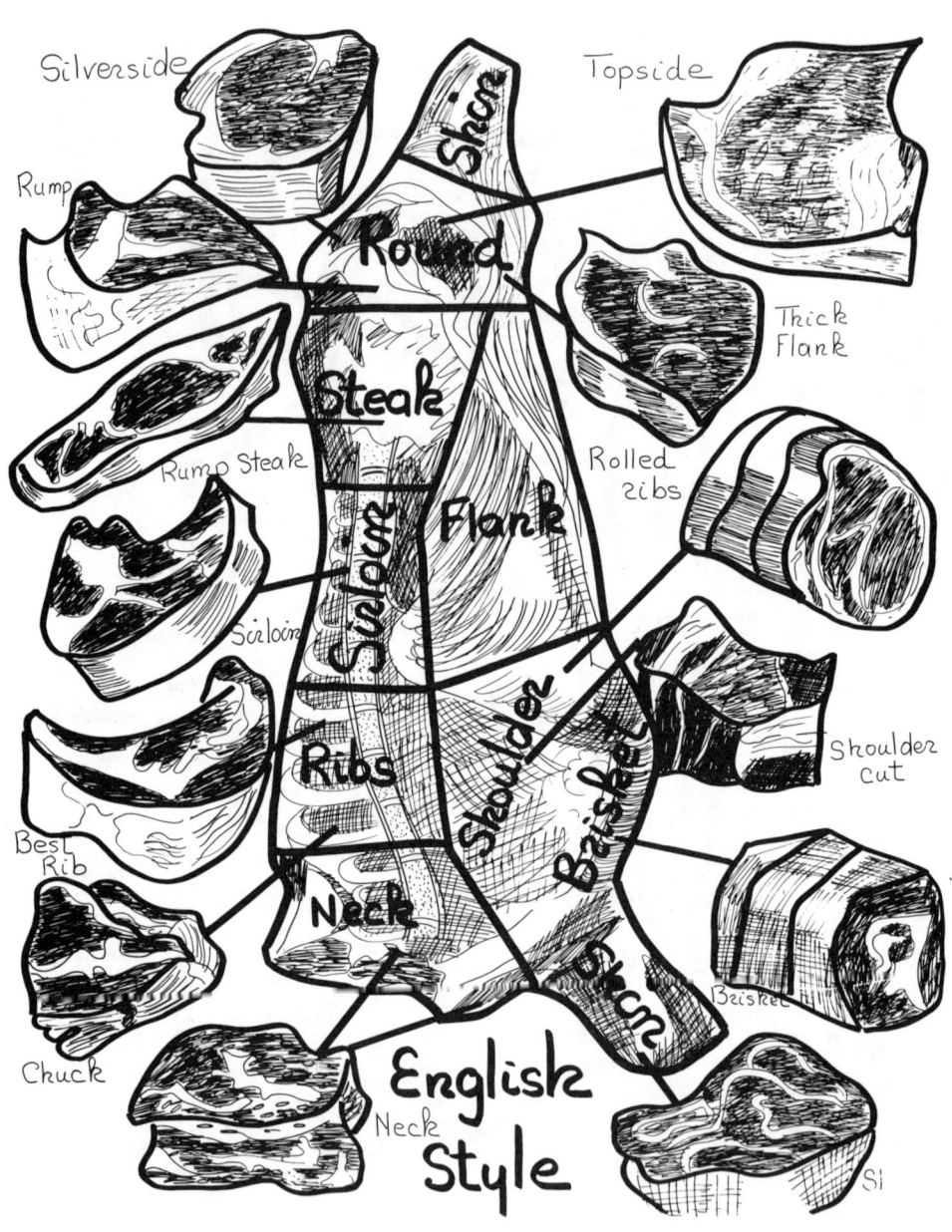

Tournedos Argenteuil
Sirloin Strips
6 servings

2½ lbs asparagus
¼ cup margarine
4 tomatoes
1 tbsp mustard
1 tbsp brown sugar
2 tbsps bread crumbs
salt and pepper
3 to 4 lbs top sirloin of
  beef, 1½-inches thick
several strips of back fat
  or bacon
6 slices of bread for
  croutons

Béarnaise sauce:
  ¼ cup vinegar
  ¼ cup white wine
  2 chopped shallots
  1 tbsp herbs: tarragon,
    chives, parsley, thyme
  salt and pepper
  3 beaten egg yolks
  ½ cup butter

Wash asparagus and break off stalks with fingers. Peel slightly. Tie asparagus tips together in small bunches and cook in salted boiling water for 10 minutes; drain (never leave in the hot water as they will continue cooking). Set aside.

Cut ends of asparagus into pea-size pieces. Cover and cook in margarine on low heat for 10 minutes.

Cut tomatoes in half. Mix mustard and brown sugar, then dip tomatoes in it, then in bread crumbs. Add salt and pepper and dot with butter. Place in a buttered dish and broil for 5 minutes.

Cut tournedos in 4-inch strips. Wrap fat or bacon around them. Sear on one side for 5 minutes on a greased sheet. (Recipe can be done ahead to this point, but do not put in the refrigerator. They can be frozen if necessary and used later.) Broil other side for 5 minutes. Remove strip of fat or bacon before serving.

Serve meat on the croutons, fried in butter until golden brown. Arrange on a platter with tomatoes and asparagus tips on either side. Pass with **Béarnaise sauce** (recipe follows).

Béarnaise sauce. Combine wine, vinegar, shallots, and herbs in the top of a double boiler until mixture has reduced to 2-3 tbsps. Add the egg yolks and stir until thickened. Beat in butter, cut into pieces. Remove from heat.

Emincés de Boeuf Paloise
Minced Beef with Mushrooms and Wine

2 lbs thin-sliced
  strips of beef
½ lb sliced mushrooms
6 tbsps butter
1 tbsp oil

8 oz dry white wine
1 tbsp chopped parsley
salt and pepper
chives or chopped green
  of scallions

Remove all fat from beef. Heat 3 tbsps of the butter with the oil; when hot, add beef and cook a few minutes at high heat. Add salt and pepper and stir. Add wine and mushrooms and cook a few minutes more. Add chives or scallions.

Arrange on platter and pour over meat the remaining 3 tbsps of butter, browned. Sprinkle with parsley and serve.

Coquettes au Gratin

3 lamb or veal kidneys
2 lamb or veal brains
1 lemon (rind and juice)
6 tbsps butter
¼ lb mushrooms
1 clove garlic
2 tbsps parsley, chopped
3 onions, chopped
1 chicken (2½ to 3 lbs)

Mixed Meat au Gratin
6 to 8 servings

1 bay leaf
1 sprig of thyme
2 tbsps flour (rounded)
1 cup chicken broth, warmed
$1/3$ cup sherry
salt and pepper
1 cup cream
bread crumbs

Soak the brains and kidneys in cold water for 10 to 20 minutes. Remove the pellicule (small skin) from the brains and the fat and nerve from the kidney. Put the brains in cold water with the lemon rind. Bring to a boil, reduce the heat and simmer for 5 minutes. Remove, reserving the cooking liquid, and cool.

Chop the stems of the mushrooms, reserving the caps. Chop the garlic. Sauté the mushroom stems in 2 tbsps butter. Add the garlic and 1 tbsp of parsley and set aside.

Slice the kidneys and sauté quickly in 2 tbsps of hot butter with 1 chopped onion.

Poach the chicken in water with the 2 remaining onions, bay leaf, and thyme, for 25 minutes. Remove and cut in medium-sized pieces. Reserve broth.

Make a light roux with the remaining 2 tbsps butter and flour. Stir a few seconds, then add warm broth, the sherry and ¼ cup of the brains cooking liquid. Let it simmer about 10 minutes. Add cream, salt and pepper and the remaining tbsp of chopped parsley. Add the mushroom stems and the kidneys, brains and chicken.

Grease a fireproof dish and arrange all the meats with sauce poured over. Sprinkle with bread crumbs and dot with butter.

Bake in a 375° oven for about 20 minutes. If too dry, moisten with a little broth and melted butter. Then, put under the broiler until lightly brown.

Note: Eggplant au gratin is delicious with this dish. Other vegetables such as peas, carrots, spinach, string beans, or any member of the turnip family also go well.

Rognons Sautés au Champagne

Sauteed Kidneys in Champagne
4 to 6 servings

6 to 8 lamb kidneys
  or 3 veal or 1 – 2 beef kidneys
4 tbsps butter
2 tbsps oil
¼ lb mushrooms, sliced
1 clove of garlic, minced
1 tbsp parsley, chopped
½ tsp aromatic herbs: thyme, rosemary, marjoram, and winter savory
2 egg yolks
¼ cup cream
parsley for decoration
fleurons or bread triangles if desired
1 cup champagne

Wash the kidneys and remove their skin. Remove the nerves and fat from the center and cut the kidneys in thin slices.

Heat the butter and oil in a frying pan until very hot. (Kidneys have to be sautéed very quickly so as not to get tough.) Sauté the kidneys about 4-5 minutes, remove from the pan and keep them warm.

In the same fat, sauté sliced mushrooms, garlic and parsley (the mushrooms should also be sautéed very quickly). Add the champagne and the herbs and simmer 5-6 minutes. Add the kidneys and warm, but do not boil.

Mix the egg yolks with the cream and add to sauce. Serve at once, sprinkled with parsley. You can surround the kidneys with fleurons (puff paste crust) or triangles of toasted or fried bread.

Rognons de Veau Robert

Veal Kidneys Robert
4 to 6 servings

4 to 6 veal kidneys
1 cup butter
salt and pepper
¼ cup brandy or cognac
juice of 1 lemon
1 tsp mustard
2 tbsps parsley, chopped
⅓ cup white wine
additional parsley
triangles of puff paste or toasted bread

Cut the kidneys in half lengthwise and remove the fatty nerve in the center. Sauté the kidneys in half the butter and cook them briskly. Add salt and pepper and ignite with warmed cognac. Put in a casserole in a 375° oven for 15 minutes. Baste with remaining butter, mixed with lemon juice, mustard, and chopped parsley. When cooked, slice the kidneys in thin slices and put on a warm platter; keep them warm while preparing the sauce.

To the pan juices add white wine and reduce a little, simmering about 15 minutes. Pour the sauce over the kidneys. Sprinkle with additional parsley and serve hot with triangles of puff paste or toasted bread around the kidneys.

Grenadins de Veau au Citron — Veal Tournedos with Lemon

1 grenadin of veal per serving: 1" thick x 4" diameter
juice of 2 or 3 lemons
6 to 8 lemon slices
1 cup white wine
½ cup chicken or veal broth

several strips of bacon or fat back
2 shallots, finely chopped
1 carrot, finely chopped
1 egg yolk
salt, pepper
2 or 3 tbsps butter

Wrap tournedos with strips of bacon or fat back and sauté in butter until brown on both sides. Remove to a covered casserole. In the same pan add the shallots, wine, lemon juice and broth and reduce to one third. Pour over grenadins and add the carrot and the lemon slices. Cover and braise 30 minutes in a 350° oven.

Before serving, make a liaison of egg yolk with the juice of the veal. Pour some of the sauce over and serve the rest separately. Serve on a bed of creamed spinach and sorrel, mixed. Or, you may wish to serve with **Sauce Chateaubriand** (recipe follows).

Sauce Chateaubriand

4 tbsps butter
4 shallots, chopped
¼ lb mushrooms, chopped
2 cups white wine
1 clove garlic, minced
1 tbsp parsley, minced

juice of 1 lemon
2 cups veal broth
1 tbsp tarragon, minced
1 tsp cornstarch
salt and pepper
parsley, chopped, to garnish

Melt 2 tbsps butter. Sauté the chopped shallots until translucent but not brown. Add the chopped mushrooms and the wine. Cook slowly until volume is reduced to one-half the original. Add the garlic, parsley, lemon juice, veal or chicken broth. Reduce again.

Mix the remaining 2 tbsps of butter with the tarragon and the cornstarch. Add to the sauce. Let it come to a boil and pour it over veal tournedos. Sprinkle with more parsley and serve hot.

JOSEPHINE SAYS:

I prefer using coarse ground black pepper because it gives a very good flavor. Once I used it in a Béchamel sauce, and my employer looked at the sauce and then said to me, "What are those black spots in the sauce, Josephine?" "Why," I said, "black elephants, of course!"

Galopins de Marseille

very thin slices of
   veal scalloppini
equal amount of slices of
   Italian ham (prosciutto)
chives or chopped green onions
chopped parsley
mushrooms, sliced (canned or fresh)

Scalloppine Marsala
6 servings

4 tbsps meat seasoning sauce
2 tbsps Worcestershire
8 oz Marsala wine
   (more or less to taste)
1 large onion, chopped
Parmesan cheese, grated

Place the scalloppine on a board. Pepper them only. Lay the prosciutto on top, then a thin layer of chives and parsley. Sprinkle with Parmesan cheese. Roll up and fasten with toothpicks. Roll in flour and brown in oil or shortening — not too quickly — and take out.

In the same oil brown the onion. Add some meat stock, the meat sauce, and the Worcestershire. Cook gently for about 10 minutes. Add the Marsala wine.

One half hour before serving, place the scalloppine in a baking dish. Pour sauce over, and add mushrooms and juice. Cook on a slow flame or in the oven at 350° for ½ hour. Marsala should never be cooked too much or not enough — 30 minutes should be just enough time.

If the sauce is not thick enough, add 1 level tsp of cornstarch dissolved in broth or Marsala.

Queue de Boeuf Sainte Menehauld

oil for sautéeing oxtails
2 ox tails
1 tbsp flour
1 carrot, sliced
1 onion, sliced
2 cups broth
salt and pepper

Braised Oxtails with Bread Crumbs

aromatic herbs: rosemary,
   thyme, bay leaf (1 tbsp in all)
½ qt champagne
1 – 2 egg yolks
$1/3$ cup cream
¼ cup bread crumbs
butter

Preheat oven to 300°.

Heat oil and sauté all sides of oxtails until golden brown. Add the flour, stir well and add the vegetables, broth, salt, pepper and herbs. Bring to a boil, then bake in the oven at 300° for 2 hours. Add the champagne and bake 30 minutes longer.

Remove the oxtails and place them side by side on a fireproof dish. Reduce the cooking liquid a little, add egg yolk and cream. Do not allow it to boil any more. When thickened, pour the sauce over the oxtails, sprinkle with bread crumbs and dot with butter. Set in a 400° oven or under the broiler until lightly brown.

Langues de Boeuf Braisées Champenoise
Beef Tongue Braised in Champagne

To begin cooking the tongue:

1 beef tongue	1 stalk celery
12 small onions	thyme
2–3 cloves	bayleaf
1 carrot	a few grains of allspice
1 leek, if available	salt, pepper

Rub the tongue with salt 24 hours before cooking.

Place the tongue in a soup kettle large enough to hold it comfortably. Add water so that it is several inches above the tongue. Bring to a boil. Remove the scum on top and reduce the heat to simmer. Add the vegetables (cut up), the herbs, and spices. Simmer for about 2 hours, covered, leaving slightly ajar for air. Maintain the heat at a simmer.

Reserving the liquid, remove the tongue, trim and skin it. Remove small bones and fat. You are now ready to braise the tongue:

Sauce for braising tongue:

2 tbsps butter	thyme
2 tbsps oil	bay leaf
2 tbsps flour	½ tsp aromatic herbs:
1 carrot, diced	rosemary and oregano
1 onion, chopped	⅛ tsp cloves
1 stalk of celery, chopped	⅛ tsp allspice
½ cup tomato purée	⅛ tsp cumin
1 cup broth from the tongue	salt and pepper
	4 oz champagne
	1 tsp cornstarch, if needed

Heat the butter and oil and brown the tongue on all sides. Remove the tongue, stir the flour into the butter, adding more if necessary to make a sauce consistency. Stir until the flour is light brown, then add the vegetables, tomato purée, broth, spices and herbs. Put back the tongue and bring it to a boil. Simmer on top of the stove or in a 300° oven for ½ hour. Then add the champagne and cook another ½ hour, or until tender. Remove the tongue. If the sauce is too thin, thicken with one tsp cornstarch dissolved in a little water.

Slice the tongue and pour the sauce over it.

JOSEPHINE SAYS:

Pellaprat used to say, "Mushrooms without garlic aren't worth the fart of a rabbit!"

Sauté de Veau au Cresson

Veal Sautéed with Watercress
6 to 8 servings

2 lbs veal (shoulder or breast)
3 tbsps oil
2 tbsps butter
1½ cups bouillon
2 to 3 medium onions, coarsely chopped
salt and pepper
1 large bunch of watercress
2 tbsps extra butter
1 tsp cornstarch
½ cup cream
⅛ tsp nutmeg

Cut the meat into fairly large pieces and sauté in the oil and butter until golden brown. Moisten with the broth and let it simmer for 20 minutes. Add the coarsely chopped onions and continue simmering for ½ hour. Add salt and pepper.

Clean and wash the watercress, drain and cook in the extra butter. When the watercress is cooked, remove from the heat and add the cornstarch mixed with the cream and nutmeg. Add this mixture to the veal and let it simmer for a few minutes without allowing it to boil. Serve on a warm platter.

Note: Sautéed potatoes are good served with this dish.

Grenadins de Veau Ambassadeur

Tournedos of Veal Ambassador
4 to 6 servings

1 fillet or boned roast of veal
strips of bacon or back fat
1 tbsp oil
1 tbsp butter
2 to 3 shallots or the white part of scallions
1 small onion, chopped
1¼ lb mushrooms, fresh or canned
1 clove garlic, minced
1 tbsp parsley, chopped
1 cup bouillon
1 pinch of thyme
1 lb dried green peas or 2½ lbs fresh peas
salt and pepper
1½ lbs potatoes
additional chopped parsley

Cut round pieces of veal like tournedos. Put a slice of bacon or back fat around each and sauté in a pan with the hot oil and butter until brown. Remove and keep warm.

Chop the shallots and onion and sauté in the same fat, adding a little more if necessary. If using fresh mushrooms, sauté them in another pan with a little butter and add the chopped garlic and parsley. Add the shallots and onions. Deglaze the mushroom pan with the broth and add to the onion mixture. (If using canned mushrooms, add the juice along with the broth). Reduce heat a little, add the veal and simmer for 25 minutes. Add salt, pepper and thyme.

Boil the peas until tender. Purée and add salt, pepper and butter. Do the same with the potatoes.

Put the two puréed vegetables in the middle of a warm platter side by side.

Lay the tournedos on top and pour the sauce over. Sprinkle with parsley and serve hot.

Escalopes de Veau Morandi

Veal Scallops Morandi

6 servings

6 veal scallops, 4 ozs each, and pounded thin
6 thin slices ham
6 slices Swiss cheese

black olives, cut in half
butter and oil for frying
½ cup consommé, Madeira or white wine
chopped chives (optional)

Preheat oven to 375°.

Lay veal pieces flat and season with salt and pepper. Then place on top a ham slice, trimmed to the size of the veal, followed by a slice of cheese. Finally, put on an olive half and tightly roll them up and secure with a toothpick or string.

In a frying pan melt butter and oil and brown scallops on all sides. Remove and place in a casserole. Deglaze pan with wine and pour over veal. Arrange more olives and some chives on top, if desired. Braise, covered, in preheated oven for 30 minutes and serve with braised lettuce and rice.

Tournedos Benjamin

4 to 6 servings

beef fillet or sirloin top, cut in rounds, 1½ to 2-inches thick
4–6 slices of bacon or back fat
1 large clove of garlic
2 tbsps olive oil

½ cup butter
a few drops of Worcestershire
2 tbsps minced parsley
juice of 1 or 2 limes or lemons
salt and pepper
4 to 6 toasted rounds of bread the same size as the tournedos

Cut the meat neatly into round pieces 1½ or 2-inches thick and surround each with a slice of bacon or back fat. Mash the garlic and add it to the oil in a heavy frying pan. Heat the oil very hot and fry the tournedos 3½ minutes on each side. Remove and keep warm.

Melt the butter, add the Worcestershire. When it comes to a boil add the parsley and the lime juice. Salt and pepper the tournedos, put them on toast, and pour the butter over them.

 **JOSEPHINE SAYS:**

A lot of cooking is imagination. The recipe is meant as the general rule, but you have to adjust it to your own preference.

Tournedos au Poivre

Pepper Steak Fillet

4 to 6 servings

2 tbsps green peppercorns (see note)
¼ cup butter
6 steak fillets, 1½-inch thick
salt
1 small liquor glass of cognac
1 cup cream
2 or 3 tomatoes

Mash the pepper to a pulp and mix half of it with the butter. Melt the butter in a heavy frying pan and sauté the steaks until brown on both sides. Salt the steaks, remove from pan, and keep warm. Deglaze the pan with the cognac. Add the rest of the pepper and the cream.

Cut the tomatoes in half and sauté them in butter. Pour a little cream sauce over. Put one steak on each tomato half and pour sauce over or serve separately. Serve with baked potatoes or french fried potatoes.

Note: The pepper can also be put on the steak, without mashing it. If green pepper is not obtainable, use crushed black pepper.

La Brioche de Ris de Veau au Champagne
Sweetbread Brioche with Champagne Sauce

6 to 8 servings

2 lbs veal sweetbreads
salt and pepper
4 thin slices of pork fat
4 tbsps butter
2 tbsps oil
2 carrots, finely chopped
1 medium onion, finely chopped
1 bay leaf
2 or 3 sprigs parsley
¼ tsp fresh thyme, chopped

3 tbsps butter
⅓ cup flour
½ bottle of champagne
¼ cup heavy cream
1 recipe of brioche dough (*see recipe*)
1 egg beaten
½ recipe of sabayon sauce made with champagne and no sugar (optional)

Soak the sweetbreads in cold water and let them stand for 1 hour or more. Drain and put them in a pot of cold water. Bring to a boil, add salt and reduce the heat. Cook for 5-6 minutes. Drain, reserving the cooking liquid. When the sweetbreads are cold, trim away all the gristle and other tough parts. Put them on a board or a platter and press them under a weight. Cut the fresh pork fat in small strips and lard the sweetbreads with them.

Heat the butter and oil in a heavy pot and add the sweetbreads, carrots, onions, bay leaf, parsley, thyme, salt and pepper. Cover and cook over low heat for 30 minutes. Take off the fire and set aside.

Melt 3 tbsps butter and stir in the flour. Cook, stirring, for a few minutes until the mixture just begins to color. Add the champagne and the cream. Add the sliced sweetbreads and gently heat them through in the sauce.

Fill buttered round, fluted brioche mold with brioche dough, filling it within ½ inch of the top. Brush with egg glaze. Let it rise and bake for 10 to 12 minutes. When the brioche is cooked, cool a little, carefully remove the top and scoop out the center. Fill the brioche with the sliced sweetbreads. Adjust the seasoning of the sauce, then pour sauce over the sweetbreads. Replace the top and pour the rest of the sauce over. Run under the broiler to brown.

If desired, make a sabayon with 3 egg yolks and ½ cup of champagne, beating continuously in top of a double boiler until it becomes thick and falls in a ribbon from beater. Pour around the brioche before serving.

Pâté de Foie en Croute

Liver Pâté in a Crust

1 recipe of brioche dough
    (see recipe)
1 can of liver pâté or
    homemade pâté (see below)

¾ cup beef jelly
1 egg beaten with 2 tbsps
    milk, for decorations
    (see note)

Homemade Pâté:

1 lb goose, chicken, or
    pork liver
¾ lb chicken or pork fat
1½ tsps salt
½ tsp pepper
¼ tsp cloves
¼ tsp allspice
1 onion, chopped fine

1 clove garlic, chopped fine
¼ cup cognac
2 eggs, slightly beaten
1 cup cream
1 cup milk
2 rounded tbsps flour
1 pork **caul (crèpine)** or
    strips of back fat

If homemade pâté is to be used it is generally made the day before. To prepare it, preheat the oven to 350°. Mix the ground liver and fat together; add the spices, onion, garlic, cognac, eggs, cream, milk, and flour. Mix well. Line meat loaf dishes with the caul or with strips of back fat criss-crossed. Put the pâté mixture into the pans and set them in a pan of hot water. Bake, covered, at 350° for 1½ hours. Let the pâté cool.

Roll the brioche dough and set the pâté in the center. Fold the dough over and seal edges well. Cut the excess dough and form a chimney in the center to let the steam escape. Let it stand in a warm place for 1 hour. Preheat the oven to 375°. Bake the pâté for 30 minutes. If it gets too brown, cover with foil. Serve cold.

When cold you can pour beef jelly through the hole in the crust, using a funnel.

Note: You can make decorations with leftover dough before baking and glaze with beaten egg mixed with 2 tbsps milk.

Le Saucisson en Croute
Sausage Wrapped in Pastry
8 servings

1 recipe pâte brisée, pâte brioche, or any non-sweet pastry
1 large **saucisson** (or any desired sausage)
3 cups broth or wine
bay leaf
1 egg mixed with cream, or cream alone

Prepare pastry dough in advance.

Prick **saucisson** and barely cover with broth or wine in pot. Add bay leaf and simmer for 45 minutes; cool in the broth until ready to use.

Roll dough thin. Remove the skin from the sausage and place sausage in the center of dough. Make a package, sealing dough with water. Turn so the seam is on the bottom and place in a greased shallow baking pan. Make several slashes in top of pastry. Allow it to rest in the refrigerator for 10 minutes.

Before baking, brush dough with the egg glaze or cream. Bake according to the temperature of the dough you are using. To serve, slice sausage and serve with juices thickened with a tsp of cornstarch mixed with a little water.

Saucisson Toulouse
Spiced Sausage

2 lbs fresh pork, ground
½ lb back fat, ground
1 tbsp salt
½ tsp pepper
pinch each allspice and cloves
1 bay leaf, crumbled
¼ cup cognac
5 cloves garlic, minced
2 tsps **Spice Parisienne** *(see below)*

Mix all the ingredients together and stuff casings. Hang by a string in a cool place for 2 days. Keeps 2 weeks refrigerated.

Épice Parisienne
Parisian Seasoning

2 bay leaves
1 tbsp savory (winter or summer)
1 tbsp cloves
1 tbsp mace
1 tbsp paprika
1 tbsp marjoram
1 tbsp cinnamon
½ cup white pepper
1 tbsp red pimiento or red pepper
1 tbsp coriander
1 tbsp fennel
1 tbsp cumin
1 tbsp thyme
1 tbsp oregano
1 tbsp sage
3 cups salt*

Grind and mix all ingredients together (*the salt may be added when making the spice or, according to taste when using it). Dry herbs can be used and blended with the rest of the ingredients. The proportion of the various herbs and spices can be increased or diminished as desired.

Use ½ tsp **Parisian Seasoning** for each ½ lb meat.

Carré d'Agneau en Couronne

Crown Roast of Lamb
6 to 8 servings

1 16-rib crown roast of lamb
2 medium sized tart apples, chopped fine
1/3 cup celery, chopped
2 tbsps mint leaves, chopped
3 to 4 tsps poultry seasoning
½ cup melted butter
14 to 16 slices of bread, cut into cubes

Trim excess fat from the lamb. Put the roast on a rack, rib bones up, in an open shallow pan. Combine the remaining ingredients to make a stuffing. Fill the center of the roast with the stuffing. Wrap the rib ends with foil to prevent charring. If using a meat thermometer, insert it into the ribs at the thickest part of the meat. Roast in a preheated 325° oven, allowing about 40 minutes per pound or until the thermometer registers 170° – 180°, about 2½ to 3 hours, depending upon the desired degree of doneness.

Remove the foil and top each rib with a paper frill.

Gigot d'Agneau Pondichery au Gingembre
Leg of Lamb with Ginger and Garlic

1 leg of lamb (4 to 5 lbs)
2 tbsps oil
3 – 4 cloves garlic
1 tbsp powdered ginger
salt and pepper
¼ lb fresh ginger or dried ginger root
½ cup port or sherry
1 whole carrot
1 whole onion
bouquet garni of thyme, sage, fennel, bay leaf
½ cup strong broth or consommé

The day before you plan to serve, rub the leg of lamb with powdered ginger, pepper, and oil (no salt — it tends to draw the blood out of the meat). The next day, make 3 or 4 incisions in the meat and insert pieces of ginger root and garlic in each incision.

On top of the stove, brown the lamb in oil on all sides. Place in roasting pan and add carrot, onion, broth, port or sherry, **bouquet garni.** Roast it uncovered at 325° for 1½ hours for a rosy, not rare, roast. For well done, cook 30 minutes longer, then remove cover and cook 15 minutes.

Remove roast from pan and keep meat warm. Reduce juices to 1½ cups. Add a piece of **beurre manie** (1 tbsp butter mixed with 1 tbsp flour) and simmer juices for 10 minutes in the pan or a double boiler. You can also thicken the sauce by adding 1 tsp cornstarch mixed in broth or sherry, cooked for 2-3 minutes.

Carve lamb and arrange on a hot platter. Surround with parsley or watercress. Glaze meat with some of the sauce and serve remaining sauce separately. Serve with parsley or roasted potatoes, glacéed carrots, string beans amandine, or flageolet beans with chervil.

Côtelettes Marinées Grillées   Grilled Marinated Lamb Chops

juice of 2 lemons
3 tbsps oil
1 bay leaf
thyme
salt and pepper
1 small onion, chopped
2 lamb chops per serving
bread crumbs

Make a marinade with the lemon juice, oil, salt, pepper, onion and herbs. Marinate the chops in this marinade for at least one hour.

Remove from the marinade and roll in bread crumbs. Put in a fireproof dish, sprinkle with melted butter, and bake in the oven at 375° for 15 minutes. Put under the broiler for a few seconds to brown.

Serve with apple sauce and, if desired, with rice. The seasoning from the chops can be used in the rice.

Carré de Mouton Saigon   Lamb Shanks Saigon Style

6 servings

Marinade:
  1 cup soy sauce
  ¼ cup brown sugar
  ½ cup sherry
  ¼ cup anise seed, tied in a cloth
1 tbsp parsley, chopped
½ tbsp rosemary, chopped
1 sprig thyme, chopped
1 onion, chopped
1 clove of garlic, chopped

6 lamb shanks
flour – enough to coat the lamb
2 tbsps butter
2 tbsps oil
2 cups ouillon
1 tsp cornstarch, mixed with ½ cup broth
additional parsley for decoration

Marinate the lamb shanks for several hours or overnight in the soy sauce, sugar, sherry, anise seed, herbs, onion and garlic.

Drain the lamb, reserving the marinade. (Do not dry the lamb with a towel as that would absorb some of the marinade.) Roll the pieces in flour and brown the lamb shanks in the butter and oil in a large skillet. Add all the marinade, bring to a boil and simmer for 15 minutes.

Add the bouillon and simmer, covered, for 1 hour or until the lamb is tender. Remove the lamb and keep warm.

Mix the cornstarch with ¼ cup broth and stir into the lamb. Cook over low heat until the mixture thickens and boils gently for 5 minutes. Remove the anise seed. If the sauce is too thick, add a little more bouillon.

Place the lamb in a serving dish and pour the sauce over it. Sprinkle with parsley and serve with rice or buttered noodles with fresh chopped basil.

Épaule d'Agneau à la Menthe

Minted Shoulder of Lamb

6 to 8 servings

1 lamb shoulder, boned and rolled
2 tbsps butter
2 tbsps oil
salt and pepper
1 tbsp mustard
2 cloves garlic
½ cup mint leaves, chopped

Sauce:
½ cup currant jelly (apple or plum may be used)
2 tbsps vinegar
¼ cup mint leaves, chopped
1 tbsp mustard
juices from the meat

Preheat oven to 325°.

Brown the lamb shoulder on all sides in the hot butter and oil. Put the meat on a rack in a roasting pan. Make 2 incisions in the meat and insert the garlic cloves. Sprinkle with salt and pepper and rub with mustard. Pat the chopped mint leaves onto the lamb shoulder (they will stick because of the mustard). Bake in a preheated oven, covered, 20 minutes to the lb (about 1½ hours), until done. When you insert a knife the juices will appear clear, depending upon the degree of doneness.

Let the lamb stand about 10 minutes before carving so that it can be sliced into even, uniform slices.

Make a mint sauce by combining the sauce ingredients. Bring to a boil and serve with the lamb.

Carré d'Agneau à l'Orange

Roast Rack of Lamb with Orange Sauce

2½ lbs rack of lamb, (about 9-10 chops)
1 tsp salt
½ tsp pepper
½ tsp powdered ginger
2 cloves of garlic

Sauce:
½ cup orange juice
½ cup orange marmalade
½ cup bouillon or water
½ tsp powdered ginger
fresh orange slices

Preheat oven to 375°.

Sprinkle the rack of lamb with salt, pepper, and powdered ginger. Slice the garlic and insert pieces between the chops. Place the meat in a roasting pan and roast in 375° oven. Roast 45 minutes if you prefer the meat medium-rare or 1 hour if you prefer it well-done.

Prepare the sauce with the orange juice, orange marmalade, bouillon and powdered ginger. Simmer in a saucepan for about 10 minutes.

When the roast is done, place the rack on a serving platter. Surround it with fresh orange slices and serve with the sauce.

Ragoût d'Agneau Provençale   ## Lamb Stew Provencale

1 lb lamb neck, sliced
  in ¾-inch pieces
1½ lbs lamb breast, sliced
  in ¾-inch pieces
⅓ cup olive oil
2 tbsps flour
2 cups bouillon or water,
  heated
2 small onions, chopped
2 cloves garlic, minced

¼ cup pimientos, diced
3 large tomatoes, chopped
1 small green pepper,
  cut in strips
2-3 large potatoes, quartered
½ tsp sage
salt and pepper
a **persillade:** parsley chopped
  with 1 clove of garlic

Preheat oven to 375°.

Heat the olive oil in a dutch oven or deep-sided pan and brown the pieces of lamb on all sides in the oil. Stir in the flour and add the hot bouillon or water. Add the vegetables and the seasonings. Bring to a boil, cover and cook in a 375° oven for 1 hour. Add more broth or water if it becomes too thick while cooking.

Test for doneness. When tender, serve on a serving dish and sprinkle with the **persillade**.

 **JOSEPHINE SAYS:**

To have an easier time peeling garlic cloves, first drop them into boiling water for one-half minute.

Jambon à la Crème   ## Ham with Madeira and Cream

10 to 15 servings

1 medium-sized ham
Mirepoix:
  1 stalk of celery
  1 onion
  1 carrot

thyme
1 bay leaf
2 cups Madeira or Sherry
broth, if needed
½ cup of heavy cream

Soak the ham overnight in water and drain. Put in a large flameproof casserole and add water to come about halfway up the side of the ham. Bring to a boil and set in a preheated 300° oven for 1½ to 2 hours.

Remove the ham and drain the liquid from the bottom of the dish. Spread the diced vegetables over casserole bottom, put the ham back and pour the warmed Madeira or Sherry over it. Cover and set in a 300° oven for 45 minutes. Check to see that it doesn't get too dry; otherwise, add a little broth. When the ham is done, drain the braising liquid into a saucepan. Reduce it by ⅔; add the cream, and warm. Serve with the ham.

Côtes de Porc à l'Armoricaine

4 pork chops
flour
2 tbsps butter
2 tbsps pork fat (lard)
salt and pepper

Pork Chops Brittany Style
4 servings

4 slices of Gruyère cheese
1½ cups tomato sauce
thyme
1 bay leaf
1 dozen or more fresh
    figs (white or black)

Flour the pork chops on both sides. Melt the butter and lard in a heavy skillet and sauté the chops until brown on both sides. Put the chops in a fireproof dish, add salt and pepper and place them, covered, in a 375° oven for 15 to 20 minutes. Uncover. Place cheese on each chop and put under the broiler until the cheese is golden brown. Sauté the fresh figs in butter until warmed. Warm the tomato sauce and pour over the chops and arrange the figs around them.

Note: Dried prunes and apples may take the place of the figs. Prunes and apples should be cooked; the figs are only sautéed.

 **JOSEPHINE SAYS:**

Pork should be cooked until well done to be digestible. When broiling **choose meat with some fat between the tissues; brush often with butter or oil during cooking; allow about 6-7 minutes a side.** When frying, **choose pork steak or chops. Brush with oil or butter and cook over moderate heat 8 to 10 minutes; cover after browned to simmer a little longer.** To braise, **cook covered, 30 minutes to the lb, for very tender meat.** To roast, **brown on all sides, then cook at low temperature (250°) for 30 minutes to the lb (at least 2 to 3 hours). Moisten with 1 cup of broth after 15 minutes to prevent drying. Or, backfat may be tied to the roast and removed before serving.**

Cassoulet du Languedoc

1½ lbs dried white beans
½ lb pork rind
½ lb lean salt pork
1 onion, studded with
    4 cloves
1 carrot
1 stalk of celery
¼ tsp thyme
1 bay leaf

Bean Casserole with Pork and Lamb
6 to 8 servings

1 lb garlic sausage or
    1 **saucisson**
1 lamb breast
3 tbsps oil
1 onion, chopped
1 lb pork filet
salt and pepper
bread crumbs for topping
parsley

Continued

Wash the beans and soak them overnight. Cook them in a large pot with the pork rind in the same water they soaked in. Bring them to a boil and simmer for 30 minutes. Add the salt pork, onion studded with cloves, the carrot, celery, thyme, and bay leaf, and simmer 30 minutes longer. Then add the sausage or the **saucisson.**

Sauté the lamb until brown, add 1 chopped onion, and add to the beans. Sauté the pork filet on all sides and add to the beans. Simmer ½ hour longer. Remove the pork filet and slice.

In a baking dish make a layer of beans and one of meat until all is used. Cover and bake in the oven for another 30 minutes. Taste and adjust the seasoning. Top with bread crumbs and allow it to brown. Serve in the same pot or on a serving platter, all mixed together. Sprinkle with chopped parsley.

Cassoulet de Castelnaudary   Beans with Duck or Goose

Every province in France has its own method of cooking the cassoulet. This is one of the best.

Prepare in the same way for **Cassoulet du Languedoc,** substituting roast duck or goose or *confit d'oie* (see note) for the filet of pork. Add 2 minced cloves of garlic. Serve in a casserole or deep serving dish.

Note: Confit d'oie is a goose that is cooked in its own fat with the addition of pork, seasoned with salt, pepper, thyme, and bay leaf. It is stored in an earthen crock, covered with goose fat (2 inches above the meat), and kept from year to year.

 **JOSEPHINE SAYS:**

If you want pork meat to be white when cooked, rub with salt 12 hours prior to cooking time. When ready to cook, rub off excess salt. To keep meat tender, moisten with 1 oz cognac or brandy 15 minutes before roasting.

Meat will brown evenly if you rub the juice of a lemon over the surface before placing in the oven. To improve the flavor, add a shallot and 2 to 3 tbsps of vinegar to the baking pan after it has cooked 10 minutes.

Cochon Saoul — Civet de Porc

Drunken Pig Stew

4 to 6 servings

Marinade:
- 2 cups red wine
- 1 finely chopped carrot
- 2 tbsps oil
- thyme, bay leaf
- 1 onion, chopped
- 2 cloves garlic

- 1½ lbs pork shoulder
- 1 lb pork spareribs (ask butcher to cut into cubes)
- 2 tbsps flour
- 2 tbsps butter
- 1 onion, chopped, 1 carrot, sliced
- 1 cup broth
- 2 cloves garlic
- 1 big pinch cloves, allspice
- 1 tsp herbs: rosemary, sage, marjoram
- 2 tbsps oil
- salt and pepper
- 1 tbsp apple or other jelly

Prepare marinade with red wine, oil, thyme, bay leaf, onion, and carrot. Marinate pork for at least 12 hours (even 3 to 4 days if possible), turning meat from time to time, once or twice a day.

Cut pork into generous 1" cubes. Melt the butter and oil and brown meat that has first been dusted in flour. Add all marinade and broth and stir well. Add the sliced carrot, onions, herbs, and spices. Bring to a boil then simmer, covered, on low heat (or in a 300° oven) for 1½ to 2 hours; test meat after 1½ hours. If tender to the fork, it is cooked.

Mix in the jelly. Set on a service dish and sprinkle with parsley.

JOSEPHINE SAYS:

High quality pork is pink, very firm, with very white fat. Even lean pieces have about 18% fat; therefore, a small portion (less than ½ lb) will give you all the fat you need in one day. Choose meat that is not too fat and remember that meat cooked with the bone is always more succulent.

Pieds de Porc ou de Veau Ste. Menehould
Grilled Pigs' Feet or Veal Trotters

Two Ways

The *Pieds de cochon truffes* have made the reputation of many a charcutier and restaurateur in France, and can be bought in most of France and Europe ready to cook or already cooked. Although it seems a very humble kind of food, it is appreciated by gourmets and gourmands alike and is considered quite a luxury in France.

Continued

1 foot or trotter per
   serving
1 onion, chopped
2 carrots, sliced
celery leaves

bouquet garni of bay leaf, thyme,
   and strip of lemon peel
salt and pepper
a few whole cloves
1 leek, sliced

Buy the feet or trotters one day ahead of time if possible. Sprinkle them with salt (coarse salt is best) and leave them overnight. When ready to cook, rinse salt off and put into large pot with the vegetables, herbs, **bouquet garni,** and enough water to cover. Bring to boil, reduce heat to simmer, remove top scum and cover. Allow to simmer for 3 to 3½ hours, until skin and meat are coming loose from the bones. Take out and let meat cool.

Strain the stock, and if you wish, clarify it to make jelly. Cook it once again with either some raw ground beef or white of egg with the shell; simmer for 15 to 20 minutes. When it cools, it will be very thick, clear jelly you will want to use in other recipes.

Ste. Menehould Garnish #1

chopped pork or leftover
   meat of any kind (add ⅓
   chopped fresh pork to every
   1 lb of leftover meat)
2 cloves garlic, chopped
½ cup chopped parsley and/or
   tarragon, chervil, and a
   little basil

1 small onion, chopped
1 caul of pork
½ cup butter or margarine,
   melted
1 truffle (optional)
bread crumbs
Tartare or Remoulade sauce

Remove bones from the feet or trotters.

Mix garlic, onion, leftover meat, and herbs. Taste for seasoning, then add salt, pepper, and truffle. Stuff mixture into the cavities left by the bones in the feet or trotters. Wrap each in a piece of the caul. Then dip each first in melted butter, then coat in bread crumbs.

Set in a warm oven until feet are warmed through. Pour some melted butter over them and then brown under the broiler until outsides are brown and crisp. Feet must be served sizzling hot with or without a sauce. The sauce should be highly seasoned, such as a Tartare or Remoulade sauce (see recipes).

Ste. Menehould Garnish #2

In this method, leave the bones in. While the feet are still warm, coat them with melted butter or margarine and bread crumbs. Grill as in method #1.

With the bones removed, the feet or trotters may be grilled as described above and served as delicious appetizers. Cut them into bite-size pieces and serve on toothpicks.

LIGHT SUPPER OR
LUNCHEON IDEAS

SONG TO BEAT EGGS AND SAUCES TO:

Et pendent ce temps la
Je tournais la manivelle
Et monsieur jouait de la
   prunelle
Comme un gros pacha.

And all the while
I am turning the crank
He is making eyes at me
Like a fat pasha.

— M. Pellaprat song

"Use Your Imagination"

Imagination is important to cooking. These recipes for light suppers or luncheons may show you some new ways of preparing a light meal. Always alter the recipe to suit your own taste.

Light Supper or Luncheon Ideas

We have one daughter, Jacqueline, who lives here in San Francisco with her husband Jack and their four boys. When Jacqueline was just a baby, I worked for the Figgenbaum family. I decided I wanted to spend more time at home with my baby, so I looked for another job with less-demanding hours, but which still paid well. At the time, the Figgenbaums were paying me $90 a week ~ $50 of that was going to pay for a woman to look after Jacqueline while I cooked.

Since I'll always try anything, I took a job in the shipyards in Oakland. There weren't many women working there then, but those of us who did wore overalls just like the men. This was during the very early part of the war, and the shipyards were extremely busy. My first day on the job, the manager took me over to the hull of an enormous ship. And he showed me a very narrow ladder that hung down the side, going all the way to the bottom of the ship. I was supposed to climb down into that black hole and clean the ship. I was scared, but that didn't stop me! I did it anyway, and I was a good worker. From then on, it was always Josephine who went into the bowels of the ships.

Meanwhile, I'd told Charles not to say anything to the Figgenbaums ~ I didn't want to them to know what I was doing. Sometimes Mr. Figgenbaum would drop by and ask where I was, and Charles would say I was "in the country." And sometimes I would be right there, hiding on the porch!

The shipyard was very tiring work, even though I got home early in the afternoons. It became too much for me and I decided to quit. My next job was with Mrs. Tobin. She paid me very well, and gave me one day off every week ~ when I wouldn't have to get up for a thing!

 **JOSEPHINE SAYS:**

No matter what the size of your garden, there's always room for herbs.

The measurements in my recipes are usually for fresh herbs, straight from our garden. Reduce the amount called for if you are using ground or dried herbs.

Crêpes Saint-Cloud   St. Cloud Crêpes

6 to 8 servings

*1 recipe crê*pes (see recipe)	salt and pepper
8 oz cream cheese	½ tsp nutmeg
2 chopped shallots	1 pinch cayenne
1 tbsp chopped parsley, tarragon, watercress, chives	**beurre noisette**

Prepare basic crêpe dough. Let it rest at least 20 minutes. Try one crêpe — if batter is too thick, add a little more milk. Make the crêpes and stack; keep warm in the oven.

Mix the cream cheese, shallots, and herbs. Add salt and pepper to taste, along with the nutmeg and cayenne. Spread this mixture across each crêpe and roll. Place them in a fireproof dish cover, and put in a 375⁰ oven until warm through, about 10 to 15 minutes. Pour **beurre noisette** over them and serve.

Crêpes   *for 16 to 18 crêpes*

3 tbsps of flour	⅛ tsp vanilla or 2 tbsps of rum or cognac*
3 eggs separated	½ tsp cinnamon*
⅛ tsp salt	⅔ cup milk, mixed with ⅓ cup of water
3 tbsps sugar*	2 tbsps melted butter or oil

*For dessert crêpes only

This batter should be made in advance and allowed to stand at least 15 minutes before it is used.

Mix flour, salt and sugar together. Moisten flour with a little milk, add the egg yolks and the whites beaten slightly, add vanilla or liquor, cinnamon, the melted butter and the rest of the milk. Let it rest a while.

When ready to use, grease a hot skillet, 8 to 9 inches in diameter, with a little butter on a piece of absorbent paper. Pour in a small amount of dough, just enough to cover bottom of pan. Swirl pan around to spread dough evenly. Brown on the underside (when crêpes are ready to turn, bubbles form over the top and sides are brown), turn and brown the other side. Stack crêpes on an ovenware plate and keep warm.

Crêpes Bohemiennes

Bohemian Crêpes
6 to 8 servings

1 recipe of crêpes
¼ lb onions, minced
3 tbsps butter
1 tbsp oil
¼ lb green pepper, minced
2 cloves garlic, minced

2 tomatoes, peeled and chopped
salt and pepper to taste
parsley, chopped
chervil, chopped
3 eggs, beaten

Prepare the crêpes according to the recipe.

Mince the onions and cook them in butter and oil until softened. Add the minced green pepper and garlic and the peeled tomatoes. Season to taste with salt and pepper and add the herbs.

When the vegetables are cooked, bind the filling together with 3 beaten eggs. Fill the crêpes and serve very hot.

Crêpes Berthil

Shrimp-Filled Crêpes

These are shrimp-filled crêpes, topped with a Béchamel sauce made with fish court-bouillon and enriched with cream and egg yolks.

1 recipe crêpes
1 lb small cooked shrimp
½ cup Béchamel sauce using fish court bouillon and milk
2 egg yolks, mixed in a little cream

1 cup Swiss cheese, grated
2 to 3 tbsps butter
½ cup additional fish court bouillon or clam juice

Make a thick Béchamel sauce. Prepare crêpes and keep warm in the oven.

Melt butter in top of double boiler and add shrimp, coating them completely. Add 2 to 3 tbsps of the Béchamel and stir to coat shrimp. Keep mixture warm.

Grease a fireproof dish. Put 3 tbsps shrimp mixture in each crêpe and roll up; place side by side in dish. Add fish court bouillon to Béchamel; then stir in egg yolks and remove from heat. Pour sauce on top of crêpes and sprinkle with the grated cheese. Brown under the broiler and serve.

 **JOSEPHINE SAYS:**

My hands can be much more useful than a spoon when working with food. As Pellaprat would say, "The hand of the chef is cleaner than the utensil, because his hand is in water all the time."

I had an employer who liked to sit in the kitchen and watch me prepare the meals. One time she said to me, "Josephine, I see you like to use your hands an awful lot in my food." I told her I was sorry, but I couldn't use my feet! I thought sure I would be fired, but I worked for her for two more years. She said I was a tonic for her nerves.

Tomates Farcies Gabrielle

Stuffed Tomatoes Gabrielle
6 servings

6 medium tomatoes, washed and dried
½ cup mayonnaise, well seasoned with Dijon mustard
½ tsp salt

1 avocado, diced
juice of ½ lemon
6½ oz can of tuna
1½ tsps parsley, chopped
pepper and paprika to taste
lettuce or watercress leaves

Cut off tomato tops and remove pulp. Turn tomatoes upside down on a plate or towel to drain.

Season mayonnaise with Dijon mustard, salt, pepper and paprika. Add the avocado sprinkled with lemon juice along with tuna and 1 tbsp chopped parsley.

Fill tomatoes with this mixture, sprinkle with remaining parsley and serve very cold on a bed of lettuce leaves.

Salade Forestière

Mushroom Salad
6 servings

1 lb mushrooms (white if possible)
3 cloves garlic, chopped
1 tbsp chopped parsley

juice of 1 lemon
½ cup oil
salt and pepper
1 tbsp of mustard

Mushrooms should be washed in lemon or vinegar-water, dried and seasoned with the juice of one lemon, the oil, mustard, salt and pepper, garlic and parsley. (If brown mushrooms are used, they should just be peeled.) Mix well, put on a bed of watercress or other greens, sprinkle with a **persillade** (chopped garlic and parsley). Serve at once. If you're not ready to serve, leave mushrooms in lemon or vinegar-water until ready.

| |

Céleri-Rave Rémoulade

Celery Root Salad
6 servings

1 large celery root or 2 small
2 egg yolks
1 cup of oil
juice of 1 lemon
1 tbsp **fines herbes:** parsley, chives, tarragon, chervil or sweet basil

1 tbsp capers
a few black or green olives
salt and pepper
1 tbsp mustard (Dijon preferred)

Blanch the celery root in boiling water for 10 minutes, peel and cut in match-like strips. Prepare a mayonnaise with the egg yolks, mustard, salt and pepper as follows: Stir yolks with mustard and seasoning, then pour the oil in by droplets until it begins to stiffen, then add more oil until all has been added; add all the herbs and chopped capers. Mix chopped olives with celery, then season it all with the mayonnaise. Serve on a bed of greens, sprinkle with more herbs.

Topinambours en Salade — Jerusalem Artichoke Salad

In the summer, Jerusalem artichoke salad makes a refreshing dish at suppertime.

1½ lbs Jerusalem artichokes
1 red sweet pepper
6 to 10 green olives
1 **cornichon,** chopped

1 small onion, chopped
1 recipe vinaigrette
   (see recipe)
few lettuce leaves

Mix vegetables and toss with the vinaigrette. Serve on lettuce leaves. If desired, add 1 stalk of celery (chopped) and ½ cup of green beans or peas.

Salade de Pois Chiches — Garbanzo Bean Salad

6 to 8 servings

1½ cups uncooked garbanzo
   beans
½ cup string beans, cooked
   and cut into ½ inch
   pieces
1 clove garlic, minced
¼ green pepper, finely
6 olives, green or black,
   chopped fine
2 green onions, chopped fine
3 tbsps fine herbs,
   chopped fine

1 recipe vinaigrette
6 anchovy fillets, soaked in
   water to remove salt
¾ cup olive oil
1 tbsp mustard (Dijon or
   dry preferred)
5–6 radishes, grated
   and seasoned with salt
   and pepper
salt and pepper
¼ tsp nutmeg

Soak the garbanzo beans overnight in enough water to barely cover. Simmer for two hours in this water. Drain well. Prepare the vinaigrette and add the fine herbs, green onions, and garlic. In a separate bowl, crush the anchovies and mix with the mustard. Slowly add oil to the anchovies (as you would in making mayonnaise). Season with salt, pepper, and nutmeg.

Stir the green beans and garbanzo beans into the vinaigrette. Add the olives, peppers, and radishes. Stir in the anchovy mayonnaise and correct seasonings if necessary.

Salade Niçoise   Nicoise Salad

6 to 8 servings

This salad originates from Nice, Provence.

2 large boiled potatoes (about 1 lb)	½ lb string beans, cooked
1 cup vinaigrette *(see recipe)*	1 large can tuna fish
	12 pitted black olives
	1 lb tomatoes
herbs: parsley, fresh basil, tarragon or chervil	4 hard-cooked eggs
chives or green onions, chopped	1 small can anchovy filets
	salt and pepper
	6–8 lettuce leaves

Boil the potatoes, peel and cut them into ¼ inch slices. While they are *still warm*, season them with ½ cup of the vinaigrette and with several of the herbs listed above. Arrange the potatoes in the center of a platter and sprinkle with chopped chives or scallions. Surround with lettuce leaves.

Toss the cooked, drained string beans with vinaigrette and arrange them in clusters around the potatoes. Drain the tuna and place at each end of the platter. Cut the tomatoes in quarters and arrange around the potatoes. Cut the eggs in half and place around the platter, with pieces of anchovy filet criss-crossed on top of each.

Pour the final ½ cup vinaigrette over all; sprinkle with herbs and serve.

Note: This salad can be served as an entrée for dinner or as the main dish for a luncheon.

Mousse au Saumon   Cold Salmon Mousse

4 to 6 servings

1½ lbs salmon (bones and skin removed)	1 tbsp gelatin
salt and pepper	fish or meat aspic (fish preferred)
⅛ tsp nutmeg	pimientos or olives for decoration
½ cup butter, softened	watercress for garnish
2 egg whites, beaten	
1 cup whipped cream	

Grind the fish twice with the finest blade of a grinder or in a Cuisinart. Put into a large bowl; season with salt, pepper, and nutmeg to taste. Set this bowl over ice in another bowl. Add the softened butter, and the egg whites very slowly, beating all the while with a wooden spoon until light and fluffy. Volume should increase by one third. Fold in the whipped cream little by little, beating continuously.

Soak the gelatin in cold water and set over hot water to dissolve. Fold it into the fish mixture.

In a fish mold, pour ¼ inch of fish aspic and let it set. Pack the mousse into the mold, pour over another layer of the fish jelly and chill until set. Unmold on a large platter. Use pimiento or olive for the eye. Garnish with crescents of aspic and watercress. Serve with a Remoulade sauce.

 **JOSEPHINE SAYS:**

Take advantage of the abundant local foods and their freshness. They may involve more work, but what else are you going to do?

Les Delices de l'Ete

Summer Delight Salad
6 servings

6 to 7 Belgian endives	1 egg
16 oz cream cheese	3 tbsps oil
8 oz cottage cheese	1 tbsp vinegar
1 cup chopped nuts	salt and pepper
10 oz fresh gooseberries, blueberries or strawberries	½ pt sour cream
	1 tbsp paprika
	chopped parsley, chives or tarragon

Remove a few outer leaves from endives and arrange them on a plate with ends touching in center to form a star.

Cream the two cheeses together thoroughly, fold in nuts and chill. When almost ready to serve, add the berries.

Beat egg with oil and vinegar until slightly thick. Season with salt and pepper. Mix in sour cream and paprika thoroughly and set aside.

To serve, mound cheese and berry mixture on top of endive star. Cut endives lengthwise and set them upright against the cheese. Spoon some of the sour cream dressing over the salad, sprinkle with parsley and top with a berry. Serve cold with the remaining sauce passed separately.

Scarole en Croûte

Escarole Salad in Crust
4 to 6 servings

1 recipe of pâte à tourte (see following recipe)	1 tin of anchovy filets (about 12) cut in small pieces
1 large head of escarole	3 egg yolks (two for mixture and one for the glaze)
3 cloves garlic	
2 tbsps butter	
6 to 8 black olives, pitted	
1 tbsp capers	2 tbsps cream

Prepare the pâte à tourte and let it rest for 20 to 30 minutes. Preheat oven to 375º.

Cut the escarole in half and wash. Cook in boiling water for 10 minutes. Drain and squeeze out the water. Peel and chop the garlic and sauté lightly in the butter. Add the escarole, then the olives, capers, and the anchovies. Add two egg yolks and mix well.

Continued

Roll out the dough and line a glass pie plate. Fill with the mixture and cover with leftover dough. Glaze with the remaining egg yolk, mixed with the cream. Bake for 40 minutes at 375°.

Pâté à Tourte — Dough for Tart

1 lb flour
1 cup butter, melted
4 tbsps shortening
1 tsp salt
1 tbsp yeast
¼ cup water or more, as needed

Put the flour in a large bowl and add the melted butter, shortening and salt. Dissolve the yeast in ¼ cup of water and add to the flour. If not soft enough to roll, add a little more water. Knead the dough until it no longer sticks to the hands. Roll in a ball and let it rest for 20 to 30 minutes.

Mousse au Jambon — Ham Mousse with Claret Sauce

6 to 8 servings

2 tbsps butter
1 tbsp flour
1 cup cream
1 dash cayenne pepper
1 pinch nutmeg
grated rind of 1 lemon
salt and pepper
3 eggs, separated
2 extra egg whites
½ cup fine bread crumbs
2 lbs lean ground ham
1 onion, grated

Make a roux with the butter and flour. Add the cream and stir; then set aside and cool. Add the seasonings: Cayenne pepper, nutmeg, lemon rind, salt and pepper. Add the three egg yolks and mix well. Next add the breadcrumbs, ham and grated onion.

Beat the egg whites until very stiff, but not too dry. Fold them very carefully into the ham mixture. Grease a pyrex dish and pour in the mixture — it should be about ¾ full. Set in a pan of hot water, and bake in a preheated 375° oven for 25 to 30 minutes. Check for doneness with the point of a knife (it should come out dry). Let it rest a few minutes and then unmold on a warm serving dish. Serve with claret sauce (see below).

Claret Sauce:

3 tbsps butter
1 onion, finely chopped
2 tbsps flour
2 cups red wine
1 tbsp brown sugar
¼ lb mushrooms, minced
1 clove garlic, minced
1 tbsp parsley, chopped

Combine the wine, onion, mushrooms, garlic, and brown sugar in a saucepan; allow to reduce a little. Meanwhile melt the butter in another saucepan and stir in the flour. Then add the wine sauce and parsley and allow to simmer for 20 - 25 minutes.

Oeufs Pochés au Thon   Poached Eggs on Tuna

4 to 6 servings

3 tbsps butter
2 rounded tbsps flour
1 to 1½ cups milk
salt and pepper to taste
⅛ tsp nutmeg
½ cup grated cheese

1 can of tuna (7 oz)
1 piece of toast (round) for each serving
1 egg per serving
paprika

Make a Béchamel sauce with the butter, flour, and milk in the usual manner. This sauce should not be too thin. Add the salt, pepper and nutmeg. Stir in the cheese and set aside.

Drain the tuna and moisten it with some of the sauce so that it makes a stiff paste. Toast the bread rounds or muffins and coat with the creamed tuna. Top each with a poached egg. Pour the remaining sauce over all and sprinkle with a little paprika.

Asparagus and tomatoes may be served around the dish.

Couronne de Champignons aux Oeufs Brouillés
Mushroom Ring with Scrambled Eggs

4 to 6 servings

1 lb mushrooms, minced
1 onion, grated or finely chopped
2 pieces of bread, soaked in milk and squeezed dry
2 tbsps butter
1 clove garlic, chopped

1 tsp parsley, chopped
2 eggs, well beaten
½ cup sherry
salt and pepper
nutmeg
scrambled eggs for 4 to 6 servings

Sauté the mushrooms and onions together lightly; sprinkle with the chopped garlic and parsley and set aside.

Beat two eggs in a bowl. Add the soaked bread, mushrooms and onion, along with the sherry. Season with salt, pepper, and nutmeg and mix well. Place in a well-greased ring mold, set in a pan of hot water and bake in a preheated 350° oven for 40 to 50 minutes. Allow mold to set 5 minutes before unmolding. Then fill the center with scrambled eggs, which can be flavored with fine herbs. An elegant late breakfast or light lunch.

Boeuf Bouilli en Salade

Leftover Beef in Salad

2 servings

¾ to 1 lb leftover boiled or braised beef
3 or 4 green scallions or chives
2 tbsps chopped parsley
1 or 2 boiled potatoes

1 tbsp vinegar
few drops Worcestershire
1 tbsp prepared mustard (Dijon preferred)
3 tbsps oil
salt and pepper

Garnish: Hardcooked eggs, tomatoes, avocado, asparagus.

Eliminate all the fat from the meat and dice into large pieces. Dice potatoes. Prepare French dressing with the oil, vinegar, Worcestershire, mustard, salt and pepper. Beat a few minutes and add the chopped scallions or chives. Mix in the meat, potatoes and parsley. Allow 1 hour to marinate, then arrange on serving dish. Garnish with the above suggestions.

DESSERTS

"One for the Cook!"

I use my fingers a lot when I cook ~ better than any utensil for mixing, and cleaner, too. I also taste my cooking as I go along ~ it's wasteful to use a seasoning or flavoring in a dish if you can't tell it's there.

Desserts

When I worked for the Tobins, they would spend six months of the year in New York, because Mrs. Tobin was one of the Vanderbilts. They would go every spring and fall for three months, to their home in Syosset, Long Island. The cooks and servants would stay in San Francisco to take care of the house. One spring Mrs. Tobin called from Long Island to say that Mr. Tobin had broken his hip and would have to remain there until it healed. Would I come out and cook for them? I told her I had to stay with my daughter because she was still very young and going to school. Finally they decided to pay for both me and Jacqueline to go to New York for the summer. So Jacqueline and I rode the train out to New York, while Charles stayed in San Francisco.

I ended up working very hard those few months because Mrs. Tobin entertained New York society all summer! Once she gave a luncheon for the wife of Teddy Roosevelt, Jr., the president's son. You know what I served? Leftovers! We had leftover bass, served in a cold salad. Mrs. Roosevelt complimented me on it ~ said it was very good. Later I told Mrs. Tobin ~ I didn't want to say it in front of her guest ~ that the lunch was made from leftovers. But Mrs. Tobin was a very smart woman. She said that it was wonderful, and quite a success. By the end of the summer, we were glad to get back to San Francisco. My Charles was very lonely and getting tired of keeping house by himself.

SONG TO COOK BY~

Drink a little bit, it's very good.
Drink a little bit, it's very sweet.
But you must not roll under the table.
Drink a little bit, it's very sweet.

Mousse aux Pommes   Apple Mousse

1 lb apples, peeled and diced
½ cup sugar
1 tbsp vanilla
4 egg whites

Custard cream:
4 egg yolks
½ cup sugar
1 tsp vanilla
1½ cups milk

Cook the apples in ½ cup water and drain. Mash the apples to a purée, then add the sugar and vanilla. Beat the egg whites until very stiff and fold into the apple purée.

Grease a charlotte mold or a fireproof dish. Pour the apple mixture into it, set in a **bain marie,** and bake at 350° for 25 to 30 minutes.

While the apples bake, make a custard cream. Beat the egg yolks with the sugar until lemon-colored. Heat the milk in a double boiler and when hot, pour over the eggs and sugar. Mix well and return to the double boiler. Cook, stirring, until thick enough to coat a wooden spoon. Cool and serve over the cold apple mousse.

Tarte à la Frangipane   Almond Tart

pâte brisée or pâte feuilletée (see recipe)
3 eggs
⅓ cup sugar
¼ cup butter
2 tbsps flour

1 cup milk, warmed
⅓ cup ground almonds
1 tsp almond extract
¼ cup raisins
1 small liquor glass of rum
confectioners sugar

Beat the eggs with the sugar until lemon colored. Make a roux with the butter and flour, add the warm milk and stir. When hot, mix with the eggs and add the almonds and extract. Put back on a slow fire and stir until thick. Add the raisins and rum.

Precook the crust for 10 to 15 minutes at 375°. Put the egg and almond mixture into the crust and bake 20 minutes more. Sprinkle with confectioners' sugar and serve hot or cold.

Gâteau Solange   Solange Cake

4 squares semi-sweet chocolate
4 oz (½ cup) sweet butter
4 rounded tbsps sugar
4 eggs, separated

¾ cup cake crumbs or use lady fingers, crumbled
whole lady fingers, to line the mold
coffee cream *(see recipe below)*

Melt the chocolate, butter and sugar in a double boiler. Add the 4 egg yolks, stirring occasionally. Remove from the heat, let the mixture cool and add the stiffly beaten egg whites and the cake crumbs.

Line a buttered mold with lady fingers and pour the chocolate mixture into it. Chill. To unmold, dip the mold in hot water for a few seconds. Serve the cake with coffee cream.

Coffee Cream

¾ cup strong coffee (or
   ¾ cup water and 1 rounded
   tbsp instant coffee)

4 egg yolks
4 rounded tbsps sugar
1 cup heavy cream, whipped

Beat the egg yolks and sugar until lemon-colored. Bring the coffee to a boil and slowly add to the egg yolk mixture. Put it in the top of a double boiler over hot water and cook, stirring constantly, until it has thickened and coats a wooden spoon. Let the mixture cool; fold in whipped cream, and pour over the cake.

Note: coffee cream can also be served by itself as an excellent dessert.

Compote de Rhubarbe   Rhubarb Compote

4 to 6 servings

1 lb rhubarb
½ lb sugar

½ pt whipping cream,
   sweetened with sugar

Preheat oven to 300°.

Peel and wash the rhubarb. Cut it in 2 or 3-inch pieces and lay the pieces in an ovenproof dish. Sprinkle with sugar, cover, and bake in the oven at 300° for 20 to 25 minutes. (When rhubarb is cooked in the oven it doesn't go to pieces, but remains whole.) Put the rhubarb in sherbet glasses and cover with sweetened whipped cream.

Alternate Method: Put the sugar and rhubarb in a saucepan and cook slowly until reduced to a pulp. Cool in the refrigerator. Fill sherbet glasses with the rhubarb and top with whipped cream. Serve with cookies.

Poires Almina ## Pears Almina
6 servings

From Pellaprat, 1920

1 cup sugar, for syrup	1 tsp crème de riz
½ cup water	(rice flour)
2-3 tsps kirsch or	1 tbsp sugar
Cointreau	zest of 1 orange, slivered
3 fresh pears, peeled	and parboiled until tender
and halved	or 1 tbsp orange marmalade
3 egg yolks	½ cup heavy cream,
	whipped and flavored with
	same liqueur used for syrup

Mix sugar and water over heat until syrup forms. Add liqueur flavoring, then poach pears until tender, about 15 minutes. Remove pears and set aside 1 cup of syrup.

In top of double boiler combine egg yolks, crème de riz and sugar thoroughly. Add reserved syrup and cook over medium heat until mixture thickens enough to coat a spoon, about 7 to 10 minutes. Stir in orange zest.

To serve, pour sauce over pears and top with flavored whipped cream.

Crème Mousse au Citron ## Lemon-Cream Mousse

3 eggs	1 pt heavy cream, whipped
½ cup sugar	1 env gelatin
grated rind of one lemon	strawberries, raspberries, peaches,
juice of one lemon	or other fruit

With an electric beater, beat the eggs and add sugar gradually until mixture is thick and creamy. Add grated lemon rind. Combine gelatin with lemon juice and dissolve over hot water. Add to egg mixture and beat well.

With a spatula or whisk, fold whipped cream into the mixture and pour into a 2-quart ring mold. Chill several hours or overnight. Unmold on a platter and surround with sliced fruits of your choice or berries that have been sugared and chilled.

Poires à la Savoyarde ## Caramel Pears
6 servings

6 pears (Anjou or similar	¼ cup sweet butter
type)	½ pt heavy cream
1 cup granulated sugar	1 tsp rum

Preheat oven to 500°.

Peel the pears, which should not be too ripe, and cut them into quarters. Remove the cores and poach them in simmering water for 5 minutes.

Remove the pears from the water and place the pieces close together in a shallow baking dish. Sprinkle them generously with granulated sugar. Sprinkle the rum over them and put a piece of sweet butter on each.

Place the dish on the middle rack of the oven, preheated to 500°, until the sugar has turned to a golden dark brown. Baste them once or twice with their own juice while browning. When the sugar is caramelized, pour in the heavy cream, letting it blend with the sugar to make an exquisite caramel cream.

Serve hot.

Ananas Martine / Pineapple Martine

4 to 6 servings

5 egg yolks	lady fingers or cookies
½ cup sugar	1 liquor glass of **Grand Marnier**
1½ cups milk	6 slices of pineapple
1 tbsp cornstarch	powdered sugar

Beat the egg yolks and the sugar until light. Bring the milk to a boil and mix with the yolks. Put back in a saucepan and cook slowly, stirring until it coats a spoon. Dissolve the cornstarch in a little cold milk and mix with the yolk mixture. Stir until thick.

Prepare individual dishes or sherbet glasses. Pour 2 or 3 spoonfuls of custard into the bottom of each dish. Dip the lady fingers in the **Grand Marnier** and lay one on the cream. Top with a slice of pineapple and put the remaining custard cream over it. Sprinkle with powdered sugar and cool until ready to serve. Sprinkle with hot **Grand Marnier** and ignite. Serve at once.

JOSEPHINE SAYS:

Keeping a brick in the oven is a good trick for making bread crust turn crispy and to keep cookie and pastry bottoms from burning on a tin sheet. It's also an easy way to retain heat in the oven for warming dishes.

Le Pithivier / Almond Cake

½ cup sugar	1 liquor glass rum, kirsch, or cognac
¼ cup butter	
1 egg	1 recipe puff paste *(see recipe)*
½ cup powdered almonds	1 egg, beaten with 1 tsp water
½ tsp almond extract	

Beat the sugar and butter until light. Beat in the egg, almonds, almond extract and liquor. Cover and refrigerate until chilled and firm enough to be handled easily. Prepare the puff paste. Roll out the puff paste ¼-inch thick on a lightly floured board. Use a pot cover or a cake pan to cut two large circles 9 inches in diameter.

Preheat the oven to 425°

Continued

Work the almond paste into a cake 4 to 5 inches in diameter and put it in the center of one of the puff paste disks, leaving a margin of 2 inches all around. This will prevent the almond cream from leaking out during the baking. Brush the circle with water and cover with the other disk. With your hands press the top disk to the bottom one all around the lump of almond cream.

Invert a bowl or cake pan, 8 inches in diameter, over the cake, leaving a margin of about ½-inch showing all around the edge. Use a small knife to cut a scalloped border all the way around, making it as even as possible. Remove the bowl or pan and chill the cake in the refrigerator for about 20 minutes.

Just before baking, paint the surface with egg glaze (1 egg beaten with 1 tsp of water.) Make a chimney with a pastry tube or foil and set in the center of the cake. With the point of a knife cut curving lines out from the center and down into the dough. Bake immediately, setting it in the middle of the preheated 425° oven for 20 minutes or until the pastry has puffed a little. Reduce heat to 325° and bake 25 to 30 minutes more, or until pastry sides are brown. (If the cake browns too much during the baking, cover with foil or brown paper.)

Fanchonnettes

1½ cups crème pâtissière
  (see recipe)
pâte sucrée:
  ⅓ cup sugar
  1 cup flour
  1 egg
  6 tbsps butter
  ½ tsp vanilla

Walnut Cookies

2 eggs separated
1 cup ground walnuts
1 tsp almond extract
½ cup jam, any flavor
10" quiche pan, filmed

Prepare pâte sucrée by working the flour with the butter and sugar into a fine powder. Add the egg and vanilla and work into a dough. Chill until firm enough to roll or press into the pan with your hands. Beat the yolks into the crème patissière, along with the nuts, jam, and extract. Whip the whites and fold in. Pour the mixture into the pan. Place on a cookie sheet and bake in a preheated 350° oven for 30-45 minutes, or until an inserted knife comes out clean. If the top should start to brown before it is done, place a piece of foil on top. Cut into wedges when cool.

Carnaval de Nice

1 brioche, conical-shaped
  or high mold *(see recipe)*
4 oz bitter chocolate
2 tbsps water
½ cup sugar
½ cup unsalted butter

Brioche with Chocolate and Meringue

8 to 10 servings

2 egg yolks
⅓ cup whipping cream
⅔ cup sugar for meringue
2 egg whites
1 tsp instant coffee
chocolate chips or pastilles

Make a recipe of brioche.

Melt the unsweetened chocolate with 2 tbsps water over hot water or very slow heat. Add the sugar, butter, and egg yolks. Remove from the heat, let it cool a little and then beat with an egg beater. Add the cream and beat until the mixture becomes fluffier.

Cut the brioche in slices and put some of the cream on each slice. Use leftover cream to coat the top and the sides. Put in the refrigerator to chill.

Make the meringue with the 2 egg whites, $2/3$ cup sugar, and instant coffee. Beat constantly in a double boiler over very hot water until it is very stiff. Then spread unevenly over the brioche and garnish with the chocolate chips or chocolate pastilles.

Pain aux Herbes — Herb Bread

½ cup lukewarm water
2 pkgs dry yeast
¼ cup sugar
1 cup sour cream
1 cup milk, heated until lukewarm
3–4 cups flour
2 eggs
1 tbsp fresh fennel leaves or dill, chopped
½ tsp fresh thyme, chopped
1 tbsp fresh tarragon, chopped

In a large bowl blend together the water, yeast and sugar. Heat the sour cream and milk to just barely lukewarm and add to the yeast mixture. Add 1 cup of the flour and beat with an electric mixer at medium speed, scraping the bowl occasionally. Add the eggs and 1 more cup of flour. Beat at high speed 1 minute until elastic. Gradually add the remaining flour until it makes a soft dough which leaves the sides of the bowl. Add all the herbs.

Turn out on a floured board and knead about 5 minutes until the dough is smooth. Place it in a large greased bowl, cover, and let it rise in a warm place (70°–80°) free from drafts. When the dough has risen 1 hour and is doubled in volume, punch it down and divide it into rolls or two loaves. Place in greased pans, brush with melted butter and let it rise once more until double in size.

Note: The dough may be braided or made into knotted rolls.

Bake in a preheated 350° oven for 20 to 25 minutes for rolls and 35 to 40 minutes for loaves. Remove from the pans immediately and allow to cool on racks.

Pain aux Légumes ou Fruit — Vegetable or Fruit Bread

½ cup butter
1½ cups sugar
2 eggs
2 cups flour
½ tsp baking soda
1½ tsp baking powder
½ tsp salt
1 cup milk
juice of 1 lemon or 1 tsp vinegar
rind of 1 lemon
rind of 1 lemon
½ cups of the fruit or vegetable selected *(see note)*
¾ cup ground nuts, lightly toasted (walnuts, almonds, etc.)

Continued

Cream the butter with the sugar. Add the eggs and continue beating until fluffy. Combine the flour, soda, baking powder, salt and half of the flour. Add to the butter mixture. Add the milk and lemon juice and lemon rind. Add the remaining flour, the fruit or vegetables, and the nuts.

Turn into a greased and floured bread pan (9x5x3 inches). Bake in a preheated 350° oven for 55 minutes to 1 hour, until a wood or metal skewer comes out clean. Cool 10 to 15 minutes in the pan, then invert on a wire rack. Wrap with plastic wrap when cooled. This bread can be frozen.

Note: This bread can be made with bananas, carrots, zucchini, apples or your choice. When using carrots or zucchini, they should be grated with $1/3$ cup more milk added.

Meringue Italienne — Italian Meringue

This will make a beautiful white meringue, perfect for lining a dessert mold or adding a finishing touch to a cake or mousse. A good use of extra egg whites, too!

$2/3$ cup water
2 cups sugar
6 egg whites
pinch of salt

In a heavy pan, combine the water and sugar over moderate heat until the sugar is dissolved and clear. Swirl the pan once or twice, cover and lower heat until a candy thermometer reaches 238° (or when the syrup forms a soft ball when dropped in cold water). Beat the egg whites with a pinch of salt until stiff. Pour the hot syrup by droplets into the beaten whites, and continue beating until mixture cools and forms heavy peaks.

Use a pastry tube or drop batter onto a buttered and floured cookie sheet, arranging in desired shapes, and allow to dry on the middle rack in the oven with only the pilot light on, for 6 to 8 hours or overnight. Store meringue in an airtight container.

Couronne aux Noix — Walnut Ring

1 cup milk
¾ cup butter
3 cups flour
½ tsp salt
¼ cup sugar
4 eggs
½ lb walnuts, finely chopped
1 tbsp yeast
confectioners' sugar
walnut halves

Bring ¾ cup of the milk and the butter to a scalding boil; cool. In ¼ cup of tepid milk, dissolve the yeast, adding 1 tbsp of sugar to accelerate the fermentation.

In a large mixing bowl, mix flour, salt and sugar; beat in the eggs one at a time with a wooden spoon, or use the tips of your fingers. Add the milk and butter, and yeast, and beat quickly until the dough is elastic. Add the chopped walnuts and beat again. Cover bowl with plastic and a heavy towel. Let it rise at 70°-80° until doubled in bulk.

Grease a ring mold or tube pan and arrange the pastry in it; let it rise again until almost to the top of the mold (about 1 hour). Bake at 300° for 1 hour. When done, powder all over with confectioners' sugar and decorate with walnut halves.

Crêpes Adeline

½ cup (4 oz) semi-sweet chocolate
1 tbsp water or strong coffee
1 or 2 apples
2 tbsps butter
½ cup hazelnuts

Adeline Crêpes

1 liquor glass of Calvados or brandy
1 recipe Brittany crêpes *(see recipe)*
powdered sugar

Over hot water melt the chocolate with the water or strong coffee. Peel the apples and dice them. Sauté the apples in butter until slightly soft. Chop the nuts and brown them slightly in a 350° oven. Mix the chocolate, apples, hazelnuts and Calvados.

Prepare the crêpes; they should be quite thin. Spread the chocolate mixture on each. Roll. Sprinkle with powdered sugar and serve hot.

Crêpes du Convent

1 recipe crêpes with 3 tbsps flour *(see recipe)*
1 recipe crêpes with 6 tbsps flour
butter

Crêpes with Pears
16 to 18 crepes

1 cup jam, any flavor
flavoring: vanilla, rum, or kirsch to taste
4 to 5 pears, coarsely chopped and poached in light syrup

Before beginning crêpes, poach pears in a light syrup. Reserve poaching liquid for the sauce.

Proceed as for crêpes by placing regular crêpe batter in hot buttered crêpe pan. Place a few pieces of pear on top and cover with the heavier batter. Place a dot of butter under the crêpe and quickly turn to cook the other side.

Place crêpes on a heated platter and top with sauce, made from the poaching liquid, flavoring, and jam.

Marquis au Chocolat — Rich Chocolate Cake

Cake:

2/3 cup flour, measured
   then sifted
4 eggs, separated
4 oz semi-sweet chocolate

2 tbsps rum
1/3 cup sugar
pinch of salt

Butter cream:

(handwritten: 12 oz. semi-sweet choc.)

1/3 cup sugar
3 egg yolks
3/4 cup boiled milk

1 cup butter, unsalted
2 tbsps vanilla or rum
   flavoring

Chocolate glaze:

6 oz semi-sweet chocolate
4 oz butter or margarine,
   unsalted

2 tbsps strong coffee or rum
2 tbsps sugar

To make cake, melt chocolate with the rum in the top of a double boiler. Meanwhile, with an electric mixer, beat yolks. Add small amounts of sugar and 1/3 cup flour, beating well each time until all has been added. Add melted chocolate and mix well.

Whip egg whites until almost dry, adding a pinch of salt after they begin to whip. Fold 1/3 of the whites into the chocolate mixture then sift in the remaining 1/3 cup flour, alternating with the rest of the egg whites until all has been added. Pour into a buttered round cake pan that has been filmed and dusted with flour. Bake in a preheated 350° oven for 30 to 35 minutes. The top of the cake will have cracked and the center should be moist. Cool.

To make butter cream, mix sugar and egg yolks. Stir in boiled milk and return to a double boiler.

Note: 3/4 cup hot chocolate or coffee may be substituted for milk.

Cook and stir until mixture coats the spoon; cool to tepid. With the electric mixer, start beating the butter, adding egg mixture a little at a time, until it is a smooth butter cream.

To make chocolate glaze, melt chocolate, rum, and sugar together in a double boiler. Remove from heat and add small chunks of butter, mixing each one thoroughly. Mixture should be quite glossy.

To assemble cake, split cooled cake into two layers. Spread one layer with the butter cream and place the other layer on top. Spread more butter cream on the top and sides. Then place cake in the freezer to harden frosting. This will help prevent the cream from dissolving when adding the glaze. When hardened sufficiently, place cake on a cake rack with paper or plate beneath it. Pour warm glaze over cake, tipping cake if necessary to cover all the cream with the glaze. A knife may be used to touch up the sides only.

Gratin de Cerises

Cherries, pitted
Syrup:
   1 cup red wine
   ½ cup sugar
   1 inch stick of cinnamon
     (more if stronger
     flavor desired)

Crêpe-Wrapped Cherries with Custard

Custard:
   2 cups hot milk
   ½ cup sugar
   3 eggs
   2 tbsps flour
   1 tsp vanilla flavoring
Crêpes *(see recipe)*
sweet crumbs: cake, brioche,
   cookie, etc.

Prepare syrup by combining sugar, wine and cinnamon and bringing to a boil. Make sure sugar has completely dissolved before adding cherries. Cherries will give some of their own juices to the syrup, so any amount of cherries may be added. Simmer 10 minutes. Meanwhile make the custard.

In a double boiler, mix eggs and sugar together thoroughly before slowly adding the milk. Mix well. Add flour and continue to stir until mixture thickens and custard mixture will coat a spoon.

Fill crêpes with cherries and completely envelop. Place in bottom of filmed ovenproof bowl or casserole. Poke a hole in each crêpe and pour custard over. Sprinkle top with crumbs and set the bowl in a pan of water. Bake in a preheated 375⁰ oven for 45 minutes to 1 hour, or until custard has set.

Pommes Chanoinesse

½ recipe **pâte brisèe** *(see recipe)*
1 recipe **pâte à choux** for one 10-inch pie *(see recipe)*
1½–2 cups **crème pâtissière** *(see recipe)*
4–6 small apples

Whole Apple Custard Tart

1 egg mixed with a little milk
1 cup plus 2 tbsps sugar
1 tsp vanilla or lemon juice
1 cup apricot jam, strained
decorate with glacéed cherries

Prepare **pâte brisée, pâte à choux,** and **crème pâtissière** ahead of time.

Cut a round of **pâte brisée,** the size of pie desired and place on greased cookie sheet. Prick the round with a fork to keep from puffing while baking. Around the edge make a border with the **pâte à choux,** using a pastry bag and a plain tube. This may also be done by dipping a spoon in cold water and placing small mounds next to each other around the rim. Moisten hands and smooth the paste together.

Brush the tops and sides with the egg-milk mixture for a golden glaze. Coat the exposed **pâte brisée** with a small amount of **crème pâtissière** to prevent

Continued

the crust from burning while the **pâte à choux** bakes. Bake in a preheated 400° oven for 10 minutes. Turn the oven down to 300° and bake 25-30 minutes more.

Meanwhile, peel and core apples. Poach them in a syrup of 2 cups water and 1 cup sugar, vanilla (gives good flavor but darkens apples) or lemon juice (keeps apples white); cook apples through. Avoid overcooking. When apples cool, fill the cores with **crème pâtissière** or apricot jam.

When the shell is finished baking, partially fill the center with the **crème pâtissière**. Line up the whole apples on top of the cream. Top with an apricot glaze made of remaining jam heated with 2 tbsps of sugar. Decorate with glacéed cherries.

HAUTE CUISINE

"Dressed Like a Horse on Parade"

*For a very elegant occasion, you may
want to prepare something extraordinary.
The recipes in this section may require
more time to prepare.*

Haute Cuisine

One of my best employers had a very unruly and spoiled little girl named June. But June would listen to me because she was afraid of me ~ I'll tell you why.

One time she kicked me ~ she was just seven years old. I just looked at her, took her by both arms, and marched her into the kitchen. Then I shook her just like a prune tree. She became white as a sheet of paper. No one had ever done that to her before. She was afraid of me, then, and she said, "I am going to tell my mother what you did and then she will give you a shake!" I told her that was good, because if she didn't tell her, I would.

Later that evening her mother came into the kitchen, as she always did, to thank me for dinner. This time when she came in, I asked her if June had said anything to her. No, she hadn't. When I told her what had happened, she just said, "I am so glad. That's just what she needed!" June minded me after that, and I think she even liked me, because she knew I'd done it for her own good.

But she could be a devil of a girl. Every summer that I went to Europe with my employer, I would have to look after June. When we went to Paris, they would stay at the Hôtel Lapérouse, and I would stay with my relatives for a good visit. And I would take care of June most of the time.

It is because of June that I eventually stopped working for that family. She had been sent to a private school in Switzerland, but she was breaking all the rules; finally they called her mother to tell her that June would have to leave. Off she flew, without a word to me about when she would be back, or what I was to do, as she usually did. So naturally I thought I'd better find another job, and I went to Mrs. Charles Figgenbaum to cook.

It was several months before June's mother returned. She called me up, in tears, wanting to know why I had left her. I told her I was sorry, but she hadn't asked me to stay. And of course I couldn't leave Mrs. Figgenbaum without a good reason. So that was the end of eight wonderful years with June's mother.

Cailles du Bocage

Quail with Wild Rice
8 servings

1 quail per serving
1 strip of back fat for each quail
1 grapeleaf for each quail
Mirepoix:
   1 stalk of celery, diced
   1 carrot, diced
   1 medium onion, diced

1 or 2 tomatoes, diced
1 cup white wine
½ cup chicken broth
salt and pepper
½ tsp fresh sage, sliced
1 tsp cornstarch
wild rice *(see recipe)*

Wrap each quail with a piece of back fat and a grapeleaf and tie. Place in a buttered pan and bake in a preheated 450° oven for 10 minutes. Remove the quails and keep them warm.

In the same pan sauté the *mirepoix* of celery, carrot, and onion. Sauté for about 10 minutes, stirring so it will not burn. Add the tomatoes. Then put the quails back on top of the *mirepoix* and add the wine, broth, salt, pepper, and sage. Bake for another 10 minutes. Cover if birds get too brown.

Again remove the quails from pan and keep them warm. Transfer the juices to a small saucepan and reduce a little. Strain out the vegetables and thicken the sauce with the cornstarch, which has been mixed with a little cold water. Spoon off the fat. Arrange the quails on the wild rice and pour the sauce over them.

About Wild Rice

Wild rice is a perfect accompaniment to all game and also to domestic fowl such as duck, goose, turkey, Cornish game hens, etc. It may also be served with beef, liver, and other meats.

Wild rice can be cooked with a diversity of vegetables and dried fruits: celery, mushrooms, walnuts, hazelnuts, almonds, and raisins. Try it with a good dose of Madeira. Wild rice can be prepared ahead and reheated in a double boiler or moistened a little, and kept covered in the oven.

Riz Sauvage

Wild Rice

1 cup wild rice, soaked in boiling water
1 tsp salt
2 tbsps butter
1 small onion, chopped

2 cups broth or water
salt and pepper
additional butter
1 hard-cooked egg

Rinse the wild rice thoroughly. Put it in a pot and pour boiling water over it. Let it soak until water is cold. If the rice is not sufficiently swollen, repeat, soaking with more boiling water.

Strain the rice in a colander. Melt the butter in a heavy pan and add the chopped onion. Cook until the onion is a golden brown. Then add the rice, stirring to mix well. Add the warm broth or water and salt and pepper. Bring it to a boil, then reduce heat, and simmer for 30 to 40 minutes. If the rice becomes too dry, add a little broth or Madeira.

When cooked add a piece of fresh butter the size of a walnut, and put rice into a vegetable dish. Strain the egg yolk and white separately. Sprinkle half the rice with egg yolk and the other half with egg white. Serve.

Faisan Vigneronne

Pheasant with Grapes and Sweetbreads

1½ lbs fresh grapes
2 pheasants
3 tbsps goose fat or other fat (or 2 tbsps oil and 2 tbsps butter)
1 glass cognac or brandy
1 carrot, chopped
1 onion, chopped
2 shallots, chopped
¼ cup raisins
1 cup broth
salt and pepper to taste

paprika, to taste
1 tsp aromatic herbs: rosemary, sage, winter savory, marjoram, oregano, thyme, bay leaf
1 lb sweetbreads
juice of 1 lemon
¼ cup **crème fraîche** (heavy cream) or sour cream
1 or 2 egg yolks
croutons
parsley, chopped

Crush the grapes the day before and let them stand at room temperature so they will ferment slightly.

Cut the pheasant in pieces and sauté in the fat or butter and oil. When brown, pour cognac or brandy over and ignite. Add the chopped carrot, onion and shallots. Soak the raisins in hot water for a few minutes and add to the pheasant. Add the crushed grapes and the broth. Season with salt, pepper, paprika, and the herbs. Cover and simmer for 30 minutes.

Blanch the sweetbreads, simmering in water and lemon juice for 7 to 10 minutes. Clean and sauté in a little butter.

After the pheasant has cooked 30 minutes, test with a fork. If tender, add the sweetbreads and simmer again 15 minutes longer. (This recipe calls for a well-done pheasant.)

Mix the cream and egg yolks and add to the pheasant at the last minute. Serve with triangular-shaped bread croutons which have been fried in butter. Sprinkle with chopped parsley. Strain the sauce and serve.

Note: The pheasant can also be cooked in a 350° oven for the same amount of time.

Ballotine de Volaille à la Régence

Poached Chicken Regency Style
6 to 8 servings

1 large chicken, 4 to 5 lbs boned (see below)
quenelles stuffing *(below)*
1 truffle (optional)
½ lb cooked tongue
2½ qts water
1 veal bone
2 onions, studded with cloves
2 carrots, sliced thickly

1 stalk of celery, cut in pieces
1 tbsp salt
½ tsp pepper
bouquet garni of thyme, bay leaf, celery leaves and parsley stems
½ lb mushrooms, sautéed
1½ doz artichoke hearts, cooked
1 cup supreme sauce *(see recipe)*
pitted green and black olives

Bone the chicken without breaking the skin and lay it out flat on a cheese cloth, skin side down (save bones for cooking liquid). Cover the flesh of the chicken with a layer of quenelle stuffing *(see recipe)* and sprinkle with the (optional) chopped truffle. Then place 4-inch by 1-inch fillets of cooked tongue lengthwise on top and cover with the remaining stuffing. Roll the chicken lengthwise into a firm roll and wrap the cheese cloth securely around it. Tie the cloth tightly at both ends and at intervals between so that the **ballotine** will hold its shape during the cooking process.

Put it into a large pan with the water, veal bone, and the chicken bones. Add the onions, studded with cloves, carrots, celery, salt, pepper, and the **bouquet garni.** Bring slowly to a boil and skim off skin that collects. Reduce heat and simmer for 45 minutes to 1 hour.

Remove the **ballotine,** unwrap and slice with a sharp knife. Arrange the slices in a circle on the serving dish like a crown. In the center, place the cooked mushrooms and artichoke hearts with a **supreme** sauce. Garnish with pitted green and black olives. The same **supreme** sauce can be passed separately.

Note: A brown Madeira sauce can be substituted and other vegetables can be used as garnish if you prefer.

Farce à Quenelles (Panade)

Quenelles Stuffing

1 cup bread
$^1/_3$ cup milk
3 tbsps butter, softened
salt and pepper
$^1/_3$ tsp nutmeg

5 to 6 tbsps cream
$^2/_3$ cup ground lean veal or chicken
2 egg whites

Soak the bread in the milk and squeeze dry. In a large pan mash the bread with a wooden spoon. Add the butter, salt, pepper, and nutmeg. Put the pan over a low flame and vigorously stir in the cream, a little at a time. Remove from the heat, allow the mixture to cool a little, and combine with the ground meat and the egg whites. Mix thoroughly.

Dodine de Canard

Stuffed Boned Duck

approximately 10 servings

court bouillon (meat stock may be substituted, if on hand):
- 1 leek
- 1 carrot
- 1 stalk of celery
- 1 onion, studded with 4 cloves
- 1 cup water
- salt and pepper

1 large duck (5-6 lbs)
¼ cup cognac or brandy
½ cup sherry or Madeira
½ tsp salt
½ tsp pepper
½ tsp thyme
1 bay leaf, crushed

¼ lb chicken liver
duck livers and heart
½ lb ground pork
¼ lb ground veal
¼ lb ground ham
¼ lb fresh bacon, ground
½ tsp sage
1 tbsp in all: rosemary, thyme, marjoram
1 tsp tarragon, if available
1 tsp allspice
1 tbsp Curaçao
1 tbsp cognac
2 slices of bread
1 cup wine, red or white

Simmer the ingredients for the **court bouillon** for 25 to 30 minutes; set aside and allow to cool. (The **court bouillon** is not necessary if beef or other meat stock is available.)

Bone the duck through the neck opening, using your fingers and a sharp boning knife. Slide the skin off as you proceed. Do not break the skin (the wings can be cut if you cannot skin them, and the hole closed with a needle and thread). Take the carcass out; cut all the meat into small pieces and marinate it in the cognac or brandy and sherry, seasoned with salt and pepper, thyme, and a crushed bay leaf. Let it stand in the marinade in the refrigerator.

Meanwhile sauté the reserved duck liver and heart and the chicken livers in butter, or boil for 5 to 6 minutes until firm. This will make them easier to grind. Mix the pork, veal, ham, ground bacon and the liver (ground), with the herbs, Curaçao, cognac, salt, pepper, and allspice. Soak the bread in bouillon or in the liver-poaching liquid and add to this mixture, after squeezing it dry. Fry a spoonful of the mixture and taste to test the seasoning. Adjust seasoning and add the marinated pieces of duck, along with the marinade.

Sew one end of the duck skin closed and add the filling. Then sew the other end closed. Roll in cheese cloth, tying both ends securely with string, and secure the middle with string if necessary. The duck will be like a large sausage.

Place it in the cold **court bouillon** or broth and add 1 cup of wine. Bring to a boil, lower the heat, and simmer on top of the stove or in a preheated (300°) oven for 1½ hours. Let it cool in its own stock and glaze with meat jelly. The duck and platter may be placed in the freezer for ½ hour or more, to congeal the glaze more quickly. (You may have to repeat this several times to get it well-coated.)

Serve with slices of pineapple, peaches, quinces, or other fruits, also glazed with the meat jelly.

Canard a la Tour d'Argent   Pressed Duck

This dish is usually done with wild duck. If domestic duck is used it should be killed by strangulation in order to keep its blood. For this recipe you also need to have a duck press.

1 fat, young duck (about 8-9 weeks old)	²/₃ cup Madeira
1 cup consommé, duck or game	¼ cup good brandy or cognac
liver of the duck	juice of 1 lemon
½ cup port	salt and pepper
	pinch of cayenne pepper

Make about 1 cup of consommé using the duck trimmings. Crush the duck liver and marinate it in the port, Madeira, and cognac and lemon juice. Preheat oven to 450°.

Brown the duck well on all sides on top of the stove, then roast for about 15 minutes in the oven. It should remain very rare. Slice the meat from the bones, cutting it into small pieces, reserving the legs, which can be broiled until done and served with the duck, or served separately for another course.

Crush the duck bones in the duck press in order to extract all the blood. Add ½ cup of the duck consommé to the blood and pour all this juice over the crushed liver, port, Madeira, cognac, and lemon juice. Cook this mixture over a low flame (a chafing dish is ideal) until the sauce becomes thick and chocolate-colored. Add salt, pepper, and a dash of cayenne pepper. You must stir the sauce continuously, without interruption, for about 20 minutes.

Pour the sauce over the duck and serve very hot.

Cochen de Lait Rôti   Roast Suckling Pig

25 to 30 servings

suckling pig, 22 lbs (see note)	2 cups of fresh herbs: oregano, thyme, parsley, sage, tarragon, fennel, marjoram (use ½ this amount if using dried herbs)
2 lbs pork liver	1 tbsp salt
½ lb ground ham	½ tbsp pepper
½ lb ground sausage meat	½ tsp allspice
½ lb fat, not rendered	½ tsp cloves
4 cups of bread	6 eggs
2 to 2½ lbs onions	1 bunch fennel or dill
4 cloves garlic	sufficient mustard
	½ lb butter

Boil the pork liver until it is easy to grind, about 10 minutes. Grind liver and fat, and add to ham and sausage meat. Soak the bread in milk or bouillon and squeeze dry; then add to meat. Peel onions, slice, and sauté with garlic in 2 tbsps oil and 2 tbsps of butter until translucent. Add to meat mixture along with the herbs, salt and pepper, cloves, allspice, and the eggs beaten slightly.

Dry the inside of the pig with a towel; salt and pepper. Fill the inside with the meat mixture and before closing, add a bunch of fresh fennel or dill; sew opening closed with string or skewers. Rub the outside of pig with mustard, on the top and bottom, and sprinkle with more herbs. Place another sprig of fennel or dill on top and wrap in cheesecloth, tying both ends with string or wire. Pour butter over it and roast in a preheated oven (350°) for 2 to 2½ hours, basting it often with the basting sauce (recipe follows), after the pig has had a chance to brown a little.

Before serving, you can flambé pig in ½ cup heated brandy. Then slice.

Note: A suckling pig of 12 lbs can be roasted; just cut all ingredients in half.

Sauce Aigre-Douce

Basting Sauce

This is a good barbecue sauce for suckling pig, roast of beef, lamb, chops, hamburger, or chicken.

2 tbsps mustard
²/₃ vinegar
10 oz jelly (quince, apple, or currant) *or*
²/₃ cup brown sugar

½ cup broth, chicken or beef
½ cup catsup
3 tbsps soy sauce (optional)
1 tbsp cornstarch
salt and pepper, sparingly

Mix mustard, vinegar, jelly or brown sugar, broth, catsup, soy sauce, and salt and pepper. Boil until the jelly has dissolved. Mix the cornstarch in a little broth and stir into the sauce; cook until thickened.

JOSEPHINE SAYS:

There are several varieties of mushrooms used in cooking. **Les champignons de Paris are the fresh, cultivated white mushrooms** — an almost essential element in French cuisine as a vegetable, a garnish, or in sauces and stuffings. They are generally cooked very briefly and separately and added to the dish or sauce.

Wild mushrooms (the *cèpe* and *morille*) are used in France quite a lot. You can generally find them here packaged and dried.

 **JOSEPHINE SAYS:**

We use a lot of sweet butter in French cooking. In 1971 I went to France, as I do every few years, and I visited the Cordon Bleu. I asked the chef about the difference — "Which is better to use in America, butter or margarine?" He said because the butter in America is 20% less fat than the butter in France, you might as well use margarine and save some money.

Turban de Filets de Sole

Fillet of Sole Ring with Mousse

4 to 5 servings

This recipe consists of five parts: the **court bouillon, panade,** mousse, turban (assembling the mold), and the sauce.

Court bouillon
1½ cups fish stock or
   clam juice
½ cup white wine
salt and pepper
1 small onion, chopped
1 small carrot, chopped
celery leaves
3 to 4 sprigs parsley
bay leaf
pinch of thyme, cloves

In saucepan, mix fish stock, wine, and all other ingredients. Cook 2 to 3 minutes, reduce heat, and let simmer covered for 30 minutes more. Strain and let cool. Reserve ½ cup for the **panade,** then reduce the remaining stock to 1 cup.

Panade (pâte à choux)
½ cup fish stock
¼ cup white wine
salt, pepper, nutmeg
¼ cup butter
½ cup flour
2 eggs
1 or 2 egg whites

Bring fish stock and wine to a boil along with butter. When liquid is boiling and butter melted, add flour all at once and remove from heat. Continue beating with a wooden spoon until mixture leaves the sides of the pan, and the bottom of pan has a slight film. Then break one egg in the center of the dough and beat; repeat with second egg. Add egg white and beat again. The dough should now hold its shape. Brush with butter to prevent caking and cover.

The Mousse
¾ cup fish purée
¾ cup **panade**
salt and pepper
finely chopped parsley
½ cup chilled whipping cream
   or evaporated milk
1 egg white if needed

Prepare fish purée by putting fish through the fine blade of a meat grinder. Mix with **panade** and beat with a wooden spoon until it holds its shape. Add seasonings to taste; then add cream. If mixture is too stiff, add egg white and beat again.

The Turban — Assembling the Ring Mold
6 fillets of sole
salt, pepper

Butter well the ring mold. Season fillets with salt and pepper and score the skin side of fillets with a knife to break the fibers, so that they will keep their shape. Lay fillets side by side in mold, overlapping slightly. Trim them evenly. Layer mousse on top; fold the ends of the fillets over the mousse.

(*Note:* Turban can be prepared ahead up to this point. Cover with greased wax paper and refrigerate up to 12 hours).

When ready to bake, place mold in a pan of boiling water in the lower third of oven and bake at $375°$ for 45 to 60 minutes. Turban should raise about ¼ inch. Unmold on hot platter and fill center of mold with carrots, mushrooms, broccoli, cauliflowerets, or any kind of creamed shellfish.

Coat **turban** with sauce supreme *(see recipe)*; or use a mousseline or mornay sauce. Serve the remaining sauce in warm sauce boat.

Buche de Noël   Traditional Christmas Log Cake

4 egg yolks
4 egg whites
4 tbsps sugar
4 tbsps flour
1 cup cream, whipped

Mocha Cream:
4 egg yolks
4 tbsps sugar
1 cup strong coffee
1 cup sweet butter

Beat yolks and sugar together, then add flour gradually. Fold in the egg whites, beaten stiff. Butter a jellyroll pan and spread the mixture evenly over it. Bake for 15 minutes at $350°$. Remove from oven and cover cake with a towel until cooled. Loosen cake from baking sheet.

To make the **mocha cream,** beat egg yolks and sugar together and pour in nearly boiling coffee. Stir mixture over double boiler until it becomes creamy; then let it cool slightly. Beat in the butter, stirring until it is completely absorbed.

Spread with a thin layer of mocha cream over the cake, then cover with a layer of sweetened whipped cream. Roll the cake lengthwise and slide gently onto a platter. Use the remaining mocha cream to frost the outside of the roll. Use the tines of a fork to roughen the surface in imitation of tree bark. You may use a pastry tube to add leaves and twig decoration.

THE FUNDAMENTAL DOUGHS FOR PASTRY, PIE, BREAD

"Know the Fundamentals"

The basic doughs and sauces referred to in the recipes are listed here. They are fundamental to all French cooking.

The Fundamental Doughs for Pastry, Pie, Bread

Pâte à Brioche   Brioche Dough

Ten pages in the cookbook for the average American brioche — for mine, one-half page.

Ingredients for sponge:
1 envelope dry yeast
½ cup lukewarm water or milk
1/3 cup flour
1 tsp sugar
1 pinch salt (⅛ tsp)

Dissolve the yeast with the water or milk, add pinch of salt and the sugar. Mix in the flour to form a soft ball. Put in a buttered bowl and let sponge rise until it doubles in size.

Method for Brioches:
3 2/3 cups flour
½ lb butter or margarine melted
1/3 cup sugar
4 or 5 eggs
raised sponge

Work the butter with flour, add sugar and salt, and the eggs one at a time to make a very soft dough, but not liquid. Knead until it becomes a very smooth paste (almost elastic). Add the raised sponge, mix well, and put in the buttered bowl.

Let stand for 2 to 2½ hours (at 70°–75°) until double in bulk. Punch down, cover with a plastic bag and put in refrigerator for 2½ hours at least, or overnight. *For best results, keep overnight.* Afterward, grease some fluted molds, or one large one, fill 2/3 full, make a cross with a knife and insert small ball of the dough to make the head, and let it rise again. Bake at 400°, 15 to 20 minutes for small ones; 30 to 35 minutes for larger ones.

Pâte Brisée Fine

Pastry for Pies, Pâtes, Quiches

1 cup flour
½ tsp salt
½ tsp sugar (if to be used for a sweet filling)

6 tbsps butter or margarine, cold
1 egg yolk *(see Note)*
a little water (ice water if available), about 2 to 3 tbsps

Place the dry ingredients in a mixing bowl and rub in the cold butter with the fingers until the mixture becomes granulated, like cornmeal. Beat the egg yolk with 2 to 3 tbsps of water to make about ¼ cup liquid. Add the liquid to the flour-butter mixture and blend quickly, until the dough can be pressed into a firm ball. It must not be sticky.

Place the dough on a floured board and **fraise** it. (**Fraisage** means to press the pastry with the heel of the hand, not the palm. Press away from you in a quick firm touch of the heel of the hand.) Form quickly into a round ball, sprinkle lightly with flour and wrap in waxed paper or a cloth. Place in the refrigerator for at least two hours or overnight. This pastry will keep one day in the refrigerator or a month or more if frozen. If kept any longer than a day, it is best to freeze it. When ready to use, roll out to desired thickness on a lightly floured board.

To precook pie shell; roll out and put into the pie pan. Press well against the edges. Put foil over the crust, pushing it down well against the dough. Weight it with beans and bake at 375° for 15 minutes. Remove the foil and return the crust to the oven for 10 minutes or as long as necessary to brown it slightly.

Note: Do not use the egg yolk if the crust is to be used for a filling which contains eggs. Without the eggs it is called **pâte brisée.**

Pâte à Choux

Cream Puff Paste

½ cup butter or margarine
1 cup water
1 tbsp sugar

salt and nutmeg
3 to 4 eggs
1 cup flour

Bring water and butter to a boil until the butter is completely melted and slowly add seasoning. Pour in all the flour at once. Beat vigorously for 1 to 2 minutes until it forms a ball and leaves the sides of the pan. Remove from heat. In center of dough, break an egg. Beat thoroughly before adding the next. The last egg will be absorbed more slowly (sometimes three eggs will suffice). The dough should be able to hold its shape.

Pâte à choux can be made into puff crackers and hors d'oeuvres. It can also be refrigerated and warmed slowly when needed, but it will not rise as much as when the dough is fresh.

Crème Pâtissière — Pastry Cream

1½ cups milk
¼ cup butter
3 egg yolks
⅓ cup flour
2 tbsps cognac or rum, or 1 tsp vanilla
½ cup sugar

Scald the milk. Beat the sugar and egg yolks until lemon in color and runs like a ribbon. Add a little milk and the flour. Mix well. Gradually add the rest of the hot milk, and place over heat in a double boiler. Stir with a small wire whip or wooden spoon. Continue to stir over heat (to cook flour) for 5 or 6 minutes. Remove from heat; add butter and flavoring. Let it cool before using. Stir once in a while to prevent skin from forming on the surface. This cream will keep a few days in the refrigerator, or can be frozen for 3 to 4 months.

Variations:

Crème Chantilly

Add about 1 cup of whipped cream to completely cooled Crème Pâtissière. Use for pastry, desserts, petit fours. For a topping in puff pastry, add ½ cup sugar, 1 tsp vanilla to the whipped cream.

Crème Saint Honoré

Add two stiffly beaten egg whites to the Crème Pâtissière. Add the egg whites when the cream is hot, as this will set the whites. Stir them quickly. Use to fill cream puffs or cake.

Crème Bourdaloue

To the Crème Pâtissière, add ¼ cup unsalted butter, 1 jigger of Kirsch and 1 tsp of almond extract. Good base for fruit.

Crème Frangipane

To the Crème Pâtissière, add ½ cup almond paste or powdered almond.

Pâte Feuilletée — Puff Pastry, for Turnovers, Patty Shells, Dessert Pastries and Cookies

4 cups flour (sift before measuring)
1½ cups water, more as needed
1 lb butter or margarine at room temperature
⅛ tsp salt if using unsalted butter or margarine

Put flour in a bowl and add enough water to make a dough soft enough to roll. Knead dough until it is smooth and elastic, 10 to 15 minutes. Slam down on board three times and let rest, covered, in refrigerator 10 minutes. Mold butter into one large cube. Roll the dough into a circle on a well-floured board and place the butter in the center. Fold over four flaps of dough to completely envelop the butter. Turn dough over and roll again, first in one direction and then another in order to form a large one inch thick square. Butter might leak through while rolling, but it will eventually be incorporated correctly.

Continued

Do not turn dough over while rolling it out. It will be necessary to flour the board often to keep the dough from sticking. After forming the square, fold into thirds by folding first the left flap and then the right flap on top of that. Roll dough again and fold into thirds. This operation is termed a "turn." The dough will now have two "turns." Dent with two finger marks to mark the turns, and place in plastic bag and refrigerate an hour or more to chill dough completely. This prevents it from becoming too elastic and difficult to work with.

Remove it from the refrigerator and give two more turns. Dent with four marks and refrigerate until ready to use. This paste is better when made a day or more before you intend to use it. It will keep ten days in the refrigerator and up to six months in the freezer. When ready to use, give the dough two final turns.

Roll out dough and shape accordingly. Seal edges with water and prick top for turnovers. In general, the baking temperature is 400° for 10 minutes, 300° for 30 minutes. Remember this is in general: if necessary, adjust timing, not temperature.

Alternate Method:

Same proportions as above. Take three cups of flour and make the dough soft enough to roll. Amalgamate the butter in the fourth cup of flour and proceed as above — same way — same folds.

Note: Dampen the baking sheet with cold water. It is not necessary to use grease unless there is a filling in the paste that will touch the sheet.

THE FUNDAMENTAL SAUCES

"The Winning Tricks"

These are the fundamental sauces you will need for French cooking. I have included variations that I have referred to in the cookbook, but there are hundreds more. (A more complete list of sauces can be found in Josephine's first book, "Cooking with Josephine.")

The Fundamental Sauces

SONG FOR MIXING SAUCES:

Mary, dip your finger
Come dip your finger
Mary, dip your finger in the sauce.
Mary, dip your finger
Come dip your finger
Mary, dip your finger in the wine.

Fundamental Sauce:

¼ cup butter
⅓ cup flour   1/4 c. or less flour
1½ cups chicken or veal broth
   (fond blanc) — less if juices
   of the dish are to be added

Velouté Sauce

salt and pepper to taste
nutmeg to taste
1 egg yolk, beaten
⅓ cup cream

Make a white roux by melting the butter in a double boiler or heavy pan over low heat and blending in the flour. *Do not allow it to brown.* Pour in the hot broth and beat until smooth and well blended. (Use less broth if juices of the accompanying dish are to be added later.) Add the seasonings to taste and cook over hot water on very low heat for 45 minutes to 1 hour.

The sauce may be cooled and refrigerated for several days or it may be frozen. When ready to use, heat, adding the egg yolk mixed with the cream at the last moment. *Do not allow the sauce to boil after adding the egg yolk and cream.*

Fundamental Sauce: Béchamel Sauce

This sauce is made in the same way as the Sauce Velouté, but hot milk is substituted for the broth. Use the same method, proportions and cooking time. The juice of the dish to be served may be used for part of the liquid.

Sauce Béchamel and Sauce Velouté are good with poultry, lamb, veal, fish, eggs, and vegetables such as broccoli, cauliflower, asparagus, spinach, Brussel sprouts, and onions.

Derivatives of Béchamel and Velouté Sauces

These sauces can be made from either of the basic sauces, unless otherwise specified in the recipe.

Aurore:
To 1½ cups sauce, add 1 tbsp tomato paste and 1 egg yolk. Serve with chicken, lamb or fish.

Mornay:
To 1½ cups sauce, add ¾ cup grated cheese and ½ cup white wine. Serve with fish, any meat or vegetable.

Moutarde:
Add 1 tsp dry mustard to 1½ cups sauce. Recommended with grilled herring.

Nantua:
Add cayenne pepper or 1 tbsp paprika and shrimp butter (chopped shrimps mixed with butter) to 1½ cups sauce. Sauce should be pink in color. Serve with fish.

Ravigote:
Add chervil, tarragon and chives to taste with 1 tbsp mustard, along with a chopped shallot or the white part of a green onion. This sauce can be served cold on vegetables, fish and cold meats.

Riche:
Add chopped truffles or black olives. Good with lobster, fish, lamb, veal, pork, or steak.

Soubise:
To 1½ cups sauce, add 2 to 3 onions which have been puréed. Serve with braised lamb, poached eggs, veal, cabbage, fish, string beans, cauliflower.

Suprême:
Follow Velouté recipe, using one part fish stock to three parts chicken stock, and adding juice of half lemon with the seasonings. Just before serving, mix in two beaten egg yolks mixed with ½ cup heavy cream and 2 tbsps butter. Do not reheat or let the sauce boil after the butter has been added. Makes 2 to 2½ cups.

 **JOSEPHINE SAYS:**

I prefer to use a double boiler when I make sauces, and not worry about burning or sticking. It is not so professional but Pellaprat always told me, "Forget professional — use the double boiler and take an extra headache out of your head!"

Fundamental Sauce: Hollandaise Sauce

4 egg yolks
salt and pepper to taste
2 tsps lemon juice

½ cups butter
cut in small pieces

Beat the egg yolks thoroughly with the lemon juice and salt and pepper. Put mixture in the top of a double boiler over hot water (not boiling). Stir the mixture constantly until it starts to thicken slightly. Then add the butter (cut in small pieces) and beat the sauce until it is the consistency of mayonnaise. Up to ¼ cup more butter can be incorporated, if desired, but it is better to have less than risk separating the sauce.

Remove the sauce from the heat. It will keep warm for half an hour on the side of the stove.

Béarnaise:

Boil ¼ cup vinegar and ¼ cup dry white wine (Chablis or Sauterne) with two chopped shallots, 1 tbsp tarragon, parsley, chives, salt and pepper in the top of a double boiler until the liquid has been reduced to 2 to 3 tbsps. Put over hot (not boiling) water, and add 3 beaten egg yolks and stir until slightly thickened. Beat in ½ cup butter, cut into pieces, and proceed as for Hollandaise. Sauce Bernaise is good with vegetables, fish, steak, and other broiled meats.

Curry:

Add 1 tbsp curry powder to sauce. Serve with fish, shellfish, eggs, lamb, chicken.

Maltaise:

To 1½ cups sauce, add the juice of a small orange (or about ½ cup) and 1 tbsp grated orange peel. Good with fish, meat, vegetables or eggs.

Mousseline:

Fold into sauce, 2 egg whites stiffly beaten, and pinch of nutmeg. Serve warm with poached salmon, cauliflower, asparagus, or broccoli.

Fundamental Sauce: Mayonnaise

2 egg yolks
1 tbsp mustard
 (dried or prepared)
salt and pepper to taste
1½ to 2 cups vegetable oil
1 tbsp vinegar

Mix the egg yolks, mustard, and salt and pepper together. Add the oil, little by little at the beginning. As the mayonnaise starts to thicken, the flow of oil can be gradually increased until the amount needed has been absorbed by the egg yolks. Add about 1 tbsp vinegar, according to taste. Stir and put in a closed jar.

Derivatives of Mayonnaise:

Aioli:
Pound 2 to 6 cloves of garlic (using mortar and pestle) and add to 1 cup mayonnaise little by little while stirring.

Chantilly:
To make a very thick mayonnaise, add lemon juice instead of vinegar, and 3 tbsps whipped cream. Very good with asparagus, cauliflower, artichokes, and white fish. Also good with chicken and veal.

Oscard:
To 1 cup mayonnaise, add 1 cup chopped sweet red pepper, 1 tbsp vinegar, and 1 tbsp chopped tarragon. Mix well. Add salt, pepper, and 1 tbsp chili sauce (or pinch of cayenne) to taste. Serve with cold or hot broccoli, cauliflower, cabbage, turnips, cold fish or roast meat.

Remoulade:
To 1 cup mayonnaise, add 1 tsp chopped capers, 1 tsp sour pickles, 1 tsp mustard, one green onion chopped coarse, pepper to taste, and a pinch of cayenne. Good with cold meats and fish.

Tartare:
Follow recipe for **Remoulade Sauce,** adding 2 hard-cooked egg yolks (strained) and 2 raw yolks.

JOSEPHINE SAYS:
For sure-fire results in mayonnaise, when mixing the egg yolk and mustard, add a tsp of hot water or hot vinegar before adding the oil. Pour oil slowly until the mixture thickens, then you can add a little more at a time without fear of catastrophe. Do not forget when making a *liaison* (thickening) with egg yolk, it should never boil.

To bring back a curdled mayonnaise, take another bowl and add 1 tbsp ice water. Add the curdled mayonnaise by the spoonful and stir constantly.

When making mayonnaise, make in quantity, as it will keep a long time and is always good to have on hand. To keep it longer, add 1 tbsp boiling water when mayonnaise is made, and store in a well-covered jar on the bottom shelf of the refrigerator.

Fundamental Sauce: Brown Sauce

Note: The **Brown** sauces have *glace de viande* (brown beef concentrate) for their base. They are usually used for meat and game.

2 tbsps shortening	3 tsps tomato paste or puree
1/3 cup flour	1/8 tsp pepper
1½ cups brown broth	½ tsp *glace de viande (see recipe)*

Make a *roux* by melting the shortening in a saucepan, adding the flour and stirring over moderately low heat until it has turned a brown color. Add the broth and stir. Then add the tomato paste or puree. Let it come to a boil. Add the pepper and simmer on a very low fire for about 2 hours. This sauce should not be too thick. If it thickens too much while cooking, add a little more broth. Skim off as much of the fat and scum which rises to the surface as possible.

After it has cooked long enough, add the meat extract. Strain the sauce, cool, and keep in a covered jar in the refrigerator for future use. (It will keep at least two weeks.) Make enough so that you won't have to make it each time you prepare a sauce of the same order. Makes about 1½ cups.

Glace de Viande   Concentrated Meat Extract

The **glace de viande** plays a great part in the flavoring and cooking of soups and sauces. Our ancestors made the extract from a great many ingredients, and compressed it into cubes to use as needed. Today such extravagane preparation may not seem worth it, but commercially prepared meat extract, made mostly of water, cannot compare to the extract that you make yourself. Made in quantity, the **glace de viande** can be stored in the refrigerator or freezer for several months. Lean beef is preferred for this recipe because it yields more juice than other meats and has a stronger flavor. Use other meats and bones to supplement the beef.

2 lbs lean beef	2 carrots
2 lbs veal neck	2 onions
2 lbs veal bones	2 stalks celery
2 lbs beef bones	1 tsp thyme
1 calf's foot (optional)	2 bay leaves
1 chicken or chicken parts	1 tsp salt per quart of water
any extra bones, roasted in the oven until well browned, then added to the stock to give color	1 tsp pepper

Remove all fat from the meat and bones. Dice meat into big cubes and cover meat and bones with water, 6 to 8 inches above meat. Bring to a boil, skim surface and add all the vegetables and seasonings. Bring to a boil again and

Continued

simmer for 6 hours. Skim surface from time to time to remove as much of the fat as possible. Strain and press meat to extract the juice, then transfer back to the pot and simmer for 6 more hours, skimming frequently, until the broth reaches the desired consistency. It should coat the back of a spoon. Transfer the stock to a smaller saucepan and reduce heat as the sauce thickens. Pour the extract into jars and store in the refrigerator. It will keep at least a month this way, and longer if it is reboiled every week. Or, freeze in an ice cube tray, cut into cubes, wrap, and store in the freezer. Use as needed; glaze melts quickly when heated.

Fundamental Sauce: Vinaigrette (French Dressing)

1½ cups olive or vegetable oil
½ cup vinegar
  (wine vinegar preferred)
¾ tsp salt
½ tsp pepper

1 tbsp prepared mustard
  (Dijon)
1 tsp Worcestershire sauce
1 clove garlic, crushed

Mix all ingredients thoroughly, dropping the crushed clove of garlic into the dressing.

Derivatives of Vinaigrette:

Aromatic Herb:
To 1 cup of Vinaigrette add 1 tbsp total of the following herbs: basil, dill, fennel, winter savory, thyme, rosemary, oregano, and sage.

Chapon:
To 1 cup of Vinaigrette, add 5 or 6 croutons rubbed with 1 or 2 cloves of garlic. Add to the salad and toss at the last minute before serving.

Fundamental Sauce: Tomato Sauce
Makes about 1 qt

¼ cup butter
2 tbsps olive oil
2 cloves garlic, minced
1 large onion, chopped fine
1 tbsp chopped parsley
rosemary, chopped

1 tsp sweet basil or *pesto*
oregano or marjoram, to taste
salt and pepper to taste
1 qt tomato puree (or 5 to 6 lbs
  fresh tomatoes, peeled, seeded)
1 can tomato paste

In butter and oil sauté together the garlic, onion, and spices. Add the tomato puree and tomato paste. Cook over low heat for two to three hours. Add basil or pesto (basil and oil) when cooking is finished so its flavor will be preserved.

Tomate Coulis

Tomato Sauce
Yields 3 cups

1 large onion, chopped
3 tbsps oil
4 tbsps butter
2 cloves garlic, minced
2 tbsps flour
1½ cups **fond brun** (or 1
1½ cups **fond braun** (or 1 bone roasted or **glace de viande** and then use water)
1 lb fresh or canned tomatoes

bouquet garni:
 thyme, bay leaf, celery, oregano, fennel
salt, pepper
1 tsp sugar
1 tbsp basil or pesto
¼ lb mushrooms, chopped

Melt 2 tbsps butter with 2 tbsps oil and sauté the onion. Add 1 clove of garlic and the flour. Stir and add the **fond brun,** the tomatoes, and **bouquet garni.** Season with the sugar and salt and pepper to taste. Simmer 2 hours. Sauté the mushrooms in 2 tbsps butter and 1 tbsp oil. Add the second clove of garlic and continue to sauté briefly. Just before serving, stir the mushrooms and garlic into the tomato mixture along with the basil.

Sauce au Persil

Parsley Sauce

1 cup parsley, chopped
1 tbsp finely chopped walnut
½ onion or 3 scallions, chopped
2 cloves of garlic, chopped
2 yolks of hard-cooked eggs, chopped fine or reduced to a paste

¼ cup oil
2 tbsps wine vinegar
1 pinch sugar
salt and pepper
1 tbsp mustard
1 tsp Worcestershire

Mix all ingredients well. Serve with boiled corned beef, boiled beef, or with pasta.

Sauce Smitane

Sour Cream Sauce

½ lb red or yellow onions
1 cup white wine
juice of ½ lemon

salt and pepper
cayenne
1 pt of sour cream

Peel the onions and chop them fine. Cook them in the wine and lemon juice until reduced by half. Add all the spices and the sour cream. Let it simmer 5 minutes.
Serve with fish, mousse, poached eggs, chicken and other meat.

Beurre Blanc   Butter Sauce with Shallots

Makes about ½ cup

¼ cup shallots, finely chopped
¼ cup white wine
¼ cup white distilled vinegar or white wine
½ cup butter, cut in small pieces

Put the shallots, wine, and vinegar in the top of a double boiler and cook to reduce until the liquid is almost evaporated, with only about 1 tbsp left.

Over hot water, add one piece of butter at a time to the double boiler, whipping with a whisk until it is totally incorporated before adding the next piece. Repeat until all the butter is incorporated into the sauce.

Note: The butter should not melt but should be beaten in, otherwise the sauce will have an oily film to it.

This sauce will keep several weeks. To reheat, melt 1 tsp butter and add the rest of the sauce slowly, beating constantly.

Derivatives:

Raifort:

To 1 cup butter, add 3 tbsps horseradish and a little mustard. Store until firm.

Beurre de Homard   Lobster Butter

Use ½ cup commercial lobster spread to 1 cup butter. Or make your own lobster spread from the coral, colored with some of the red lobster shell cooked with it. Use same proportions as above.

GLOSSARY

Glossary

Termes Culinaires   Culinary Glossary

Aïoli:
Sauce for vegetables made of six to seven cloves of garlic, pounded with a mortar and pestle, and added to one cup of mayonnaise, homemade or commercial.

Anglaise:
Any preparation cooked mostly in water or white stock. Also, bread crumbs coated with an oil, egg and milk mixture.

Amalgamer:
To amalgamate or mix thoroughly without stirring too vigorously.

Arroser:
To baste a roast or other foods with butter, broth, or the fat and juices of the roast.

Aromatic herbes:
Strong seasoning made by chopping and combining any or all of the following: oregano, winter savory, marjoram, sage, chives.

Baba:
Cake made of raised dough, with or without raisins and soaked in rum or kirsch syrup after baking.

Bain-marie:
A vessel of hot water in which sauces and dishes can be set to stay hot, usually kept on top of the stove.

Ballotine:
Boned, stuffed and rolled meat, fowl, or fish molded into a cylinder shape and wrapped in cheese cloth or skin. Normally served hot as a first course.

Barder:
Wrapping a piece of meat, poultry, game or fish with strips of fresh or salted pork fat known as fat back, in preparation for braising.

Bardes:
Slices of fat back used for barding meat, poultry, game.

Baveuse:
Term for describing the desired consistency of a properly made omelet; it means "mellow" or "moist."

Béchamel:
Fundamental sauce made of butter, flour and egg yolk added to a cream base.

Beignets:
Fritters, or any food dipped in batter and deep fat fried.

Beurre manié:
Thickening agent for sauces made of equal parts flour and butter, mixed into a paste and brought to the boiling point.

Beurre noisette:
Drawn butter, lightly browned.

Binding:
Process of thickening a sauce that is too thin.

Blanc:
A mixture of flour and water in which various vegetables and meats can be cooked to keep them white (cauliflower, sweetbreads, etc).

Blanch:
To submerge any ingredient in boiling salted water for varying amounts of time in order to cook or harden it.

Blondir:
To brown very lightly in butter, oil or fat; also, to cook flour and butter together to form a light roux.

Bouilli:
Boiled beef.

Bouillie:
Pulp or gruel.

Bouillir:
To boil rapidly in salted water.

Bordure:
Dishes that are served in a ring or crown-shaped mold. The mold may be made of Duchesse potatoes, rice, semolina, etc. for hot dishes; jelly, custards, cream, riz à l'Impératrice, etc. for cold or sweet dishes.

Bouchées:
Small patty shells or cream puffs, filled, and served as hors d'oeuvres, before or after the soup course.

Bouquet garni:
A packet of herbs tied together and added to the dish while cooking, usually made of thyme, bay leaf, and parsley. Amount should be judged sparingly, but according to the size of the dish being prepared. For some dishes, bouquets are

made of highly scented herbs, such as basil, celery, tarragon, rosemary, sage, etc. The bouquet is removed from the sauce or dish before serving.

Canapés:
Toasted or fried bread cut into round, rectangular or other shapes and spread with various mixtures. Served as appetizers or luncheon entrees.

Cassoulet:
A casserole composed of beans and meat.

Chiffonade:
Chopped lettuce, sorrel, spinach and other herbs added to soups at the last minute as a garnish.

Caul:
Or crepine is the membrane enclosing the belly of the pig. It is boiled and used to line and cover pâté, or to wrap meats for cooking. Strips of fresh pork fat can be used as a substitute.

Chapeler:
Preparation of bread crumbs from bread that has been dried, crushed with a rolling pin or bottle, and passed through a metal sieve.

Chevaler:
The symmetrical arrangement of various ingredients of a dish, placed to overlap one another.

Coagulate:
To thicken or congeal fats and jellies.

Coquetier:
An egg cup.

Corder:
An excess of water mixed into pastry dough, causing it to bake leatherhard, and be unpalatable.

Cornichons:
Small sour pickles.

Coulis:
A light tomato sauce.

Court bouillon:
A cooking liquid made by simmering together vegetables, wine, and stock.

Crème à l'anglaise:
A custard cream made of egg yolks, sugar, milk or cream thickened in a double boiler.

Crème Frâiche:
Stir 2 tbsps sour cream or buttermilk into 1 cup whipping cream. Let stand at room temperature for 24 hours. If very warm, refrigerate after 12 hours.

Crepine:
Same as caul.

Croustades:
Thick slices of bread, hollowed out and toasted in the oven until dried out and browned.

Croutons:
Dried-out bread that is toasted or fried and then cut into ¼ to ½" cubes; or can be cut to the shape of the meat being prepared, to be used as a foundation for the dish, as in tournedos.

Deglacer (or de-glaze):
A technical term for the dilution of the concentrated juice in a pan in which meat, poultry, game or fish has been roasted, braised or fried. Wine, soup stock or cream can be used for this purpose.

Degorger:
To soak food for any length of time in cold water to free it from any impurities (calves' head, veal sweetbreads, brains, etc.)

Demi feuilletée:
See Pâté.

Demi-glacé:
A basic brown sauce.

Duxelle:
A mixture of mushrooms with onion, shallots and nutmeg.

Dutchess potatoes:
Mashed potatoes with egg yolk added, used as a decorative border and garnish for meat and fish dishes.

Emince:
A dish made with leftover roast or braised meat. The meat is thinly sliced and placed in a casserole and covered with a sauce (Bordelaise, mushroom, etc.).

Emincer:
Meaning to slice very finely meats, vegetables, fruits.

Entrée:
Literally "beginning," but in the culinary sense it *does not* refer to the first course. The entrée in a full French menu follows the relève, or intermediate course, coming as the third course in the meal.

Etuver:
To cook food in a covered pan without moistening. This method of cooking is suitable for all kinds of meat, poultry, vegetables, and fruit. Butter, fat or oil is added.

Farci:
Preparation of veal, chicken or any fowl by stuffing the breast and then

roasting, frying or poaching the meat. Any kind of forcemeat can be used for stuffing.

Fat back, or pork fat:
Fat layer next to the skin from the back of a pig. Cut into strips, it is used to line pâtés or wrap meat for cooking.

Fines herbes:
The combination of these herbs is recommended for salads, omelets, soups, vegetables, chicken and fish: parsley, chervil, tarragon, chives, fennel, basil, sorrel, spinach, dill, savory.

Fleurons:
Small crescent-shaped decorations made from any kind of pastry dough or toast, served as a garnish for meat or fish.

Fond blanc:
White stock.

Fond brun:
Brown stock.

Forcemeat or stuffing (farces):
A mixture of ingredients, minced and seasoned and used in pâtés, gallantine, eggs, fish, poultry, meat and vegetables.

Fraises:
Strawberries.

Fricassee:
Preparation of poultry in a white sauce.

Fumet:
Liquid used to flavor or give body to stocks and sauces. Fumets are prepared by boiling foodstuffs in wine or stock made from meat or fish.

Gallantine:
A dish made from boned poultry or meat, stuffed and then pressed into a shape and poached in a gelatin stock. Served cold.

Galettes:
Usually refers to tartlets, or round coin-shaped cakes.

Garbure:
Substantial soup made with vegetables, pork and beef with cabbage added one half hour before serving.

Garnish:
Trimming added to a dish or placed around it; or served separately to accompany it. It should always blend with the flavor of the basic dish. Garnishes are classified as simple or composite.

Glaçage:
There is no single English equivalent for this term. It is used to refer to several quite distinct operations. Literally **glacer** means to freeze a liquid

until it turns to ice (ice cream), but it can also refer to culinary operations carried out in an excessively hot oven. Meat is said to be browned if served hot, and glazed (with jelly) if served cold.

Glacage can refer to covering fish, eggs, etc. with a white sauce.

Glacage can mean sprinkling wheels or vegetables (carrots, turnips, onions) with confectioners' sugar and subjecting them to high heat.

Glacage: term for the icing of cakes.

Glace de viande:
Concentrated beef extract.

Gratin:
The thin crust formed on the surface of certain dishes when browned in the oven or broiler.

Grenadins:
Slices of filet (sirloin) of veal, shaped round (tournedos) or rectangular, larded with bacon and braised.

Hors d'oeuvre:
There are two main types of hors d'oeuvre: cold and hot. They are sometimes called **entrées volantes,** or light entrées; generally served after the soup, but can precede it as well.

Inciser:
Making light incisions with a very sharp knife in the skin of fish to be grilled or fried.

Isigny:
A small town in Calvados, France where some of the best butter in France is made.

Jardinière:
A garnish made of fresh vegetables.

Jus:
In French, it has a wider connotation than in English: Juice pressed from an animal or vegetable; gravy made by diluting the juices of the roasting; brown stock of veal, especially that which is clear or thickened and used as gravy.

Julienne:
Any foodstuffs coarsely or finely shredded.

Kirsch:
Cherry flavored liqueur used in cooking.

Larding:
Strips of fat threaded through cuts of meat by means of a larding needle.

Lardons:
Strips of fresh bacon or fat used in larding.

Liaison:
Thickening process of adding egg yolk and cream or broth to a sauce or

liquid, removed from the heat. Arrowroot or cornstarch used as a liaison must be diluted first in a little cream or broth.

Madrilene:
A clear soup served hot or cold, flavored with tomato sauce.

Marinade:
A seasoned liquid, cooked or uncooked, in which foodstuffs (notably meat and fish) are steeped for a length of time.

Marmite:
A metal or earthenware covered pot, used for bisques and garbure and for the famous French pot-au-feu.

Mirepoix:
Sautéed mixture of celery, carrot and onion.

Mets:
A term for any food prepared for the table.

Mignonette:
Coarse ground pepper.

Mille feuille:
A pastry of a "thousand leaves;" in America, a "Napoleon."

Napper:
To cover meat, poultry or fish all at once with a thick velouté or other sauce.

Panade:
Cooked mixture of butter, flour and water used as a thickener. Adding whole eggs makes it pâte à choux.

Panure:
To coat with bread crumbs, first coating with melted butter or beaten eggs.

Parisian seasoning:
Salt seasoned with over a dozen herbs for use on beef, veal, etc.

Parmentier:
Method of preparing various dishes which always includes potatoes in one form or another.

Pâte:
Basic dough, includes pâte feuilletée, pâte brisée, bread dough, batters and sweet pastes.

Pâte demi-feuilletée:
Rises half as high as regular puff paste. Using puff paste recipe, use 6 oz butter and 2 oz water. Give only 3 to 4 turns, and continue as for puff pastry.

Pâté:
A meat "paste."

Pâté en croute:
Pâté baked in a pastry crust.

Pâté galantine:
Pâté baked as stuffing inside turkey or chicken.

Pâté terrine:
Pâté served in a baking dish.

Paupiettes:
Thin slices of beef or veal, stuffed and rolled, wrapped in slices of bacon and simmered in very little liquid.

Persillade:
Chopped parsley, often mixed with chopped garlic; also refers to leftover meat that is fried in butter.

Pesto:
A pounding of garlic, basil and Parmesan cheese with addition of olive oil. A soup base.

Petits four:
Many kinds of small fancy cakes.

Pigeon:
Squab.

Poach:
To cook meat, poultry, fish, etc. in a clear, spiced and flavored stock.

Pommes de terre:
Potatoes.

Profiterolles:
Small cream puffs, which may be filled with ice cream, crème patissière or other fillings.

Purée:
Food that is mashed and put through a sieve.

Quenelles:
Dumplings made with fish or forcemeat.

Raidir:
To sear a foodstuff quickly in very hot butter or fat.

Reduction:
To decrease the volume of a liquid by evaporation (in sauce making).

Remonter:
Addition of a spice to a sauce or alcohol to wine to strengthen or heighten its taste.

Rouleau:
Preparation that is rolled into shape; usually filled with another mixture, such as a cheese roll or jelly roll.

Roux:
Cooked mixture of flour and butter.

Salpiçon:
Several ingredients finely diced and mixed together, such as ham, mushrooms, etc.

Saucisson:
Large sausage, served sliced.

Sauté:
To cook over a high fire in butter, oil or fat, stirring frequently.

Soupçon:
A little bit; a dash.

Stock:
Liquid obtained from cooking meat, bones and vegetables together. If it is clarified, it becomes consommé.

Terrine:
Baking dish, oval or rectangular, particularly for pâté.

Timbale:
A custard containing cooked vegetables and meat.

Tomber:
This is an old French cooking term (meaning literally "to fall") to describe method of cooking meat without any other liquid in the pan than that produced by the meat itself. The moisture created in the cooking must reduce to a syrupy consistency. *Tomber a glace* means to add a small amount of liquid, and then boil down completely.

Travailler:
To beat a sauce, dough, or mixture.

Trognon:
Edible heart of a vegetable or fruit.

Truffle:
A fungus for garnish and stuffings. In France, the province of Perigord is famous for truffles.

Velouté:
A fundamental sauce made of butter, flour and egg yolk added to broth.

Vinaigrette:
Sauce or marinade of oil and vinegar; French dressing.

Zest:
Orange or lemon peel, made with a utensil called a *zesteur*.

INDEX

Index

A Demain Ma Mere, 35
Adeline Crêpes, 175
Aigre-douce Sauce, 187
Aïgo Bouïdo, 41
Aiguillettes de Boeuf à la Flamande, 130
Aîoli Sauce, 202
Almond Cake, 171
Almond Tart, 168
Ananas Martine, 171
Anchovy Pizza, 24
Apples and Celery, Braised with Walnut Sauce, 14
Apple-Applesauce Tart, 15
Apple Cake, 11
Apple Custard Tart, 177
Apple Mousse, 168
Apple Pudding with Orange Sauce, 13
Aromatic Herb Sauce, 204
Artichokes Lyonnais, 54
Artichokes, Stuffed with Pork and Spinach, 54
Asparagus and Peas in Cream, 55
Asparagus in White Wine, 55
Asperges au Vin Blanc, 55
Asperges en Petit Pois, 55
Aspic, Clams in, 92
Aspic, Trout in, 93
Aubergine à la Nîmoise, 58
Aurore Sauce, 200
Aurore Sauce with Cauliflower Soufflé, 57
Avocado Mousse, 56

Baked Eggs with Shrimp and Haddock, 103
Baking Hint, Josephine Says, 171
Ballotine de Volaille à la Régence, 184
Bar du Maréchal Joffre, Le, 94
Barbecue Sauce, 187
Bass, Striped, with Chivry Sauce, 94
Bean Casserole with Pork and Lamb, 149
Beans, Garbanzo Salad, 159
Beans with Duck or Goose, 150
Béarnaise Sauce, 134, 201
Béchamel Sauce, 200
Béchamel Sauce, derivatives of, 200

Beef, Boiled, with Piquante Sauce, 48
Beef, Braised Fillet, with Vegetables, 130
Beef, Leftover, au Gratin, 49
Beef, Leftover, in Salad, 164
Beef, Minced, with Mushrooms and Wine, 134
Beef, Oxtails, Braised, with Bread Crumbs, 138
Beef, Pepper Steak Fillet, 142
Beef, Sirloin Strips, 134
Beef Stew, Spicy, with Beer, 9
Beef Tongue Braised in Champagne, 139
Beef Tongue with Parsley Sauce, 34
Beef, Tournedos Benjamin, 141
Beignets Bretons, 26
Beignets de Foie, 45
Beuchelle de Nignon, La, 46
Beurre Blanc, 206
Beurre Blanc, derivatives of, 206
Beurre de Homard, 206
Beurre Manié, 97
Bisque de Crevettes, 37
Blettes, Frites, au Gratin, 64
Boeuf Bouilli Gratiné, 49
Boeuf Bouilli en Salade, 164
Boeuf Bouilli – Sauce Piquante, 48
Bohemian Crêpes, 157
Boiled Beef with Piquante Sauce, 48
Bouquets au Cari, 103
Bouquets au Potiron, 104
Brains of Lamb, Cardinal Richelieu, 47
Braised Fillet of Beef with Vegetables, 130
Braised Oxtails with Bread Crumbs, 138
Bread, Herbed, 173
Bread, Vegetable or Fruit, 173
Breast of Chicken Normandy, 78
Brie Canapés, 29
Brioche Dough, 193
Brioche de Ris de Veau au Champagne, La, 142
Brioche with Chocolate and Meringue, 172
Brittany Soup, 16
Brittany Fritters, 26
Broccoli with Cheese, 10

Brocoli au Gratin, 10
Broiled Tomatoes Provençale, 64
Brown Caper Sauce for Stuffed Cabbage, 12
Brown Sauce, 203
Buche de Noël, 189
Butter Cream Frosting, 176
Butter vs. Margarine, 188
Butter Sauce with Shallots, 206

Cabbabe, Red, Forestière Style with Blueberries, 56
Cabbage, stuffed, with Brown Caper Sauce, 11
Cabbage with Bacon, 56
Cailles du Bocage, 182
Cake, Almond, 171
Cake, Apple 11
Cake, *Buchede Noël* (for Christmas), 189
Cake of Beef with Tomato Sauce, 35
C¹ke, Rich Chocolate, 176
Cake, solange, 168
Calmars, 104
Calmars en Salade, 105
Calves' Liver with Orange, 46
Camembert Canapés, 28
Canapés, 27
Canapés au Roquefort, 27
Canapés aux Concombres, 28
Canapés de Brie, 29
Canapés de Gruyère, 28
Canapés Hollandaise, 28
Canard à la Tour d'Argent, 186
Canard de Pékin, Le, 83
Canard Rôti à Ma Façon, 82
Canard Sauvage ou Faisan, 82
Caramel Pears, 170
Carbonnade de Boeuf, 9
Carnaval de Nice, 172
Carottes Clamart, 57
Carottes Vichy, 13
Carrots with Purée of Peas, 57
Carré d'Agneau à l'Orange, 147
Carré d'Agneau en Couronne, 145
Carré de Mouton Saigon, 146
Carrots, Vichy style, 12
Casserole, Bean with Pork and Lamb, 149
Cassoulet de Castelnaudary, 150
Cassoulet du Languedoc, 149
Cauliflower Soufflé with Sauce Aurore, 57
Céleri-Rave Rémoulade, 158
Celery-Root Salad, 158
Céleri Scorvienne, 15
Celery and Apples, Braised, with Walnut Sauce, 14
Celery and Mushroom Vinaigrette for Egg Timbales, 13
Cervelle d'Agneau Cardinal Richelieu, 47
Champignons Farcis, 30

Champignons Marinés, 29
Chantilly Sauce, 202
Chapon Sauce, 204
Chateaubriand Sauce, 137
Cherries in Crêpes Baked in Custard, 177
Cherries, used as stuffing for Squab, 81
Cherry Soup Citron, 37
Cherry Soup Montmorency, 37
Cheese Canapés, 26
Cheese Fondue, Belgian Style, 22
Cheese Soufflé with Herbs, 8
Chicken, Breast of, Normandy style, 78
Chicken Breasts with Mushrooms and Noodles, 71
Chicken Carmen, 74
Chicken Livers Marie, 80
Chicken Marengo with Shrimp Garnish, 73
Chicken Patties, 23
Chicken, Poached Regency Style, 184
Chicken, Preparing for Cooking, 71, 75
Chicken, Roasted, with Stuffing, 72
Chicken Saigon, 77
Chicken Saint Peter, 77
Chicken Sautéed Hunter-Style, 79
Chicken with Artichokes and Mushrooms, 70
Chicken with Curry, 10
Chicken with Garlic, 14
Chicken with Herbs, 71
Chicken with Herbs and Mushrooms, 74
Chicken with Lemon, 79
Chicken with Pineapple, Papaya, and Ginger, 80
Chicken with Potatoes Marguery, 70
Chicken with Sherry and Garlic, 76
Chicken with Tomato and Cheese, 72
Chicken with Tomatoes and Almonds, 75
Chicken with Wine and Tomatoes, 75
Chiffonade for Soups, 35
Chivry Sauce for Striped Bass, 94
Chocolate Cake, 176
Chou à la Nivernaise, 56
Chou Farci – Sauce Brune aux Câpres, 11
Chou-fleur en Xephir, 57
Chou Rouge Forestière, 56
Clams in Aspic, 92
Claret Sauce, 162
Cochon de Lait Rôti, 186
Cochon Saoul – Civet de Porc, 151
Cocktail Dip, 22
Cod or Sole Epinette, 100
Coffee Cream (Sauce), 169
Compote de Rhubarbe, 169
Congre à l'Oseille, 91
Cookies, Walnut, 172
Coquettes au Gratin, 135
Coquille de Poisson, 93

Corn Soup, 36
Côtelettes Marinées Grillées, 146
Côtes de Porc à l'Amoricaine, 149
Côtes de Porc Charcutière, 16
Couronne aux Nois, 174
Couronne de Champignons aux Oeufs Brouillés, 163
Court Bouillon, 99
Crab Meat in Mushroom Caps, 30
Crab Meat Soup Josephine, 41
Crayfish au Gratin, 102
Crayfish with Tomato and Heavy Cream, 101
Cream Puff Paste, 194
Cream of Bean Soup, 40
Cream of Watercress Soup, 42
Crème Bourdaloue, 195
Crème Chantilly, 195
Crème d'Haricots Bonne Femme, 40
Crème Frangipane, 195
Crème Mousse au Citron, 170
Crème Patissière, 195
Crème Renversée à l'Orange, 10
Crème Saint Honoré, 195
Crêpes Adeline, 175
Crêpes Batter, 156
Crêpes Berthil, 157
Crêpes Bohémiennes, 160
Crêpes du Convent, 175
Crêpes Saint-Cloud, 156
Crêpes with Pears, 175
Crêpes with Shrimp, 157
Crêpe-Wrapped Cherries with Custard, 177
Croûtes aux Pêches, 16
Croutons au Fromage, 29
Crown Roast of Lamb, 145
Cucumber Canapés, 28
Cucumber-Pineapple Gelatin, 39
Culinary Glossary, 209-217
Currant Sauce for Squab, 81
Curry Sauce, 10, 201
Custard Cream Sauce, for Desserts, 168
Custard, with Cherry-filled Crêpes, 177

Délices de l'Eté, Les, 161
Dinde à la Touraine, 83
Dip, Garlic and White Wine, 24
Dodine de Canard, 185
Drunken Pig Stew, 151
Duck, Peking style, 83
Duck, Pressed, Tour d'Argent, 186
Duck, Roasted Josephine's Way, 82
Duck, Stuffed, Boned, 185
Dutch Canapés, 28

Ecrevisses Colombines, 101
Eeel with Sorrel, 91

Eggplant with Tomato and Herbs, 58
Eggs, Baked, with Shrimp and Haddock, 103
Eggs, Poached, on Tuna, 163
Eggs, Scrambled, in Mushroom Ring, 163
Eggs, Stuffed, 25
Eggs, Stuffed, on Bed of Spinach, 43
Eggs, Stuffed – Variations, 25
Emincés de Boeuf Paloise, 134
Epaule d'Agneau à la Menthe, 147
Epice Parisienne, 144
Epinards Sauce Aigre, 62
Escalopes de Veau Morandi, 141
Escarole Salad in Crust, 161

Faisan Vigneronne, 183
Fanchonnettes, 172
Farce à Quenelles (Panade), 184
Feuilles d'Oignons Farcis, Les, 26
Filet de Carrelet Bordelaise, 97
Filets de Sole Escoffier, 99
Filets de Sole ou Cabillaud Epinette, 100
Fillet of Sole Normandy, 96
Fillet of Sole Ring with Mousse, 188
Fish, a Hint when Poaching, 98
Fish, how to buy and store, 94
Fish, in Scallop Shells, 93
Fish Meurette, 98
Fish, Sauce for, 98
Fish Stock, 91
Flamiche aux Poireaux, 59
Flapjacks, 8
Flounder in Mushrooms and Wine, 97
Foie, Beignets de, 45
Foies de Poulet Marie, 80
Foie de Veaux à l'Orange, 46
Fondue, Cheese, Belgian style, 22
Fondue du Belgique, 22
Fouace aux Anchois, 24
French Dressing, 204
French Toast, 8
Fricadelle de Boeuf Sauce Tomate, 35
Fritters, 26
Fritters, Brittany style, 26
Fritters, Liver, 45
Frogs' Legs Sautéed with Sherry-Butter Sauce, 102
Frosting, Butter Cream, 176
Fruit or Vegetable Bread, 173
Fryer with Herbs, 71
Fryer with Potatoes Marguery, 70
Fryers with Artichokes and Mushrooms, 70
Fumet of Fish, 91
Fundamental Sauces, 199-206

Galettes, 8
Galettes de Pommes de Terre, 61

Galopins de Marseille, 138
Garbanzo Bean Salad, 159
Garbure de Maïs, 36
Garlic Chicken, 14
Garlic Cloves, preparation hint, 148
Garlic Soup, 41
Garlic, used with Leg of Lamb, 145
Garlic, used with Potatoes, 60
Gâteau de Pommes, 11
Gâteau Solange, 168
Gelatin Salad, Pineapple-Cucumber, 39
Gigot d'Agneau Pondichery au Gingembre, 145
Ginger, used with Leg of Lamb, 145
Glace de Viance, 203
Glossary of Terms, 209-217
Gnocchis Verts, 39
Grapes, used with Pheasant, 183
Gratin de Cerises, 177
Gratin d'Ecrevisses, 102
Green Potato Dumplings, 39
Grenadins de Veau Ambassadeur, 140
Grenadins de Veau au Citron, 137
Grenouilles Sautées à Sec, 102
Grilled Marinated Lamb Chops, 146
Grilled Pigs' Feet or Veal Trotters Ste. Menehould, 151
Gruyère Canapés, 28

Haddock, poached, 92
Haddock Poché, 92
Haddock, used with Shrimp and Baked Eggs, 103
Ham Mousse with Claret Sauce, 162
Ham with Madeira and Cream, 148
Herb Bread, 173
Herbs, Measurement of, 156
Hollandaise Sauce, 201
Hollandaise Sauce, derivatives of, 201
Hors d'Oeuvre Chaud de Tomates, 25
Hot Tomato Hors d'Oeuvre, 24

Italian Meringue, 174

Jambon à la Crème, 148
Jardinière de Légumes, 65
Jerusalem Artichokes Provençale, 55
Jerusalem Artichoke Salad, 159
Jerusalem Artichokes with Ravigote Sauce, 54
Josephine's Best Liver Pâté, 22

Kidneys and Sweetbreads Nignon, 46
Kidneys of Veal Robert, 136
Kidneys, Sautéed, in Champagne Sauce, 136

Laitue au Nid, 58

Lamb Brains Cardinal Richelieu, 47
Lamb, Chops, Marinated and Grilled, 146
Lamb, Crown Roast of, 145
Lamb, Leg of, with Ginger and Garlic, 145
Lamb, Minted Shoulder of, 147
Lamb Shanks Saigon Style, 146
Lamb Stew Provençale, 148
Langouste à la Parisienne, 104
Langue de Boeuf Bagnette, 34
Langues de Boeuf Braisées Champenoise, 139
Lapin aux Champignons, 84
Lapin Chasseur, 84
Leeks au Gratin, 59
Leek Tart, 59
Leftover Beef au Gratin, 49
Leftover Beef, Boiled, with Piquante Sauce, 48
Leftover Beef in Salad, 164
Leftover Beef with Tomato Sauce, 35
Leftover Chicken Patties, 21
Leftover Chicken Sauce with Walnuts, 43
Leftover Fish - *Poisson Especial,* 35
 - *A Demain Mà Mere,* 35
Leftover Meat in Stuffed Onion Leaves, 25
Leftover Meat used in Stuffed Rutabagas, 62
Leftover Roast Pork in Nancéenne Casserole, 36
Leftover Veal and Olive Timbale, 44
Leg of Lamb with Ginger and Garlic, 145
Lemon-Cream Mousse, 170
Lettuce Nests, 58
Liver Fritters, 45
Liver Pâté, 143
Liver Pâté - in a Crust, 143
Liver Pâté, Josephine's Best, 20
Liver with Orange, 46
Livers, Chicken, as a sauce for Pasta or Rice, 80
Lobster Butter, 206
Lobster Salad, 104

Maltaise Sauce, 201
Margarine, vs. butter, 188
Marinated Mushrooms, 29
Marmite du Jardin Potager, 47
Marquis au Chocolat, 176
Mayonnaise, 202
Mayonnaise, derivatives of, 202
Meat Extract, Concentrated, 203
Meat, Mixed, au Gratin, 135
Meringue Italienne, 174
Minced Beef with Mushrooms and Wine, 134
Minted Shoulder of Lamb, 147
Mixed Meat au Gratin, 135

Mixed Vegetables Jardinière, 65
Mocha Cream, 189
Mornay Sauce, 200
Moules, 92
Mousse, Apple, 168
Mousse au Jambon, 162
Mousse au Saumon, 160
Mousse aux Pommes, 168
Mousse, Avocado, 56
Mousse d'Avocat, 56
Mousse, Fish, for Turban of Sole, 188
Mousse (Fish) with Sole Fillets, 100
Mousse, Ham, 162
Mousse, Lemon Cream, 170
Mousseline Sauce, 201
Moutarde Sauce, 200
Mushroom and Celery Vinaigrette for Egg Timbales, 14
Mushroom Caps Stuffed with Crab Meat, 30
Mushroom Ring with Scrambled Eggs, 163
Mushroom Salad, 158
Mushrooms, Marinated, 29
Mushrooms, Varieties, 187
Mushrooms, with Rice, 62
Mussels, 92

Nancéenne Casserole, 36
Nantua Sauce, 200
Navets de Jean-Marie, 64
Noodles à la Cecilia, 39
Noodles with Marinara Sauce, 38
Noodles with Sour Cream, 38
Nouilles Cécile, 39
Nouilles d'Isigny, 38
Nouilles Sauce Marinara, 38

Oeufs Farcis, 25
Oeufs Farcis aux Epinards, 43
Oeufs Leontine, 103
Oeufs Pochés au Thon, 163
Omelet, basic recipe, 43
Omelet with Chicken and Walnut Sauce, 43
Omelette au Poulet Sauce aux Nois, 43
Onion Leaves, Stuffed, 24
Onion Soup, 42
Open-Faced Sandwiches, 29
Orange Custard Cream, 10
Orange Sauce for Apple Pudding, 13
Orange Sauce, for Roast Rack of Lamb, 147
Oscard Sauce, 202

Pain aux Herbes, 173
Pain aux Légumes ou Fruit, 173
Pain Perdu, 8

Parisian Seasoning, 144
Parsley Sauce, 205
Parsley Sauce for Beef Tongue, 34
Pastry Cream (Filling), 195
Pastry, for Cream Puffs, 194
Pastry for Escarole Salad, 162
Pastry, for Pies, Pâtes, Quiches, 194
Pastry, Puff Paste, 195
Pâte à Beignets, 26
Pâte à Brioche, 193
Pâte à Choux, 194
Pâte à Tourte, 162
Pâte Brisée, 194
Pâte Brisée Fine, 194
Pâté de Foie en Croûte, 143
Pâté de Foie Josephine, 22
Pâte Feuilletée, 195
Pâte of Liver, Josephine's Best, 20
Peaches on Canapés with Sabayon Sauce, 16
Pears Almina, 170
Pears, Caramel, 170
Peas and Asparagus in Cream, 55
Peas, buttered, 11
Peas, Puréed, with Carrots, 57
Peas with Greens, 60
Peking Duck, 83
Pepper Steak Fillet, 142
Peppers Stuffed with Seasoned Rice, 59
Perches Pochées Champenoise, 97
Perch Poached in Champagne, 97
Petits Pois au Beurre, 11
Petits Pois Bergerac, 60
Pheasant with Grapes, 183
Pheasant or Wild Duck with Sweetbreads, 82
Pieds de Porc ou de Veau Ste. Menehould, 151
Pig, Roast Suckling, 186
Pigeons Joyeaux, 81
Pigeons Montmorency, 81
Pineapple-Cucumber Gelatin, 39
Pineapple Martine, 171
Piquante Sauce for Boiled Beef, 48
Pithivier, Le, 171
Pizza, with Anchovies, 24
Poached Chicken Regency Style, 184
Poached Eggs on Tuna, 163
Poached Haddock, 92
Poached Sole Fillets Escoffier, 99
Poireaux au Gratin, 59
Poires à la Savoyarde, 170
Poires Almina, 170
Poisson de Saison Meurette, 98
Poisson Especial, 35
Poivrons au Riz, 59
Pommes Chanoinesse, 177
Pommes de Terre Marseillaise, 60

Pommez de Terre Rôties, 61
Pork Chops Brittany Style, 149
Pork Chops Charcutière, 16
Pork, how to buy, 151
Pork, how to cook, 149, 150
Pork Liver Pâté, Josephine's Best, 20
Pork, Pigs' Feet Ste. Menehould, 151
Pork, Roast Suckling Pig, 186
Pork, Stew, 151
Pork, used with Spinach to stuff Artichokes, 54
Potage Breton, 16
Potage Crème de Cresson, 42
Potage Geminy, 36
Potato and Turnip Purée, 16
Potato Dumplings with Spinach, 39
Potato, Josephine says, 60
Potato-Nut Balls, 61
Potato Soufflé, 61
Potatoes, Roasted Baked, 61
Potatoes with Garlic, 60
Potée Nancéenne (Lorraine), 36
Poularde Toulousaine, 72
Pouding aux Pommes à l'Orange, 13
Poulet à l'Ail, 14
Poulet au Cari à l'Indienne, 10
Poulet au Citron, 79
Poulet aux Amandes, 75
Poulet aux Dents du Chat, 72
Poulet Carmen, 74
Poulet de Grain Sauté aux Fines Herbes, 71
Poulet de Grains Sautés Bordelaise, 70
Poulet Exotique, 80
Poulet Marengo, 73
Poulet Parmentier, 70
Poulet Rafael Weill, 76
Poulet Reine Chasseur, 75
Poulet Saigonnaise Indochine, 77
Poulet St. Pierre, 77
Poulet Sauté Chasseur, 79
Poularde Savoyarde, 74
Praires en Gelée, 92
Prawns in Pumpkin, 104
Prawns with Curry Sauce, 103
Pressed Duck, Tour d'Argent, 186
Pudding, Apple, with Orange Sauce, 12
Puff Paste, 195
Purée Cherreuse, 16
Purée de Courgettes aux Herbes, 63
Purée of Potatoes and Turnips, 16

Quail with Wild Rice, 182
Quenelles Stuffing, 184
Queue de Boeuf Sainte Menehould, 138

Rabbit in Tomato and Rosemary Sauce, 84

Rabbit with Mushrooms, 84
Ratatouille à la Béchamel, 65
Ragoût d'Agneau Provençale, 148
Raifort Sauce, 206
Ravigote Sauce, 200
Ravigote Sauce with Jerusalem Artichokes, 54
Red Cabbage Forestière with Blueberries, 56
Rémoulade Sauce, 202
Rhubarb Compote, 169
Rice, Piémontaise style, 11
Rice, Wild, 182
Rice with Mushrooms, 62
Rich Chocolate Cake, 176
Riche Sauce, 200
Ris de Veau Lorraine, 45
Rissoles de Volailles, 23
Riz à la Piémontaise, 11
Riz aux Champignons, 62
Riz Sauvage, 182
Roast Chicken with Stuffing, 72
Roast Duck, My Way, 82
Roast Rack of Lamb with Orange Sauce, 147
Roast Suckling Pig, 186
Roasted Baked Potatoes, 61
Rognons de Veau Robert, 136
Rognons Sautés au Champagne, 136
Roquefort Canapés, 27
Rutabagas Agenaise, 62
Rutabagas Stuffed with Prunes and Meat, 62

Sabayon Sauce for Croûtes aux Pêches, 17
St. Cloud Crêpes, 156
Salad, Belgian Endive and Creamed Cheese, 161
Salad, Escarole in Crust, 161
Salade de Pois Chiches, 159
Salade du Verger et du Potager et Gelée, 39
Salade Forestière, 158
Salade Niçoise, 160
Salmon Mousse, 160
Salmon Steak with Sorrel Sauce, 96
Sandwiches, Open-Faced, 29
Sauce à la Gelée pour Pigeons, 81
Sauce Smitane, 205
Sauces:
    Aigre-douce, 187
    Airoli, 202
    Aromatic Herb, 204
    Aurore, 200
    Bagnette, 34
    Barbecue, 187
    Béarnaise, 134, 201
    Béchamel, 200

Béchamel, derivatives of, 200
Beurre Blanc, 206
Beurre Blanc, derivates of, 206
Beurre de Homard, 206
Brown, 203
Brown Caper, 12
Butter, with Shallots, 206
Chantilly, 202
Chapon, 204
Chateaubriand, 137
Chivrey, 94
Claret, 162
Coffee Cream, 169
Concentrated Meat Extract, 203
Curry, 10, 201
Currant, 81
Custard Cream, 168
Demi-Glace, 182
Glace de Viande, 203
Hollandaise, 201
Hollandaise, derivatives of, 201
Lobster Butter, 206
Maltaise, 201
Mayonnaise, 202
Mayonnaise, derivatives of, 202
Meurette, 98
Mornay, 200
Mousseline, 201
Moutarde, 200
Nantua, 200
Orange, for Lamb, 147
Orange, for Pudding, 13
Oscard, 202
Oseille, 96
Parsley, 205
Piquante, 48
Raifort, 206
Ravigote, 54, 200
Rémoulade, 202
Riche, 200
Sabayon, 17
Smitane, 205
Sorrel, 96
Soubise, 200
Sour Cream, 205
Sûpreme, 200
Tartare, 202
Tomate Coulins, 205
Tomato, 205
Velouté, 199
Velouté, derivatives of, 200
Vinaigrette, 204
Vinaigrette, derivatives of, 204
Walnut, 14
Saucisson en Croûte, Le, 144
Saucisson Toulouse, 144
Sausage, Spiced, 144
Sausage Wrapped in Pastry, 144

Sauté de Veau au Cresson, 140
Sautéed Kidneys in Champagne (Sauce), 136
Scalloppini with Marsala, 138
Scallop Shells Filled with Fish, 93
Scarole en Croûte, 161
Seasoned Salt, Parisian style, 144
Shrimp Bisque, 37
Shrimp-Filled Crêpes, 157
Shrimp, How to Prepare, 101
Shrimp Soufflé, 94
Shrimp, used with Haddock and Baked Eggs, 103
Sirloin Strips, 134
Smoked Salmon Cornucopia, 23
Solange Cake, 168
Sole, Escoffier Style, 99
Sole, Fillet, Ring with Mousse, 188
Sole Fillets with Fish Mousse, 100
Sole Normande, 96
Sole, Normandy Style, 96
Sole or Cod Epinette, 100
Sorrel Sauce for Salmon Steak, 96
Sorrel Soup, 36
Sorrel, with Eel, 91
Soubise Sauce, 200
Soufflé à la Courge, 63
Soufflé au Crevettes, 94
Soufflé au Fromage et aux Herbes, 8
Soufflé, Cheese, with Herbs, 8
Soufflé de Pommes de Terre, 61
Soufflé, Potato, 61
Soufflé, Shrimp, 94
Soufflé, Squash, 63
Soup au Crabe Josephine, 41
Soup, Brittany style, 16
Soup, Chiffonade for, 35
Soup, Corn, 36
Soup, Cherry Citron, 37
Soup, Cherry Montmorency, 37
Soup, Crab Meat, Josephine, 41
Soup, Cream of Bean, 40
Soup, Cream of Watercress, 42
Soup, Garlic, 41
Soup, Onion, 42
Soup, Shrimp Bisque, 37
Soup, Sorrel, 36
Soupe aux Cerises Montmorency, 37
Soupe aux Cerises II, 37
Soupe à l'Oignon, 42
Sour Cream Sauce, 205
Spiced Sausage, 144
Spinach, baked with Stuffed Eggs, 43
Spinach in Sour Cream, 62
Spinach, Josephine says, 54
Spinach, used with Pork to stuff Artichokes, 54
Squab Stuffed with Cherries, 81

Squab Stuffed with Liver, Bacon and Wild Rice, 81
Squash Purée with Herbs, 63
Squash Soufflé, 63
Squid, 104
Squid Salad, 105
Strawberry Delight, 9
Striped Bass with Chivry Sauce, 94
Stuffed Boned Duck, 185
Stuffed Eggs, 25
Stuffed Eggs with Spinach, 43
Stuffed Tomatoes Gabrielle, 158
Summer Delight Salad, 161
Suprême aux Fraises, 9
Suprême de Volaille Empire, 71
Suprême de Volaille Normandie, 78
Suprême Sauce, 200
Sweetbread Brioche with Champagne Sauce, 142
Sweetbreads Lorraine style, 45
Sweetbreads and Kidneys Nignon, 46
Sweetbreads, used with Wild Duck or Pheasant, 82
Swiss Chard au Gratin, 64
Swiss Chard Tarte, 23

Tart, Almond, 168
Tart, Apple, 15
Tart, Apple Custard, 177
Tart, Dough for, 15
Tart, Swiss Chard, 21
Tartare Sauce, 202
Tarte à la Frangipane, 168
Tarte aux Pommes, 15
Tarte aux Blettes, 23
Termes Culinaires, 209-217
Timbale du Roi René, La, 44
Timbale of Leftover Veal and Olives, 44
Timbales aux Champignons et Céleri Vinaigrette, 14
Tomate Coulis, 205
Tomates à la Provençale, 64
Tomates Farcies Gabrielle, 158
Tomato Hors d'Oeuvre, hot, 24
Tomato Hors d'Oeuvre, variation, 24
Tomato Sauce, 204
Tomatoes, Broiled Provençale style, 64
Tomatoes Stuffed with Avocado and Tuna, 158
Topinambours à la Provençale, 55
Topinambours en Salade, 159
Topinambours Sauce Ravigote, 54
Tournedos Argenteuil, 134
Tournedos au Poivre, 142
Tournedos Benjamin, 141
Tournedos of Veal Ambassador, 140
Traditional Christmas Log, 189
Tranches de Saumon - Sauce à l'Oseille, 96
Trempette, 24
Trout in Aspic, 93
Trout with Grand Marnier, 95
Truites au Grand Marnier, 95
Truites en Gelée, 93
Tuna with Poached Eggs, 163
Turban de Filets de Sole, 188
Turban de Sole en Soufflé, 100
Turkey Touraine, 83
Turnip and Potato Purée, 16
Turnips with Lemon and Sour Cream, 64

Veal Kidneys Robert, 136
Veal Sautéed with Watercress, 140
Veal Scalloppini with Marsala, 138
Veal Scallops Morandi, 141
Veal, Sweetbreads and Kidneys Nignon, 46
Veal Sweetbreads in Champagne Sauce, 142
Veal, Sweetbreads Lorraine, 45
Veal, Tournedos, 140
Veal Tournedos with Lemon, 137
Veal, Trotters Ste. Menehould, 151
Vegetable Marmite, 47
Vegetables, Mixed, Jardinière, 65
Vegetable or Fruit Bread, 173
Vegetables, some Consideration on Cooking, 53
Vegetables with Béchamel Sauce, 65
Velouté Sauce, 199
Velouté Sauce, derivatives of, 200
Vinaigrette Sauce, 104, 204
Vinaigrette Sauce, Derivatives of, 204
Vinegar, used as Wine Substitute, 78

Walnut Cookies, 172
Walnut Ring, 174
Walnut Sauce for Braised Celery and Apples, 14
Watercress Soup, Cream of, 42
Whole Apple Custard Tart, 177
Wild Duck or Pheasant with Sweetbreads, 82
Wild Rice, 182
Wine Substitute, what to use, 78